HOUSE ON FIRE

HOUSE ON FIRE

Fighting for
Democracy in the
Age of Political Arson

DAVID N. CICILLINE

TWELVE

NEW YORK   BOSTON

Twelve
Hachette Book Group
1290 Avenue of the Americas, New York, NY 10104
twelvebooks.com
twitter.com/twelvebooks

First Edition: August 2022

Twelve is an imprint of Grand Central Publishing. The Twelve name and logo are trademarks of Hachette Book Group, Inc.

The publisher is not responsible for websites (or their content) that are not owned by the publisher.

The Hachette Speakers Bureau provides a wide range of authors for speaking events. To find out more, go to www.hachettespeakersbureau.com or call (866) 376-6591.

Library of Congress Control Number: 2022937238

ISBN: 9781538722596 (hardcover), 9781538722619 (ebook)

Printed in the United States of America

LSC-C

Printing 1, 2022

For my family

CONTENTS

Part III
Looneyville

INTRODUCTION

It was one year since a mob of more than one thousand attacked the United States Capitol and began a bloody three-hour battle to overturn the 2020 election and keep America's first authoritarian president in power. On a somber day of remembrance, I listened to the prayers and testimony of colleagues who survived the attack and then gathered in the early-morning hours to fulfill their duty to certify the end of one presidency and the beginning of another.

This day of reflection was full of grief, fear, and hope. We grieved the officers who died as a result of the attack as well as the injuries—physical, psychological, and moral—suffered by those of us who were at the Capitol during the battle and a nation that witnessed it on television. We feared the deformed politics of a former president's Big Lie about election fraud, which his party fully promotes. And we hoped our fellow citizens would heed President Biden's call to defend democracy.

On the anniversary of January 6, President Joe Biden issued the call as part of his first full response to the antidemocracy movement begun by his predecessor and taken up by the Republican Party. Uncharacteristically blunt, Biden said of the mob, "They didn't come here out of patriotism or principle. They came here in rage—not in service of America, but rather in service of one man." Later, before ending on a note of hope, he said, "I did not seek this fight brought to this Capitol one year ago today, but I will not shrink from it either. I will stand in this breach. I will defend this nation. And I will allow no one to place a dagger at the throat of our democracy."

Throughout the day, grief, fear and hope mingled in my heart: grief as I met the parents of Officer Brian Sicknick, who died in the attack; hope as I heard the remarks of beloved colleagues; fear as I noted that House Republicans, with a lone exception, failed to attend the day's events. Representative Liz Cheney of Wyoming, that one exception, was accompanied by her father, the former vice president Dick Cheney. She and Adam Kinzinger of Illinois (absent this day due to the imminent arrival of his first child) are the only Republicans who have agreed to serve on a commission investigating January 6. I consider Liz a pro-democracy hero. Back home in Wyoming, state leaders have declared she is no longer a Republican.

Across the country one of our two major parties is all but united in its effort to erase the violence and the purpose of the January 6 attack from our memories. This process began immediately as, on January 7, Republican members of Congress Matt Gaetz, Paul Gosar, and Mo Brooks baselessly blamed the insurrection on anti-Trump provocateurs. Although this idea was thoroughly debunked, Republican Senator Ron Johnson and others continued to spread it. Representative Andrew Clyde, also a Republican, said these violent domestic terrorists appeared, to him, like individuals on "a normal tourist visit."

Of course, people on a normal tourist visit don't attack the police with clubs, bear spray, and Tasers. They don't ransack the Capitol while chanting "Hang [Vice President] Mike Pence" or occupy the Senate to prevent the certification of an election. The rioters of January 6 did all these things, but by the summer of 2021, Republicans were calling those who had been arrested "political prisoners."

By fall, pollsters found that about a third of Republicans believe we are so far "off track" that "patriots may have to resort to violence in order to save our country." Applause affirmed the comments of a man at a conference of political conservatives who asked, "How many elections are they gonna steal before we kill these people?" By winter a poll found that 79 percent of Republicans don't accept Biden's seven-million-vote victory in the country's most secure election ever.

The current myth that American elections are "stolen" goes back to at least 2010, when Republican state officials began a concerted effort to use false claims of fraud to support rules that made voting harder for people they suspected of being Democrats. (Think Black and brown people in big cities.) Donald Trump jumped on the bandwagon in 2012 but turned up the volume to ten in the run-up to Election Day 2016. "The system is absolutely rigged," he declared. "Of course there is large-scale voter fraud happening on and before Election Day. Why do Republican leaders deny what is going on? So naive."

Trump wouldn't promise to accept the election results, as all previous candidates had, and election officials girded for trouble. When he actually won, they breathed a sigh of relief, but he kept on insisting our elections were corrupt. It became obvious then that he was trying to destroy his followers' faith in the very foundation of our democracy while establishing himself as the source of truth in all things. He proceeded then to attack our allies and the other branches of government and insisted there was a mythical "Deep State" within his own administration bent on thwarting him.

Having listened and believed as their man lied and distorted the truth at least thirty thousand times during his presidency, millions of Trump's supporters decided they were entitled to their own "facts" and "truth," which he supplied and which were reinforced in the fever swamps of the internet. These supporters were not, by and large, people who lived on the margins of society. Most were white, middle- and upper-middle-class people who were vulnerable to conspiracy theories that explained their frustrations and drove them away from reliable sources of information. In short, they were the desperate sort you might find joining a get-rich-quick pyramid sales scheme or an overly controlling faith group. Among the Trump believers they found the warmth of community and the excitement that comes with thinking you possess special knowledge.

Millions of committed Trumpists were ready to accept his claim of fraud, and the vanguard responded to their president's call by joining the January 6 mob. A year later, as we marked the sober anniversary of this event, Republican leaders everywhere embraced the Trump-was-cheated myth as an article of faith, which meant they no longer believed that they lived in a functioning democracy. With Trump planning a comeback, the GOP under his thumb, and campaign donations pouring into his political organization, we face greater political peril than at any time since the Civil War.

What happened on January 6, 2021, was an orchestrated effort to subvert our democracy. This fact becomes more evident every day as investigators pore over evidence and the January 6 planners seek credit inside their cult. It now seems that while the president criminally pressured officials to change election results, veterans of his White House used lies and fraudulent claims to summon the mob and persuade members of the House and Senate to invalidate the election. They say they would have succeeded but for those who turned a protest into an attack and turned the public against the scheme.

————————

In retrospect one might say that the most surprising thing about January 6, 2021, was that we were surprised by it. Trump's capture of his base and then the Republican Party had followed the totalitarian playbook that has destroyed democracies in other places and times. The superpatriotism, fearmongering, scapegoating, and mind-bending assault on the truth are hallmarks of authoritarianism that most Americans couldn't recognize in the context of their beloved and exceptional country. To continue now to think that we are somehow immune to an antidemocracy movement would be dangerous. And yet many still don't take up the responsibility to fight against Trumpism. Instead I hear them ask, "What are you doing to defend our country?" as if public officials, or the Democratic Party, could alone form the bulwark.

I understand that it would be nice if people who practice politics for a living could take care of everything by themselves. But a democracy faced with the kind of crisis we confront today will not be saved only by the representatives elected by the people. Our democracy requires, by design, both an engaged citizenry and leaders committed to the democratic ideal. To fully grasp this design, it helps to visit its beginning.

America's founders understood that so-called "pure" democracy, in which the people voted on a nation's every action, would be unworkable in a country of 2.5 million that sprawled from Maine to Georgia. Their solution—a democratic republic—imagined that the people would be able to stay abreast of what their government was doing and wield their power during elections. The trouble was that unlike more visceral belief systems—like religious faith or nationalism—democracy is an intellectual concern that requires constant care and attention. Without this care and attention, a democracy will fall to mob rule.

By care and attention, I mean action, because in my years in government, as a state lawmaker, mayor, and member of Congress, I've seen countless times how good emerges when everyone is engaged, and bad things happen when our attention wanes. Today I am stunned that people aren't marching in the streets to express their outrage over the ongoing threat posed by the Big Lie. That's the part I don't get. Every time we hear someone say the election was stolen, we must respond with the truth. Speak up when it happens in your presence. Call the radio and TV stations that broadcast this destructive nonsense. Write letters to the editor. Take to social media. Organize email campaigns. Never stop confronting politicians who spread the Big Lie.

Of course, our defense of the American way cannot mirror the other side's approach. It may practice violence or deceive itself and others with lies. Our response must be peaceful and truthful. But it must also be urgent because as I write these words, the future of our great but imperfect national endeavor is less certain than at any moment since the Civil War.

Before you dismiss this statement as hyperbole, consider that after the 2020 election a majority told pollsters we are already in a "cold" Civil War that pits a mostly white conservative minority, which has accepted the lie that our elections are rigged, against everyone else. More recently 46 percent said that a future "hot" war is likely. This feeling is strongest among young adults, who may be listening to one of their own, Representative Madison Cawthorn, age twenty-six, who said, "If our election system continues to be rigged, then it's going to lead to one place, blood-shed." Nothing would please our doubters and adversaries more.

From the beginning, critics abroad predicted our failure. In 1839 a friend to Charles Dickens devoted an entire book, *A Diary in America*, to denigrating our experiment in equality. In his text Frederick Marryat seemed most focused on showing the American people to be naive rubes. In private he confessed his intent was "to do damage to democracy" so that it would not spread.

Like so many, Marryat believed the rule of a gifted aristocracy (to which he belonged) was the best defense against tyrants. He thought that democracy, in contrast, placed too much trust in voters who could be manipulated into enabling a dictator. Forty-five years after the *Diary*, British diplomat Sir Lepel Griffin made his case against America and democracy in a work mockingly titled *The Great Republic*. Lepel hated pretty much everything he saw on this side of the Atlantic, including Niagara Falls and St. Patrick's Cathedral in Manhattan. He concluded that in our country the best were driven from government by the incompetent and corrupt. The result was "an actual government of the worst."

It's no wonder that few Americans have heard of Marryat and Sir Lepel and that we choose instead to elevate another nineteenth-century visitor. Paris-born Alexis de Tocqueville's *Democracy in America* acknowledged our shortcomings, including the fact that as citizens Americans were "almost" but not quite equals. However, he found something to admire in every corner of our country and was especially impressed by our civic life, noting how freely and peaceably Americans debate, interact, and govern themselves.

But though we love to be loved by the likes of de Tocqueville, in every generation many Americans would agree with Sir

Lepel's negative view. Corruption and incompetence are fixtures of the human condition, which means that anyone who shouts about dishonesty in any human endeavor, from street cleaning to religion, is going to be right sometimes. Demagogues know this, which is why so many dictators begin as self-proclaimed reformers who tell "patriots" to blame their troubles on a secret cabal—usually academics, intellectuals, scientists, artists, and minorities—that's corrupting their otherwise pure and perfect country. The next logical steps involve electing the dictator and crushing the cabal.

Today, America's first would-be dictator is building another campaign for president on the foundation of his Big Lie about election fraud. Whether they truly believe or not, GOP politicians have used this lie to justify state-level attacks on voting rights. Fraud is a smoke screen for their real motivation, which is to preserve their power in a country that is growing ever more diverse. They know that the new limits on access to the polls will work mainly against Black and brown voters and immigrants, all of whom tend to favor Democrats.

The success of those who used lies to win support for voter suppression proves that with enough effort, a lie can overwhelm fact. In the case of Donald Trump and American politics, this effort includes the argument that he alone tells the truth. Those more than sixty state and federal court judgments against his claims of voter fraud? Didn't you listen as Trump attacked the judiciary as corrupt and untrustworthy? The consistent news reports showing no voter fraud? Haven't you heard the president talk about the "fake news" media? He says they are the "enemy of the people." (In a rare moment of candor about this topic he told Lesley Stahl of CBS that he smeared legitimate reporters "so when you write negative stories about me, no one will believe you.")

This kind of propaganda is a form of psychological warfare, and it has never been used against the people of the United States by a president, or a former president who stands as the leader of a major party. Trump has done this by using both his evil type of charisma and a sinister ability to make others believe that like him, they are victims who must rise against supposed enemies. Ever since his defeat, he has called for them to restore him to his rightful place of power and to trust in his promise of a white Christian nationalist utopia where they will be rewarded and everyone else—Democrats, liberals, Black and brown people, LGBTQ people, feminists, journalists, the Deep State, etc.—will be punished.

In various states, Republican lawmakers who control election administration are making it hard for people to vote. They are also revising laws and regulations to give themselves power once held by nonpartisans. They are positioning themselves to overrule the voters if they don't like the outcome of an election. I expect to see Republicans in some states use this power in the 2022 election to try to give their party enough House or Senate seats to dislodge the Democratic Party's majority and, consequently, halt inquiries into January 6. By 2024 they may be able to do this in enough states to return Trump to the White House no matter what people decide in the voting booths. He could lose by ten million votes and still, through such manipulation, regain the Oval Office.

While we mobilize to defend our democracy, we must also remind ourselves that it is the very best system for organizing society that humanity has ever known. As a form of self-governance, it allows us to live peaceably, balance freedoms and responsibilities, and pursue happiness in all its forms. It doesn't always work well. (Much more about that later.) But when people of goodwill commit to practicing it in a devoted way, it produces the greatest good for the greatest number of people while serving as an example others may want to follow.

My devotion includes this book, in which I share my experience, at different levels of society, with democracy in crisis and in recovery. This includes my work as a citizen, a lawyer, a state lawmaker, a mayor, and a member of Congress, where I have worked to check Trump's threat as a member of the House Committee on the Judiciary and as a member of the team of managers that nearly won his conviction in his second impeachment trial. I also stand as someone who, despite deep experience with some of the most corrupt officials in America, sees far more virtue than vice in every level of society. Indeed, at a time when cynicism is the order of the day, I am unshaken in my feeling of hope for our country.

My optimism is based not on a simplistic patriotism, but on a realistic assessment of my experience. I know that corruption and self-dealing are real, but I also know that these are sins practiced by the few and rejected by the many. Whether you consider Republicans like Dwight Eisenhower or Democrats like Barack Obama, we have had many more sincere and devoted presidents than corrupt and divisive ones. Of course there have been times when those who would pit us against each other have prevailed, but they have eventually been defeated.

Part I of this book describes our current emergency and places it in context. In the 1980s the right began to destroy the norms of compromise and mutual respect that had made our political institutions work. A campaign of sabotage made it nearly impossible for Congress to function, and many of the country's big problems were not addressed. Aided by religious zealots and amplified by extremist media, a new kind of Republican treated politics as anything-goes warfare. Less and less committed to genuine conservative values, they made power their goal and used divisive, apocalyptic messages to get it.

Part II of this book relies on my personal experience to explore how our potential for both corruption and breathtaking goodness are expressed in politics. The narrative in this part is set in Rhode Island, where I served first in a state legislature that suffered from the power games common to Washington and then as mayor of Providence. In that election the voters chose me to replace the last of the old-fashioned corrupt big-city mayors who ruled in the twentieth century.

Part III covers the battle between the most potent authoritarian movement America has ever seen and those individuals and institutions—especially the Congress where I serve—sworn to uphold our democracy. Many Americans have bemoaned the slow and sometimes inept effort to counteract Trumpism. As someone who played key roles in *both* impeachments and serves on committees that Trump's aides defied when subpoenaed to testify, I feel just as distressed as anyone. I have come to believe that even when we fail, and even when we're deemed inept, the effort to hold the Trumpists accountable is necessary. However, it must be accompanied by a brand of politics and governing that proves democracy works. But most important, we need to understand the fight ahead.

———

Throughout this book I use stories of my own life, and of my native Rhode Island, to illuminate and humanize the issues.

Though tiny, my state is a microcosm of America. A diverse place with a deeper history than most of the rest of the country, we have a legacy that includes both the best and the worst, including the early stirrings of our Revolution; experiments in liberty, religious freedom, and equality; and national sins like slavery that affect us even today.

My own life story is one of fighting against the powerful who abuse the public trust and betray their fellow citizens to advantage themselves. These people often pose as patriots or public servants, and they enjoy both the trappings and the power of their positions. From the first time I saw that officials sometimes acted in abusive ways—whether it's a prison warden arbitrarily denying a family visit or a corrupt politician accepting a bribe—it has enraged me and driven me to oppose it whenever possible. Were the times different, my preference for doing over talking would mean that I would leave the writing to others. But this is a unique moment. Our political house is ablaze, and it's up to each of us to sound the alarm and to help put out the fire in every way we can.

PART I

CONFLAGRATION

In which we learn how certain people set the conditions for the fire of January 6. (Yes, there are people to blame.)

1

HOUSE ON FIRE

This is the sergeant at arms.

"There has been a security breach.

"Secure the premises.

"Shelter in place."

It is a little after 2:00 p.m. on January 6, 2021. I'm at my desk in the Rayburn House Office Building when I hear the emergency alert come from a loudspeaker that I have never heard activated. My chief of staff, Peter Karafotas, immediately closes and locks the heavy door that opens onto the public hallway. By the look on his face, I can tell he's shocked by what's going on. With his talents he could earn triple what he makes on Capitol Hill but won't leave because he's devoted to public service. Now, unimaginably, the public is practically raging at our door.

Peter and I look at the television to see a vast mob, mobilized by the lies of Donald Trump, attacking police officers who stand between them and the Capitol. Rioters, some in combat gear, swing bats, batons, and ax handles as they surge against the vastly outnumbered police. Projectiles fly. Clouds of chemical gas, including sprays used by the rioters against police, hang in the air.

Intent on halting the certification of the 2020 election because their man falsely insisted the count was rigged, violent Trumpists are staging the first-ever coup attempt against the United States government. Skirmishes occur on three sides of the building. With their banners waving, attackers race from spot to spot to reinforce those struggling to break through police lines. Screams echo off the walls of the building that is the seat of our democracy. As one officer will later describe it, the scene is one of "medieval combat."

On every news channel I see images of shouting rioters on the Capitol steps spraying police officers with toxic bear repellent, beating them with everything from metal rods to fire extinguishers, and fighting them hand to hand. On the east front, rioters mouthing Trump's antipress slogans—*Fake news! Enemies of the people!*—attack journalists, smashing their cameras and putting matches to piles of equipment. On the west front, attackers tear apart the grandstand built for incoming president Joe Biden's inauguration.

The Capitol is first breached on the west front. A middle-aged man with long scraggly hair and a bushy gray beard uses a shield stolen from the police to pound the left side of a big window. Beside him a younger man in a red Trump "Make America Great Again" ball cap hammers on the right side of the window with a two-by-four. The safety glass breaks away, and people start hopping through. The second person in wears full military combat gear, including a helmet, and carries a baseball bat. Dozens of the attackers are similarly outfitted and charge in after him.

Once inside, the rioters force open the doors. Attackers wearing combat gear and Trump regalia stream into the building. Many carry Trump banners. Several wave Confederate battle flags. This is the first time the infamous Stars and Bars, synonymous with treason, has been unfurled inside the Capitol. Some of the attackers begin hunting for the vice president, chanting,

"Hang Mike Pence!" Others vandalize priceless artworks, carve "Kill the Media" into a door, and smear their own feces on the walls and floors.

In the House Chamber, my colleagues scramble to safety as security officers pile furniture in front of the door to the Speaker's Lobby. If the mob attempting to smash through it succeeds, it could quickly reach the members inside. There rioters could attack and kill those they consider their enemies. (Later it will be revealed that some had brought guns and bundles of zip ties that would have allowed them to take such drastic measures.)

As the rioters kick and hammer on the lobby door with flagpoles and helmets, one of the plainclothes officers raises his pistol. On the other side of the door, people shout, "Fuck the blue!" and "Break it down!" The shatterproof glass first cracks and then begins to break away. The wooden framing around the panes starts to splinter.

With the chamber nearly evacuated, the officers who had been holding back the attackers outside the Speaker's Lobby learn that a special tactical team is poised to clear the hallway. They leave their post to make room, and in the moment the rioters rush the door again. A woman wearing a Trump flag like a cape leaps up like a superhero in an attempt to reach the lobby. An officer who stands inside fires a shot. The bullet hits her in the shoulder. The group trying to smash its way into the chamber falls back in stunned silence. The tactical team rushes to her aid as she lies on her back on the marble floor. Ashli Babbitt, whose faith in wild conspiracy theories drew her to Washington, believes that Trump's side will prevail in its drive to reverse the election. She will die of her wound before the day is out.

———

With the shocking events still unfolding—it would take hours to clear the Capitol—I sat down with a pen and legal pad and began making notes on the possible impeachment of the president. As I did this work, nearly three hours would pass with the violence continuing and the world watching. I knew that Trump's actions and his speech that day had incited the attack and that his inaction confirmed his culpability. He could not be allowed to escape accountability.

Donald Trump had already been impeached once, as Congress approved articles of impeachment, which described the alleged crimes that the Senate considered as it conducted a trial. In this process, which is set out in the Constitution, a conviction would lead to a president's removal from office. In this case Trump escaped conviction only because members of his own party denied the evidence of his crimes, which was overwhelming, and deprived the prosecution of the two-thirds majority required for his removal.

Having prevailed in his Senate trial, an emboldened Trump had quickly applied his autocratic methods to the unfolding COVID-19 pandemic. He lied about the seriousness of the threat, wasted time on racist talk about its origin in China, and undermined his own experts with political grandstanding. According to many studies, Trump caused tens of thousands of excess deaths, which explains why, under his abysmal leadership, America led the world in COVID fatalities per capita.

Trump's failures, his thousands of well-documented lies, and the record-setting corruption of his administration had brought about his defeat on Election Day 2020. But in typical fashion he immediately began a furious campaign to persuade his seventy-five million supporters that widespread voter fraud had stolen the presidency from him. Despite recounts that changed nothing and more than sixty failed court actions, Trump and his allies continued to undermine the public's trust in democracy with their Big Lie. In fact, he would never drop it. Instead he bullied GOP officials across the country to support harebrained efforts to overturn the results. Each one failed.

Although just weeks remained in his presidency, I was certain Trump deserved to be held accountable and the shame of a second impeachment and the punishment that would come in the unlikely event that Republican senators dropped partisan politics for a moment and voted to convict. One beneficial outcome of a conviction, also delineated in the Constitution, would be that henceforth, Trump would be barred from all federal offices. This would deny him the chance to retake the White House, which he was already contemplating. To my mind, this sanction alone was worth the effort to impeach him again, even if the trial came after he left office.

As soon as I began sketching out the impeachment proposal, Representative Ted Lieu, whose office had been evacuated, came to shelter with us. Ted had emigrated to America from Taiwan with his family when he was just three years old. The Lieus had settled in California, where his parents had opened a business. Like that of so many immigrants, Ted's love for this country is unshakable, which he demonstrated when, after law school, he opted for military service over joining a high-paying firm. After four years' active duty in the Air Force's Judge Advocate General's Corps, he remained in the reserves, where he rose to the rank of colonel. Ted, who was my colleague on the Judiciary Committee, also thought a second impeachment was necessary and sat down to work with me. Soon we settled on the charge of incitement of insurrection. It's hard to imagine a worse crime for a president to commit.

Trump was an arsonist who was hostile to democracy and

willing to set our nation's political house on fire. After his defeat in the most secure election in history, he spent weeks riling up his supporters with lies about election fraud. In December he had called on them to come to Washington en masse on the day when Congress would fulfill its duty to ratify the election. "Big protest in D.C. on January 6th," he told his eighty-seven million followers on Twitter. "Be there, will be wild!"

The rage among Trump's followers grew until their online forums were filled with calls to violence. On January 4, Trump summoned Vice President Mike Pence to the Oval Office to meet a law professor who presented a six-step plan for Pence to over-turn the election. (Later this scheme would be recognized by many, including a federal judge, as a coup attempt.) A fringe figure who had been elevated by the right-wing media and a powerful conservative legal lobby called the Federalist Society, Professor John Eastman had had a previous moment of fame with his false claim that Kamala Harris was not native born and thus couldn't serve as vice president. This time he insisted that on January 6, as Congress formally accepted the election results, Pence could use his largely ceremonial role as presiding official to reject the results from seven states and throw the contest to Trump. All of this Eastman justified with baseless claims about Democrats who had rigged the election, even in states run by Republican officials.

Later, on January 4, Trump went to Georgia to promote his election fraud lies and incite outrage. "They're not going to take this White House," he said of the Democrats who had won the election by seven million votes and by 306 to 232 in the Electoral College. "We're going to fight like hell, I'll tell you right now."

On January 5, Trump's former White House adviser Stephen Bannon told those who listened to his online podcast, "All hell is going to break loose tomorrow." He likened the moment to a "revolution," adding, "It's all converging, and now we're on the point of attack tomorrow." Whether Bannon knew details of an attack plan wasn't clear, but his status as a Trump insider would prime the most rabid in his audience to react to what sounded like a call to arms. On the same day, Bannon went to the Willard Hotel, which is between the White House and the Capitol, for a prerally meeting also attended by Trump's infamous lawyer Rudy Giuliani and the fringe law professor who had given Trump a harebrained theoretical justification for overturning the election.

On January 6, Trump was the featured speaker at the preriot rally where more than ten thousand cheered his call to "fight," which they had already heard from other speakers. Law professor Eastman had declared that the republic itself was in danger. Former New York mayor Rudy Giuliani had called for "trial by combat." Congressman Mo Brooks called on "American patriots to start taking down names and kicking ass." Trump began his speech with a lying attack on the press and technology companies, which he accused of having rigged the election. (This despite overwhelming evidence that tech companies had facilitated Russian efforts to help Trump get elected by flooding social media platforms with misinformation.) He then devoted himself to winding up supporters who had come to Washington after he promised the day would "be wild."

"We will stop the steal," he declared before then telling the crowd, "History is going to be made" because his followers were going to march on the Capitol to "fight like hell, and if you don't fight like hell, you're not going to have a country anymore." This incitement pushed the country to a level of crisis not seen since the Civil War. No president had ever violated his oath to "preserve, protect and defend the Constitution" in such a publicly destructive way.

Read a transcript of the speech, which lasted more than an hour, and you will discover the maddest performance ever made by an American president. He began to lie from the very beginning, claiming hundreds of thousands stood before him and dispensing with the boring requirement that his statements make sense. Hence he announced, "They came from all over the world, actually, but they came from all over our country."

After a five-year effort to understand this autocrat's methods, I knew he would choose dramatic lies over boring truths and create fearsome enemies with conspiracy theories. "Big Tech," an ominous force comprised of the major firms in the business of internet platforms such as Facebook, he never defined, had "rigged an election. They rigged it like they've never rigged an election before." And then, in a seeming non sequitur, announced, "I'm honest."

Where before I would have thought it was all gibberish, I had come to recognize neofascist rhetoric. Like the original fascists, he wanted only to stir anger and fear with emotional phrases like "Our country has had enough" and "It's a disgrace." These phrases didn't need to be attached to ideas or tethered to concrete reality. Ideas and reality only got in the way. So it was that Trump praised his followers for devising the slogan "Stop the Steal" when in fact it had been coined by his brain trust and registered as an internet domain name before people even voted.

Trump knew that his supporters were mostly uninterested in facts and that if for some reason they experienced any doubt, he could give them another lie, another conspiracy theory, to dispose of their concerns. It's easy to do once you commit to it. I'll show you. Let's say you saw derogatory information about me in the *New York Times*. "Of course you did!" I would exclaim. "The Big Tech companies and the lying media want to take me down because I'm a threat to them. Are you one of those sheep who meekly trust mainstream sources, or are you brave enough to think for yourself?" Notice I'm not really asking you to think for yourself. I'm asking you to think *like me*. Standing in a crowd of thousands of believers already committed to me as a leader, you're likely to do it. And after you hand over your heart and mind once, it'll be easier for you to do it again, and again, until you are thrilled to be part of something that feels exciting and purposeful.

Anyone who has practice trying to motivate others with speeches has felt, in some small way, the energy Trump summons reflexively. It is a frighteningly easy thing to bring a group of people to think with a single mind. As someone expert in these ways, Trump transfixed even those he horrified—for this, see the TV coverage of his 2016 campaign—which is what makes him an especially dangerous demagogue.

We haven't had a Trump before now because our presidents have declined to use this power as he does. This is why most of us struggled to see what he was doing. But by the end of the 2020 election campaign, I understood what was happening, and so did most people who lived outside Trump's cult. But if we still respected our own values of freedom of speech, freedom of conscience, and freedom of assembly, all we could do was argue against Trumpism and hope that it wouldn't be converted to violent action. But this hadn't been enough, and now we had to act ourselves, in defense of democracy and the rule of law, with a unity of purpose. The question was: Could we?

2

THE COWARDS' RESPONSE

In the immediate aftermath of the riot, even our Republican colleagues seemed shaken. In brief speeches on the Senate floor, Majority Leader Mitch McConnell denounced Trump and said, "The mob was fed lies." Senator Lindsey Graham, previously an abject sycophant, said of Trump, "Count me out. Enough is enough." He also called the attackers "domestic terrorists." House Minority Leader Kevin McCarthy publicly blamed Trump for January 6 and said that his efforts to delegitimize Biden's election were "not the American way."

For a moment it seemed that the attack on the Capitol had finally awakened Republicans to the acute emergency brought about by Donald Trump. For more than four years, American democracy had been set ablaze by a demagogue whose followers believed his grimly brilliant con. I say brilliant because he had harnessed the frustrations and anxieties of millions and then, through rhetorical jujitsu, led them to believe that he alone—a slippery billionaire who had cheated and exploited working people for decades—could help them.

Why did they believe Trump was the one who would ease their suffering? Because he had confirmed their worst fears and fantasies about the corruption in the world and in the process told a simple, easy-to-grasp story that replaced all the confusing complexities of modern life. He declared them victims of the government, the press, the Democratic Party, some mysterious Deep State, and everyone who wasn't like them—an American-born white conservative. But he was going to save them like Jesus in his Second Coming, which tied into apocalyptic preaching so many knew from their churches.

Trump's pose meant that he could swat away his critics by declaring them all to be part of a vast conspiracy and reminding the faithful that his many opponents were "evil" and "corrupt" and that "I alone can fix it." Organized religion has used a similar method for centuries, warning of grievous, invisible spiritual threats to keep the faithful in line.

Before January 6, Republicans in the House and Senate had been unable to break Trump's con and had nearly all converted or at least pretended to. They had seen how Trump used his social media might to attack, humiliate, and even drive out of office fellow Republicans who failed to show sufficient loyalty. Even Senator Ted Cruz, who had declared he wasn't a "servile puppy" after Trump insulted his wife, fell in line, praising him in a write-up he published in *Time* and welcoming the man he'd once called a "sniveling coward" to campaign for him in Texas. If it came down to a choice between remaining in office and high-minded concerns like the truth and national unity, remaining in office generally won.

Then January 6 brought the danger of Trump's reign to them personally. They had been chased by a mob that was literally calling their names and they knew the world had seen it all on live television. Angry, frightened, humiliated, and alarmed, some of the timid found their voices. I let myself hope, for the sake of the country, that they would finally join in the defense of democracy before Trump and his followers burned it all down.

It is, of course, noteworthy that the response to January 6 depended on the likes of McConnell, Graham, and other powerful Republicans who had spent decades clearing the way for Trump. Indeed, they had, themselves, risen to power on the same gloomy energy that Trump had exploited to become president. The main difference was that their appeals to racism, religion, and greed had been subtly calibrated to allow what Central Intelligence Agency officials would call "plausible deniability." Trump dropped the pretense, lacing the old nastiness with new conspiracy theories and calls to action and delivering it from a lectern decorated with the presidential seal. His followers were quickly hooked. Those who could traveled the country to mainline the rage at live rallies. Millions more accessed the stuff via online sources where they could get an adrenaline high whenever they wanted it.

The end product of all the craziness would be heard in the voices of the January 6 attackers. After he was arrested for shooting Capitol police officer Michael Fanone in the neck with a Taser, the January 6 rioter Daniel Rodriguez explained to the FBI that he'd believed the government was trying to bring down the country and he had a duty to respond to Trump's call to action. As a result, he'd joined the gang that attacked Fanone. The officer, who believed he would die during the melee, suffered a heart attack, a concussion, and a brain injury.

How had the thirty-eight-year-old Rodriguez become a man who would travel from California to Washington to commit such horrendous crimes? Well, first he had been born into a society of grossly unequal opportunity where cuts in education and job training programs made it hard for him to enter the middle class. Desperate for answers, he began tuning in to extreme-right-wing media like InfoWars shows hosted by Alex Jones. There he absorbed paranoid conspiracy theories that congealed into a vision of a satanic cabal of liberal politicians, government workers, scientists, artists, and even Bill Gates controlling everything from the weather to human fertility. Six years later, Donald Trump was himself appearing on InfoWars, assuring viewers that he would be their champion against those bent on world domination. When Trump won in 2016, it seemed the savior had come. When Trump lost his bid for reelection, Rodriguez had to believe the fix was in.

"We thought we were saving the country," said Rodriguez when he was interviewed by federal agents. "There could be casualties. That, like, if this was another Civil War, this was another 1776, another Fourth of July or something, that could be a possibility." Referring to a common trope among his confederates, Rodriguez considered himself part of the 3 percent of citizens who, like those who fought in the American Revolution, were willing to fight and die for a cause. Of course, as it was with so many historical claims made by the right-wing extremists, the 3 percent thing was not remotely accurate. In 2017 political scientist John Tures of LaGrange College published an article that outlined the facts as recognized by academics who have studied the matter. They estimate that more than 25 percent of colonial American men served on land and at sea. Considering that a 6 percent wartime service rate is considered exceptional, the 3 percent notion is a ridiculous basis for a claim of a special status that points to a much greater number of supportive citizens. But then ridiculous claims devoid of facts seem to be the norm among this crowd.

————

Rodriguez represented tens of millions of Americans who had been abused by Trump and his enablers, including, prior to January 6, Mitch McConnell, Lindsey Graham, and virtually the entire Republican establishment. For the party's leaders in Washington, condemning Trump fully and following through in the effort to hold him to account would mean opening themselves to a similar kind of accountability.

Although Trump was the champion of hate-based politics, he had not invented the game, which had been played for decades by the GOP. The original practitioners had included Richard Nixon, Ronald Reagan, Newt Gingrich, and others such as the right-wing propogandists at Fox News who had toyed with the themes Trump later pursued with heedless glee.

I can't claim to have recognized this when it was occurring. Like most people, I had been busy with my own life, and, though that included politics, my focus had been on my city and my state. Besides, no one knew that the right's turn toward an anti-government message and the reckless rhetoric of fear and anger would endure and grow. However, both had proven so effective that over time they had been adopted by nearly every Republican candidate and officeholder. Those who were interested in using government in positive ways and who remained open to bipartisanship were found in isolated spots like my state of Rhode Island, where, in 2007, Senator Lincoln Chaffee became a Democrat because he felt the GOP had abandoned him.

Decent, kind, civilized, and positive, Chaffee was, in every way, the opposite of Donald Trump. But it was Trump that the Republican Party had created as it scorned the politics of mutual respect. I felt that in order to fully repudiate him and what he had done, our GOP colleagues would have to acknowledge their party had created the conditions for his rise. This option wasn't really viable for politicians like McCarthy, McConnell, and Graham, who wanted to retain the power they held and, if possible, expand upon it.

3

THE GOP ORIGINS OF TRUMP'S TRIBALISM

As much as we might wish it weren't true, race and its implications have always been part of American politics. At our founding, southerners fought to have slaves who were not citizens be nevertheless counted as such because seats in Congress were apportioned by population. Recognized as equal to "three-fifths" of a white citizen, each slave included in the census helped the South gain more power. Slave labor contributed vastly to the rise of the American economy. In 1820, Congress determined that new states would be admitted in pairs, one slaveholding and one free, thus preserving the existing balance for decades to come.

Racism was also the driving force behind the filibuster rule in the US Senate, which allows 40 percent of the senators to kill anything that doesn't win 60 percent support. The filibuster rule is best known for letting southern senators, who were in the minority, block civil rights legislation for much of the twentieth century. In this way it is similar to the Electoral College system, which determines the outcome of presidential elections. The system apportions electors based on the number of senators and House members in each state. Because states with the largest populations have no more senators than the smallest states, the small states are overrepresented. Since less populous states are also far whiter than big ones, this means that white Americans are at an advantage in both the Senate and the Electoral College.

In the distant past, it was southern Democrats who exploited racism, which is why, for nearly a century after the Civil War, the GOP, the so-called party of Lincoln, appealed to many African Americans, as Lincoln had brought about emancipation. Southern Democrats sustained segregation. Allegiances began to change as Black southerners moved into northern cities controlled by Democrats and found that they had easier access to voting and were less threatened by violent white racists. On the national level President Lyndon Johnson cemented the bond between Black voters and the Democratic Party when he persuaded Congress to pass the Civil Rights Act of 1964 and his Voting Rights Act of 1965. With these sweeping laws he did more for the case of racial equality than anyone since Lincoln.

Johnson understood that with his two big civil rights initiatives, the party might lose the South and the support of prejudiced white voters across the country. Richard Nixon knew this too. In his successful 1968 campaign for the White House and his winning bid for reelection in 1972, his Southern Strategy involved using so-called dog-whistle terms like *welfare* and *states' rights* to signal his alignment with white voters who opposed civil rights and hated African Americans. They associated social programs with minority citizens, especially in big cities, even though the majority who depend on these programs are white.

On the heels of Nixon's success, Ronald Reagan offered his own racist signaling in 1976 and 1980. He kicked off the 1980 campaign in Philadelphia, Mississippi, a place infamous for the murder of three civil rights workers by Ku Klux Klan members in 1964. Then during the campaign he offered racist references to a Cadillac-driving "welfare queen" and a mythical "young buck" who took advantage of federal food stamps. Though they came from a grandfatherly figure with a sunny disposition, these remarks were the first shots in what would later be called the "culture war" of Republicanism.

The GOP under Reagan abandoned its long-standing commitment to a host of moderate positions. From 1940 to 1980, for example, the party had favored the proposed Equal Rights Amendment to the Constitution, which would guarantee women's equality under the law. The 1976 party platform referenced many ways women suffered discrimination and backed remedies including childcare assistance. In these positions they resembled the Democrats. In reversing this stand, Reagan drew a bright line that defied compromise. He did the same as he abandoned the bipartisan project of defending the environment, which Republican Teddy Roosevelt had begun, and replaced it with hostility toward environmental protection. And in his antiabortion fervor, the man who before *Roe v. Wade* had widened access to abortion as governor of California suddenly ended debate inside a party that was evenly divided on the subject. From 1980 forward pro-choice Republicans became a dying breed, and the opportunities for dialogue and compromise receded.

Reagan weakened our ability to work together by stressing political differences. This encouraged people to form strong identities as members of a political tribe. On his side were those who favored jobs over trees and taxpayers over welfare recipients. They thought America was just fine the way it was and that women and minorities needed no help to find equality. And of course they were for controlling women's bodies from the moment a fertilized egg divided into a handful of cells. On the other side were those of us who believed government should address serious problems that private enterprise could not. We wanted to protect the environment, the rights of women to choose abortion, and an expansive vision of equality that included people of every sexual identity, racial group, and economic status. We of course saw Republicans as heartless politicians in service to big business and religious extremists. To them we were tree huggers who hated America and wanted to give advantages to people who didn't deserve them. If this wasn't enough to kick off a culture war, nothing would be.

(When the culture war sides were being drawn, I *felt* the effects in my life before I understood them from a political perspective. As a gay man living in a time before most felt free to come out, I knew that much of the country rejected me simply because of my sexual orientation. While some Democrats might support equality, they did so with care because, like racism, anti-gay bigotry was so widespread that standing against it could mean defeat at the polls.)

After Reagan it was George H. W. Bush who, despite his Yankee, patrician bearing, exploited bigotry by using a mug shot of a Massachusetts prisoner named Willie Horton to rev up white anxiety about crime and Black men. In 1986, Horton had committed rape and armed robbery while on a weekend furlough. Bush's opponent, Michael Dukakis, had been governor during the Horton scandal. The message in the ominous TV ad featuring Horton was that evil Black men were poised to attack but George Bush could stop them.

Soon after Bush won, his campaign manager, Lee Atwater, was diagnosed with a fatal form of cancer and gave a sort of deathbed confession to a political scientist named Alexander Lamis. Lamis made public the recording of that interview, in which

Atwater revealed the knowing way in which his party played on racial division to motivate bigoted white voters. Atwater said,

> You start out in 1954 by saying, "N***er, n***er, n***er." By 1968 you can't say "n***er"—that hurts you. Backfires. So you say stuff like "forced busing," "states' rights" and all that stuff. You're getting so abstract now [that] you're talking about cutting taxes, and all these things you're talking about are totally economic things, and a byproduct of them is [that] Blacks get hurt worse than whites. And subconsciously maybe that is part of it.

As Atwater seemed to acknowledge that racism had its downside, GOP operatives looked for other forms of prejudice to inflame. In 1992 and 1996, Pat Buchanan's campaigns for the Republican presidential nomination primary brought a more openly anti-LGBTQ and anti-immigrant contender to the field of GOP hopefuls. Buchanan was proudly homophobic, and his immigrant bashing was easy to recognize. He also subscribed to conspiracy theories about a "New World Order" planned by international figures and spoke ominously of the US military planning to participate in attacks on Americans.

We all should have taken it as a seriously troubling sign when, in 1992, Buchanan captured nearly a quarter of all the primary votes cast by Republicans nationwide. In 1996 he took first place in the New Hampshire primary and also won Alaska, Missouri, and Louisiana. Although he failed to get the nomination, he proved that attacks on immigrants and the LGBTQ community plus paranoid conspiracy theories was a viable political strategy. Buchanan would eventually say that "Trump stole my playbook." Trump, who had once called out Buchanan as a bigot, would, as president, embrace him. In 2019 he even used a Buchanan quote to inflame anti-immigrant feelings, saying that our southern border "is eventually going to be militarized and defended or the United States, as we have known it, is going to cease to exist."

Take apart the warning that our country "as we have known it, is going to cease to exist" and you can see how Trump and Buchanan were playing to fear and the culture war. When they refer to the country "as we have known it," they are evoking a time when white, heterosexual Christian men predominated and enjoyed every advantage, whether they were applying to college or seeking employment. Today they still get a head start in life, but others who were once heavily penalized—immigrants, women, LGBTQ people, etc.—are less burdened. After noting what their followers had lost, Buchanan and Trump upped the ante by saying the result would be a kind of apocalypse as the country ceased to exist. This message would resonate with conservative Christians, who heard doomsday talk all the time. It would also energize believers to turn politics into an all-or-nothing war as they tried to save their country.

The mix of religion and politics became irresistible, even to more staid personalities. In 2002 the George W. Bush campaign spied the antigay feelings rampant among conservative Christians and stressed his opposition to both marriage equality and stronger hate crime laws to protect gay, lesbian, and transgender people. Bush went so far as to call for a constitutional amendment to ban same-sex marriage. He also took advantage of state-level campaigns to ban marriage equality. As conservative Christian pastors rallied the faithful to go to the polls in greater numbers, they naturally picked Bush and other Republicans running for office.

In Washington, Congressman William Dannemeyer, a Republican from California, made antigay hate the centerpiece of his politics. He published a book called *Shadow in the Land: Homosexuality in America* in which he calls gays and lesbians "the ultimate enemy" and writes that equality for the LGBTQ community will "plunge our people, and indeed the entire West, into a dark night of the soul that could last hundreds of years." Dick Armey of Texas, the number two GOP House leader, called Representative Barney Frank of Massachusetts "Barney Fag." In the Senate, Majority Leader Trent Lott, a Republican from Mississippi, said gay people are like alcoholics, all but helpless in the face of their addiction to an unacceptable sexual orientation. All of these things were expressed in the open, which meant these Capitol Hill figures thought it was to their advantage to speak this way.

When Bill Clinton, a Democrat, decided to improve things he imposed a "don't ask, don't tell" policy on the military, which supposedly put discussions of sexual orientation off-limits. Of course it also reinforced the shame attached to being gay. Otherwise, why wouldn't homosexuality be discussed? This may have been Clinton's clever way of steering clear of controversy and consequences. It's also possible that he believed he was doing something significant. Either way, it offended people like me and affirmed the bigots.

On the rungs below the presidential line on the ballot, other Republicans tried their hands at using hate and bigotry to motivate certain voters. In the House of Representatives, Newt Gingrich, Tom Tancredo, Michele Bachmann, and Steve King were the most recognized in this group as they used scaremongering rhetoric about LGBTQ people, minorities, and immigrants. GOP Senator Strom Thurmond of South Carolina was so courtly in his prejudice that his biography was titled *Strom: The Sweet Old Bigot*. His colleague from North Carolina, Jesse Helms, could also seem a man of gentle manner, but then he would call gay people "weak, morally sick wretches," and you knew who he really was. (In his first foray into politics, as a campaign aide, he helped a candidate who won with a racist appeal summarized in a handbill titled "White People Wake Up," which warned of the dangers of "negroes working beside you, your wife and daughters.")

Watching from the sidelines, Donald Trump couldn't help but notice how well bigotry worked. He tested it in public appearances, where he complained about the supposed job-market advantages of Black people and whined that tribal leaders who run casinos don't really "look like Indians." When five Hispanic and Black teens were arrested in the so-called Central Park Jogger assault case, he took out huge advertisements calling for their execution. His final test came with the presidency of Barack Obama, whom Trump worked hard to delegitimize with repeated suggestions that he was not American born and was therefore ineligible to hold the office. This birtherism, as it was known, energized those who wanted to delegitimize Obama. It proved to Trump that he could be more overt with his racism when he finally ran for office himself.

No campaign since segregationist George Wallace's had featured the racial bigotry the Trump campaign displayed in 2016. He announced his candidacy with a diatribe against brown-skinned immigrants and never stopped pressing this issue. His anti-Muslim attitude was plain to see as he spread lies about how American Muslims celebrated the 9/11 terror attacks and announced that "Islam hates us." Trump's speeches and the slogans chanted at his rallies dripped with misogyny directed at Hillary Clinton. Once he was in office, his bigotry became more evident. A Black football player who knelt to protest racism became, in Trump's words, "a son of a bitch," and African nations were, he said, "shithole countries." When he was vexed by a few Black and brown members of Congress, he declared they should "go back" to the countries they came from even though nearly all were American born.

Having prepared the political ground with their own less overt expression of hate, most GOP leaders chose not to criticize their president as he wounded the country with his racism. Those who did speak against Trump found themselves targets of his counterattacks, which were then taken up by his followers, who did their best to make life miserable for Republican dissenters. As Trump voiced aloud the bigotry that had simmered beneath the surface of too many previous GOP political campaigns, he put the presidential seal of approval on the racism we'd hoped was in decline. So it was that Confederate battle flags were waved at Trump rallies and his supporters screamed racist slogans as they descended on a historically Black university outside Philadelphia. In North Carolina his loyalists cried, "White power" at an antiracism rally in North Carolina, and reports of hate crimes rose 20 percent during his term in office. Researchers found that local incidents of racial violence jumped dramatically in places where Trump held a rally. After an anti-immigrant gunman killed twenty-two in El Paso and Trump said, "My rhetoric brings people together," ABC News reported on a dozen hate crimes whose perpetrators had "hailed Trump" either before or during their crimes.

The intense loyalty of Trump's followers demonstrated that what he was doing could work, if all you were interested in was partisan politics. Yes, his divisive talk and actions made others feel distressed and angry and made governing in a way that could solve America's problems impossible. But Republicans had made doing nothing the hallmark of their party for nearly forty years. They had devised a long-running strategy that called for complaining about how Washington failed to act, winning office based on this complaint, and then blocking every effort made to clear the logjams that frustrated the American people. There was something diabolically brilliant in this approach, and all it required was a willingness to see everyday Americans struggle and suffer, year after year, while you ignored your responsibility to help and actively thwarted those who tried.

I had seen the effects of this in Rhode Island, where insufficient federal funding for education, economic development, health care, and childcare meant that people who lived in places that had been abandoned by jewelry and textile manufacturing companies seeking cheap labor abroad were left to fend for themselves. Without the taxes that had been paid by mills and factories, places like Pawtucket and Central Falls lost revenues for schools, police, and other services. But while they had been hurt by events beyond their control, many of the residents in these places heard that government couldn't help them and took the message personally. They were made to feel that they were responsible for their situation and they should be ashamed to seek help. Outside these communities, among my middle-class and wealthier friends, I heard from many a kind of heartlessness that shocked me. They didn't just blame less fortunate people, they rejected the idea that the rest of us had much of an obligation to them as fellow Americans.

Before some life experiences changed her mind, my sister Roberta felt much like this. (This made her such an anomaly in the family that we joked about her being dropped on her head as a baby.) Roberta had worked from the time she was fifteen and was always committed to her work. She and her husband had devoted every penny they made to their family. She always assumed a person's situation was mostly the product of their own decisions. She had advantages as a white person who came from an upper-middle-class family and who lived in a community where jobs were plentiful and people like her got them. If she hadn't been guaranteed success, she had at least been guaranteed a shot at it. But in talking with me about, for example, cases where the courts paid me to represent poor defendants even after they lost their appeal, she resented what she regarded as handouts.

"Why am I paying to defend him?" she asked back then, and nothing I said about constitutional rights or freedom moved her. In fact, court-appointed lawyers are generally underpaid, and their clients often receive the bare minimum of attention because their lawyers are overwhelmed. If this is a handout, it's not much of one. The same was true of most programs to aid the poor, but after Reagan, people felt free to accept that the poor were undeserving and that everyone in America had an equal chance. As a gay man who saw in his work lots of people who had been set back again and again by forces they didn't even understand, I knew this wasn't true.

4

LET'S ALL HATE THE GOVERNMENT

The American people first heard, from a voice of great authority, that they should hate the United States government in the 1980s. The voice was Ronald Reagan's. Having gained office with repeated attacks on the very idea of government, he blamed it for almost every problem faced by the nation as a whole and by individual citizens. His attitude was captured in a witticism he offered in 1986: "The nine most terrifying words in the English language are, 'I'm from the government, and I'm here to help.'"

The fact that Reagan ran the government at the time, and that it had achieved much under his leadership, meant little to most who supported him. Forgotten were his job training program, his efforts against organized crime, his administration's aid to victims of hurricanes and wildfires and the federally led advances in highway safety that had reduced deaths per mile in every year of his presidency but one. Under Reagan the government had funded research that would yield the first drug to treat AIDS (despite his initial resistance) and usher in the age of the internet. Instead of celebrating what we could accomplish together, Reagan played on the distrust many feel for big, distant institutions while flattering people with the suggestion that they could do just about everything on their own if only what many called the "damn government" would get out of the way.

No one liked the antigovernment message more than a growing number of conservative, probusiness activists who had taken to heart a call to arms issued by tobacco industry lawyer—and future United States Supreme Court justice—Lewis Powell back in 1971. In a memo requested by the chamber of commerce, Powell announced that free enterprise itself was under attack from many quarters and that major corporations were losing public support. Powell urged business leaders and the superrich to infiltrate the press, universities, branches of the government, and a host of other institutions in order to increase their influence. Where they couldn't gain a foothold, he suggested, they should fund alternatives, like their own press outlets, that would relentlessly promote their own biased views.

Powell's memo inspired explosive growth in political donations by the superrich, a flourishing of right-wing policy groups, and an astounding rise in the number of lobbyists in Washington. In the 1970s only a handful of corporations and organizations paid full-time lobbyists to try to influence Congress and the White House. Those who favored causes like the environment and consumer rights were roughly equal in number to the ones representing business. Today more than 11,500 officially registered lobbyists work in Washington. Thousands of additional people—lawyers, public relations people, think tank analysts—also pressure lawmakers, but in ways that don't meet the legal definition of lobbying. About 95 percent of these people work on behalf of business interests, and the $2.6 billion spent on this effort every year exceeds the $2 billion spent to run the House and Senate. It's no wonder. The lobbyists employ more people than work for the government on Capitol Hill and pay them higher salaries.

What do the companies get for their money? Well, since they measure everything on a profit-and-loss basis, I believe they must profit from this effort because otherwise they would stop doing it. But they don't. Time and again I have heard from companies, and corporate political action committees, that make it clear there are campaign donations to be had if only I would accept them. No one ever says that I would then owe them my vote on one issue or another, but at the very least they want access to me.

The lobbyists aren't necessarily bad people. (And my colleagues who accept their donations don't generally consider them a problem.) But the lobbyists are not concerned with what happens outside their industries, and so they often use highly questionable talking points about, say, how much their drug company invests in research and how therefore they shouldn't have to negotiate prices with Medicare and Medicaid. When they make this point to me, I remind them of the federally funded basic science they get for free and ask them just where fairness comes in when they charge three or four times the price of production for a product like insulin, which was patented a hundred years ago.

I don't hear much from corporate lobbyists, but I have noticed their wily ways and can show you how they don't just want protection from regulation. They want us to create programs that will pour federal money directly into their coffers. Consider the example of the drug industry's lobbying for the prescription benefit called Part D that was added to Medicare as George W. Bush was beginning his reelection campaign. (The bill to create this benefit was going down in defeat when the Republican Speaker of the House decided to stop the clock for hours. He then twisted enough arms to win.)

Part D was dreamed up by the pharmaceutical industry and

the Bush White House to accomplish three goals: provide medi-
cation to seniors, bond a bloc of them as voters to Bush, and create
a massive profit stream for the drug industry. The last part was
guaranteed by a passage in the law that barred the government
from using its buying power to negotiate lower prices. The result
was a $20 billion annual windfall for the pharmaceutical industry.
This is an astounding rate of return on the roughly $23 million
per year big drug companies spend on lobbyists. And every time
some of us in Congress attempt to change the arrangement, the
companies mobilize to defeat us with the aid of members of the
House and Senate who accept their campaign donations.

The corporations and superrich individuals who donate to
Republicans generally want the tax cuts that are skewed to benefit them the most, insisting that as the wealthy invest their gains,
others benefit from a "trickle-down" effect. This never happens.
Instead, for example, Reagan's cuts began a decade-long period
when the wealthy made big gains in income and net worth while
everyone else was left behind. Instead of the boom in tax revenues predicted by the GOP's economic fantasists, we got a drop
in revenue, and the federal debt rose. With cries of "Socialism!"
the GOP blocked national health care and childcare subsidies of
the sort available around the world. As you might expect, everyone but the wealthy found themselves on a treadmill of working
harder just to stay even.

Too busy to sort through the details of tax policies and how
corporations were shifting the costs of health care and retirement
onto workers (bye-bye pensions!) many people simply cast the
blame at Washington, where the GOP's new devotion to wrecking the machinery was making it impossible to get things done.
With Reagan's nine words in mind, more and more Americans
wondered if the government created, as Lincoln said, "of the

people, by the people, and for the people," which had produced
the freest, most prosperous, and most powerful nation in history,
could be trusted. It worked. As Reagan began his second term,
reliable polls found that 44 percent of Americans trusted government to generally do the right thing. By his last year in office, the
number was 40 percent. During the Trump administration, it fell
to 17 percent. Political conservatives were least confident in the
government, and by 2021, just 5 percent said they trusted it would
do the right thing.

How had trust fallen so far? Politicians had persuaded many
that the government was at best incompetent and at worst
malevolent. Where possible they had starved it of the resources
it needed to function, and then, whenever scandal arose, they
reacted with glee. Lost in their declarations about corruption was
the fact that since 1961, Republican administrations had suffered
thirty-eight times—yes, thirty-eight times—more corruption
convictions than administrations run by Democrats. It wasn't the
government per se that people should evaluate warily, it was government in GOP hands.

It was, of course, too much to ask that everyday citizens keep
track of corruption scorecards or research every claim made by
an affable, even genial leader like Reagan. Many simply believed
him and, with the aid of biased outlets like Fox News, accepted the
government-can't-be-trusted argument. Add repeated, unfounded,
and hysterical claims about voter fraud, and it's easy to see why
much of the country was willing to abandon its faith in the system
of voting and elections that determined how government would
be formed and run. Thus, by the Trump era, it wasn't just Washington that people mistrusted, but also democracy itself.

In June 2021 a *Washington Post* poll found that slightly more
than one-fifth of Donald Trump's supporters disagree with the

statement "Democracy is the best form of government." Nearly 60 percent said they were pessimistic about the future of American democracy. These findings came after their man Trump had issued countless claims that our voting system is "rigged" and every investigation and legal review of the 2020 election had determined it had been the fairest in history. Later in 2021, some of the former president's most fervent supporters believed that he would somehow be restored to power, despite there being no mechanism for such a thing to occur. Millions subscribed to extreme theologies and spiritual concepts that made them believe this would be accomplished by supernatural means. How could so many Americans believe such a thing, and pray for it to occur, if they hadn't been trained in a kind of political paranoia?

5

NOW LET'S HATE EACH OTHER

It is, sadly, a fact that political appeals to negative emotions like fear and hatred are generally more powerful, and effective, than those featuring love and hope. In 1964, Lyndon Johnson had to use his nuclear apocalypse TV ad only once to make huge numbers of people terrified of trusting the hawkish Barry Goldwater with the nation's nuclear arsenal. However, after the Cold War ended in 1989, with no existential threat looming overseas, those who practiced the politics of fear had to energize their side with warnings about domestic enemies who were not true Americans.

Ronald Reagan was too old-fashioned and decent to turn Democrats into the kind of enemy—*They're communists! They're socialists!*—that would let the GOP practice politics as war. Georgia congressman (and future Speaker of the House) Newt Gingrich never had such scruples. He began his political career as a Republican environmentalist who could talk to both Democrats and GOPers. However, after two failed campaigns for Congress, he transformed himself into a fire-breathing radical. He downplayed the policies and programs he once favored and stressed that liberals and Democrats were "traitors" and "thugs" out to "destroy our country." His long-term project was to destroy the bipartisanship that made it possible for Congress to do its work and then seek power by campaigning against a gridlocked House.

As his method worked and bipartisanship was destroyed, Gingrich pushed the GOP to "have no shame" as it chased power by exploiting everything from homophobia to religious bigotry. Under Democrats "we in America could experience the joys of Soviet-style brutality and murdering of women and children," he announced, adding that Speaker of the House Tip O'Neill "may not understand freedom versus slavery."

With his attacks Gingrich hoped to break Americans' habit of hating Congress in general but liking their particular representative. Democrats had relied on this dynamic to maintain control of the House since 1957. Gingrich became determined to break the cycle by intensifying the public's unhappiness with the institution as a whole and then attacking individual members as part of the problem. To do this he would organize colleagues to refuse to work with Democrats in any way and undermine those who did. With Gingrich and his colleagues gumming up the works, Congress couldn't deal with the problems affecting the country, and public frustration with this inaction grew. It boiled down to this: *Democrats control Congress. Congress isn't working. Let's throw them all out.*

For a while insiders wondered if Gingrich really was serious about wrecking Congress for his own partisan purposes. To demonstrate that he was, he went after Illinois Representative Robert Michel, his own party's leader in the House. Known as one of the most decent and honest people on Capitol Hill, Michel had led many bipartisan efforts to address the country's problems. The problem for Gingrich was that this success made it harder for him to prove Washington was broken and teach voters to blame Democratic politicians and to hate them and their supporters.

Certain that Michel's successes would hurt his own campaign of rage, Gingrich collected enough chits from younger members that he could use them to stop Michel. He then picked a moment to demonstrate his power. It happened in 1990 when Michel, working on behalf of the first President Bush, engineered a bipartisan effort to cut the federal deficit. Deficit reduction was a central tenet of traditional conservative Republican policy, but Gingrich rallied his troops to thwart the effort so he could continue to lambaste official Washington, including many in his own party, as feckless and corrupt.

Gingrich had sway with many of his peers because he had a plan for winning control of the House and was able to help like-minded Republicans with campaign funding and lessons in campaigning. The methods were taught in tape-recorded lessons that showed candidates how to incite voters with emotionally resonant language and claim the mantle of savior for themselves. All across the country, Gingrich's disciples used the same key words. When referring to themselves and their party the prescribed vocabulary included "truth, moral, courage, reform, prosperity, crusade." When talking about Democrats the key words included "decay, failure, collapse... destroy, sick, pathetic...shallow, traitors, sensationalists."

With the aid of like-minded agitators in the media like radio host Rush Limbaugh, Gingrich and his army of allies offered voters a continuous lineup of enemies to hate. Beginning with Democrats in office, they worked their way through various segments of society—unions, "Hollywood," academia, science, schoolteachers, civil rights supporters, feminists, etc.—until it became clear that all true patriots had an obligation to hate everyone who wasn't aligned with Gingrich-style Republicanism. People with different ideas were not well-intentioned fellow citizens. They were threats.

Observing from a distance, political scientists and historians of all stripes—conservative, liberal, nonpartisan—tended to reference bombing and arson as they described what Gingrich did. Long after his own ethics scandals and political failures forced Gingrich to resign, Princeton historian Julian E. Zelizer assessed him in a biography that was also a study of the modern GOP. The title of the book, *Burning Down the House*, said it all.

6

HATRED'S LITTLE HELPERS

The rise of Trump and the January 6 attack would not have been possible without the aid of media figures, technology executives, and religious leaders who played key roles in ruining our civic life by teaching Americans to fear, distrust, and hate each other.

The door to extremism on the airwaves was opened by pro-business deregulation campaigns that in the 1980s did away with the so-called Fairness Doctrine, which required broadcasters to offer equal time to competing views, and then in the 1990s relaxed limits that had been imposed on the owners of radio and TV stations. These regulations had, for years, represented the public's interest in a resource—the broadcasting spectrum—that was widely regarded as a public asset. With these impediments gone, broadcasters discovered great profits in inflammatory programs that kept listeners and viewers coming back, day after day.

With lies, distortions, and constant hype, the broadcasters first boosted Republicans in contests with Democrats and then began directing them on the positions they could adopt and the votes they might cast. If you were not loyal enough to the broadcasters, they declared you a RINO (Republican in name only), which was a warning that you were risking excommunication. All this began in the Reagan era with people like syndicated radio host Rush Limbaugh, who declared he was an "entertainer," and evolved to the point where a paranoid conspiracy theorist like Alex Jones, who talked of weather weapons and lizard people, interviewed Donald Trump.

In addition to the new forms of media, the politics of fear and its offspring hatred got support in the arena of crusading religion. The TV evangelist Jerry Falwell pioneered the Christian Right movement with his Moral Majority organization, which at its peak claimed four million members. Founded as Reagan began his 1980 push for the White House, the organization spent $10 million on ads benefiting him in 1980 and gave invaluable assistance by mobilizing conservative Christians to vote for him.

Adamantly bigoted against LGBTQ Americans, Falwell promoted bizarre ideas about how gays intended to "recruit" young people to become homosexual, as if homosexuality were a belief system rather than an inborn trait. He railed against efforts to repeal laws that discriminated against LGBTQ communities. All this he justified with the inflammatory call to battle against "militant homosexuals" who have plans "to transform America into a modern Sodom and Gomorrah."

With his appeals bringing in millions of dollars and his fame spreading, Falwell was joined by another Virginia-based televangelist, Pat Robertson, who added feminists to the enemies list because they supposedly encouraged "women to leave their husbands, kill their children, practice witchcraft, destroy capitalism and become lesbians." Unabashed in his partisan attachment to the Republican Party, Robertson ran for president in the 1988 GOP primaries on a largely religious platform. After he lost, he converted his campaign into a permanent political organizing force.

When Reagan left the White House, the moralizing preachers ignored Newt Gingrich's infidelities, two divorces, and three marriages and embraced him as one of their own. Gingrich and the televangelists demonstrated for a future candidate named Trump that many conservative Christians don't really care about the personal morals of politicians who support their causes. What they want is for someone to affirm their status as the truest Americans and then win elections so that the evil others—anyone who didn't share their faith and politics—will be stopped.

As Gingrich was joined by the inflammatory media and political Christians, the decorum, decency, and mutual respect that governed much of politics for the past century were gradually abandoned. A vast new subculture of right-wing entertainment, and religion, was developed and populated by millions of Americans who believed that the threat they faced was so great that they needed to engage in politics as warfare.

Planned Parenthood advocates "every form of bestiality," Pat Robertson told them, and mainline Protestants like Episcopalians and Congregationalists embrace "the spirit of the Antichrist." According to Gingrich, were the "sick" Democrats to hold power, "We may literally see our freedom decay and decline." And Limbaugh falsely reported that White House aide Vince Foster, who committed suicide, had been murdered in a secret apartment owned by Hillary Clinton.

If you hear notes that harmonize with the craziness of the Trump years, you've got a good ear. For decades those on the far right have trained much of the country to believe that America is in grave danger and only they can save it. In this context it becomes easier to understand how a man like Daniel Rodriguez might be moved to grab a knife, pack a small bag, and join tens of thousands who went to Washington to "save" their country, participating in the violent attack on the US Capitol because he felt he had no choice.

7

THE INEVITABLE RESULT

Daniel Rodriguez was born during the Reagan administration and reached adulthood amid the grief, fear, and confusion that followed the 9/11 attacks. He struggled in school, had trouble finding a job that would bring him into the middle class, and, as he considered explanations for his troubles, found them on radio talk shows.

He began with programs that suggested government conspiracies were keeping the truth about things like unidentified flying objects from reaching the public. Then came right-wing political talkers like Rush Limbaugh who delivered, every day, entertaining diatribes against liberals, feminists, and Democrats. He concluded that Democrats lacked common sense and that their programs, which always seemed to exclude him, were the source of his personal woes. The solution finally came in the person of Donald Trump, who appealed to Rodriguez with plain talk that affirmed his assumptions and fed his fear and anger. In donning a red "Make America Great Again" cap and attending events, he found acceptance, camaraderie, and a purpose.

After living in the Trump community for years, Rodriguez had trouble believing that his man had lost the election by more than seven million votes, as the media reported. Everyone he knew had voted for Trump, and didn't the president always say the press lied? It was easy for him to accept the president's claim that he had been cheated and easy for him to heed the call to come protest in Washington on January 6, and, in retrospect, it is easy to see how he wound up battling police and electrocuting Capitol police officer Michael Fanone with a Taser. Rodriguez explained it to the federal agents who interviewed him for prosecutors, and in the transcript of the interview what transpired appeared to have been inevitable. "Trump called us," he told the agents. "We thought we were saving the country. I thought I was helping to save the country."

Struck by what he had done to Fanone, who suffered a heart attack, Rodriguez said, "I'm an asshole." To a degree he was. But I also think he was a guy born into an America that had gutted education and social programs that would have helped him overcome the poverty of his youth. He then came under the influence of those who said he should blame others for his troubles and summoned him to action under false premises. He wasn't the real asshole. They were.

Although the January 6 attackers each arrived with their own story, media profiles of those in the mob suggest that many were, like Rodriguez, men who felt they were somehow victims of a society that denied them the status—good jobs, community respect, a secure future—they deserved. They blamed Democrats, liberals, and an amorphous cabal of evil actors for their plight and had agreed with Donald Trump when he surveyed America's problems and declared, "I alone can fix it."

What Rodriguez didn't understand was that the politics of the last thirty years had made life harder for most Americans. While countries like Germany responded to global competition with intensive worker training, apprenticeship programs, and increased educational opportunities, we abandoned a generation of workers who had lost high-wage jobs that had given them a sense of pride. They were told there was no money to pay for training and education even as the GOP repeatedly slashed taxes for the rich. In the meantime Republicans also killed efforts to raise the minimum wage. Hourly pay for the typical worker declined to the point where, adjusted for inflation, they made less in 2020 than they would have in 1974. In the same time period, the richest Americans saw their incomes and wealth skyrocket.

According to the RAND Corporation (hardly a liberal think tank), since 1974 the top 10 percent seized an extra $50 trillion—yes, *trillion* with a *T*—in earnings that were lost by everyone else. When the RAND scientists considered how things would be different if the pre-'74 distribution of earnings had been maintained, they discovered that instead of $36,000 in 2018, the median American income would be $57,000. The median income for the top 1 percent would drop from $1,160,000 to $549,000.

But wait, it gets worse. The same people who lost ground economically as the GOP put its thumb on the scale for the rich also suffered more under our patchwork health-care system—which the right refused to fix—and have seen the effects of climate change ravage their communities. They are overburdened by college loans, underserved when it comes to education and job training, and far more likely to be one of the 316 people who are shot (106 of whom are killed) on a typical day in America.

In my years as an official in Rhode Island, the most difficult days came when constituents' children were shot and I saw them at hospitals and funerals. Too often, children who were not even teenagers yet were caught in gang conflicts that neither they nor their families had anything to do with. In one case I'll never forget, I tried to comfort a mother whose twelve-year-old daughter had just happened to be on a sidewalk where one young man decided to shoot another and she was hit. There was no good answer I could offer as her mother kept asking: Why?

I had no good answer for anyone who lost a loved one as guns flooded our state because I couldn't explain why our legislature put firearm access ahead of the very lives of our people. For some reason the man who was then Speaker of the House was loyal to the local chapter of the National Rifle Association and just wouldn't move any legislation to regulate guns more strictly. I know there are constitutional issues, but courts have allowed some restrictions, including comprehensive background checks, waiting periods for buyers, and limits on the kinds of guns people can purchase. And there is no doubt that a majority of Americans, including most gun owners, support them. Still the years pass with deaths approaching forty thousand per year, every year, and the right to bear arms continues to trump the victims' right to live.

For decades Republicans, in thrall to the National Rifle Association, have blocked efforts to enact gun safety laws. They have done this by periodically winding up hunters and other gun owners with cries of "They're coming for your guns!" In fact, no one ever tried to take away legally owned firearms. However, this claim became a staple of their culture war. Joined with their determined effort to cut every program that helped people climb the economic ladder, the right's gun fetish politics—which some Democrats enabled because they feared the NRA—meant that poorer people would have more guns, and gun violence, but less of a chance to move up in the world.

The link between gun deaths and the lack of social mobility was proven by researcher Daniel Kim at Northeastern University, who studied firearm deaths in every census tract in the country. He found that as income and wealth drop, firearm deaths rise.

When they rise, thanks to good wages, good schools, and safety net programs to help with emergencies, gun deaths decline. The best way to find safety wasn't, as the GOP suggests, more guns for everyone. It was social mobility. Kim's research suggests that safety belongs to the upper classes.

Nothing I'm saying here should surprise anyone. No matter the time or place, those who are better off have always been able to escape the social problems afflicting everyone else. They buy access to the best schools, the safest neighborhoods, and the most pristine environments. Should they suffer a health problem or a climate event that destroys their property, they will have the means to get care when they get sick or rebuild after a storm or flood.

Historically the kind of economic and political inequality we've begun to see in America has led to oligarchy, or rule by the moneyed elite. Republicans and most especially Trump succeeded in creating an oligarch class, blocking almost everything we tried to do to help other Americans and persuading people that we were to blame for the fact that things didn't get better. We knew how to make things better: by creating a fair tax system, funding education, encouraging technology development, maintaining and improving our infrastructure, and more. They blocked us at every opportunity.

Aided by a powerful media chorus—from Fox News to the deranged conspiracy theorist Alex Jones of InfoWars—they relied on false assumptions to create a culture war to divide us and distract us from the fact that the status quo benefited them. Whether it was warnings of a "war" on Christmas or the invented threat of a global government run by the United Nations, inflammatory appeals bonded certain voters with the Republicans who spouted them.

By the time of the January 6 attack, tens of millions of working-class Americans had embraced the idea that their problems were caused by conspiracies involving the very people who had spent their lives in government service, science, medicine, and other fields devoted to the public good. Against all evidence, which shows that our government is vastly more honest, transparent, and trustworthy than private enterprises, they thought that American officials were plotting against them.

Read the FBI interview with Daniel Rodriguez and you discover a man who had, amid his own struggles to establish himself in life, come under the influence of Jones and then the QAnon conspiracy theory. He believed he was part of the "3 percent" that could overthrow a supposedly corrupt government and restore Trump to power. Toward that end he and friends practiced with firearms and supplied themselves with protective gear. Never once did he think of himself as the terrorist he proved to be on January 6. "I thought I was a good guy," he said. Here he is, in his own words:

> I just saw that there's a—there's people that have taken over this country from inside, globalist and unelected officials, elitists, you know? People who are obsessed with power and control and, you know...if you go to LA, you see homeless people and then you see a Ferrari or Rolls-Royce drive by them....
>
> They were killing Trump supporters, shooting them in the head and beating them up in school and the public, everything, right? So it's like—I kept thinking that we were going to go to, like, a civil war and it's going to go hot....
>
> So it started, like, triggering reactions in my mind that, like, you know, this country is—I mean, that's how Rome fell....

This might sound weird to you guys, but I would pray for—to God to give me the words and the wisdom and—direct me to the right path and to protect me and to help to just give me the words to help other people and to open their eyes.

Much of what Rodriguez, and millions of other Trumpists who depended on extremist media and Facebook for their facts, believed was, of course, wrong. No one was killing Trump supporters. In fact, the opposite was true. The government had never prepared for a massive assault on civilian citizens. There was no globalist cabal bent on controlling the world. And the election had not been stolen.

However, by January 2021, Republicans in Congress and in offices nationwide had formed a destructive chorus that backed Trump's claims of fraud. When Rodriguez heard Trump call for supporters to come to Washington and say that it "will be wild," he decided not to fly because "there was an idea that, if anybody needed to take anything, like, weed maybe, knife, pepper spray, that stuff's not going to be able to get on the plane. I took weed. I took a knife. I took pepper spray." Once he was in Washington, he listened to inflammatory speeches, and when Trump told people to march on the Capitol, promising to join them himself (he didn't), Rodriguez was near the front of the march. When the Trumpists began fighting police officers, he worked his way to an entry door where hand-to-hand combat was underway. He told the FBI he regretted firing the Taser and couldn't explain why he had done it:

I thought that Trump was going to stay president and they were going to find all this crooked stuff. . . . We thought

that we did something good. We were getting Nancy
[House Speaker Nancy Pelosi]—somebody was—it was
rumored that Nancy Pelosi got her laptop stolen and that
they found all this evidence on it. . . . We thought we were
being used as a part of a plan to save the country, to save
America, save the Constitution and the election. . . .

Am I mental? Am I just that stupid? I mean, yes . . . are
we all that stupid that we thought we were going to go
do this and save the country and it was all going to be fine
after? We really thought that. That's so stupid, huh?

Throughout his life, Daniel Rodriguez and people like him
had been victimized by the GOP drive, in the cause of "freedom," to burn down the government and force everyone to fend
for themselves. As the income gap between the rich and everyone else widened into a chasm and public services suffered, life
became more difficult for the middle class and the poor. Wages,
upward mobility, and even life expectancy began to decline, with
men showing the most significant losses.

As the economy demanded higher skills and education levels,
fewer men applied to college. Enrollments are now 60 percent
female. Many of the males who decline to go to college cite the
skyrocketing cost and debt burden students face because—you
guessed it—we failed to support higher education with adequate
funds. On the occasions when we Democrats controlled government, we did too little to compensate, although it should be said
that Senate Republicans used the archaic filibuster rule, which
allows a minority to block legislation, to kill most of what we
tried to do.

Although the effects of GOP policies piled up on people in
obvious ways, the party ignored it and continued to emphasize

personal responsibility. Their message was that people who suffered were responsible for their own pain and should pull themselves up by their bootstraps. Those who couldn't were shamed,
even though they lived in a country that ignored the reality of
global competition.

In recent decades, as Daniel Rodriguez tried to establish himself in adult life, we spent less government money per capita on
higher education than countries like Poland, France, Canada, and
even Turkey and less on childcare and early education than all
but two of the world's top thirty-eight developed countries. How
were Americans supposed to keep up when others had access to
schooling and childcare that made it possible for them to improve
their skills and balance work and home responsibilities? According to the Organisation for Economic Co-operation and Development, the US doesn't crack the top ten in their standard-of-living
rankings. We stand at number fourteen, well behind number ten
Canada and number one Australia.

We were last number one in health care back in 1980, when Ronald Reagan was elected and began all the cutting of taxes for the
wealthy and reductions in spending that helped everyone else.
As America fell behind much of the rest of the developed world,
Republican politicians said it was treasonous to say so. They kept
shouting, "We're number one!" even though we weren't. When
called on this deceit, they insisted that everyone should be the
sole master of his or her own fate. They killed as much of the
government as possible, called it "freedom," and said that if you
don't thrive, you have no one else to blame.

In the dog-eat-dog world he was born into, Rodriguez went
from a struggling young man burdened by all the problems
Republican politicians refuse to address to a very confused fellow

whose search for answers led him down the rabbit hole of conspiracy theories. He finally reached the place where, along with
millions of others, he believed the countless lies told by Trump.

I have met many Daniels in my travels around the country
and even some in my district. Having been taught to fear others and blame them for their troubles, most are stubborn in their
belief that America is in great peril and they could never trust
someone like me—a Democrat who serves in Congress—to
understand them and be interested in their problems. One of the
more memorable encounters for me happened a few years ago
outside a school in my district, where a woman looked at me and
said, "You don't want to talk to me."

"Oh yeah?" I answered. "Why not?"

"We don't agree on anything."

"What do you think we don't agree on?"

She told me she was upset about "illegal aliens getting everything for free." By this she meant welfare payments, food stamps,
and other government benefits for the poor or unemployed.

I think she was surprised when I said, "Well, actually, if you're
in the country illegally, you are not entitled to any government
benefits, which is actually the law. You're not entitled to Social
Security and workers' compensation, or unemployment. The one
exception is education; the US Supreme Court has said we have to
educate every child regardless of their immigration status."

Taken aback, she said she had been in a public assistance
line, heard people speaking Spanish, and concluded they must be
here illegally. This was possible, but unlikely. However, the idea
that the typical immigrant has sneaked into the country and is
now taking advantage of the "system" is widespread and held by
lots of people who fear our country can't accommodate them.
Since the woman I encountered spoke of standing in a line for

public assistance, she had struggled and likely felt self-conscious seeking help. Many Americans tend to shame anyone who can't go it alone. Those people who get assistance discover it's barely enough for them to survive. Put yourself in their place and you might think there'd be more for you if these undocumented newcomers weren't gaming the system.

Two other factors contribute to anti-immigrant feelings. The first is our silence about previous waves of immigration. Nearly every Irish American, Italian American, German American, etc., etc., is descended from someone who got some sort of help upon arriving here. They got access to free classes to learn English, put their kids in public schools, and, yes, accepted welfare. And with each wave, many of the people who were already here felt anxiety about the changes newcomers brought, and demagogues exploited this anxiety, converting it to fear and anger. In short, we have been here before and were always enriched, not damaged, by new Americans.

We are now in the demagogue phase. When considering a member of Congress named Alexandria Ocasio-Cortez, Fox News host Laura Ingraham declared, "The America we know and love doesn't exist" because of both "illegal and legal immigration." Her colleague Tucker Carlson says our country is "dirtier" because of immigrants who have made the country too crowded. These messages squawk out of televisions in countless homes and public spaces where Fox is on all day long. They are shared person to person and proclaimed by Donald Trump—he called immigration an "invasion"—until they are accepted as common sense.

In May of 2019, Trump whipped a crowd into anger as he attacked immigrants and asked, "How do you stop these people?"

"Shoot them!" shouted a man in the crowd, provoking some laughter and cheers.

Two months later a young white man took a gun to a Walmart in El Paso on a Saturday morning, when the store was typically crowded with Mexican American families. He killed twenty people, wounded dozens more, and left behind a manifesto about the "Hispanic invasion of Texas." He said that Hispanic Americans "is [sic] willing to return to their home countries if given the right incentive. An incentive that myself and many other patriotic Americans will provide." Much of the manifesto echoed Trump's rhetoric as he announced he was commencing "the fight for America."

The realities in the shooter's life did not support his claims. Was his community being invaded? No. It had been 11 percent Hispanic in the 2010 census and would be 11.9 percent Hispanic in the 2020 count. Although he scapegoated Hispanic people for his personal problems, his troubles finding work and a direction in his life were of his own making, as he himself revealed. When he was a young man, his plan had been to "go with the wind." Later, as our political atmosphere was poisoned with anti-immigrant hate, he developed a new attitude. Based on his rhetoric, he was heavily influenced by Trump and his media echo chamber. The first page of his manifesto included four statements mirroring Trump's posts on Twitter and three from right-wing media. And I consider it more than a coincidence that earlier in 2019 Trump had given a speech, in El Paso, during which he cried out, "Murders, murders, murders. Killings, murders!" as he circled the topic of immigration.

Although it takes a certain mental disturbance to move from political outrage to mass murder, it didn't help that for the first time in history we had a fearmongering, anti-immigrant president whose disturbing words were echoed continuously on television, in print, and on the internet, where others mixed them with their own bits of hate. The process seemed never-ending, with contributors continuously trying to attract attention with more and more outlandish statements.

The anti-immigrant fear, anger, and hatred at the center of right-wing politics had become so widely dispersed that even in a community that was 92 percent white and where the median income was just a little below the state average, a lot of folks were worked up about immigrants. Even though we lived in a country with more guns than people, she seemed like an ordinary person who would never turn violent. Of course I couldn't imagine that thousands who shared the same news would one day besiege the US Capitol, battle the police for hours, seize control of the building, and attempt to halt the certification of a presidential election. No. I couldn't imagine that.

PART II

THE GOOD, THE BAD, AND THE REAL

In which we discover that humans are imperfect, but we should always encourage our better angels.

8

HOPE, BUT ALSO CRIME

There's Hope Street, Hope High School, Hope Village, Mount Hope, Hope Valley, and the Wall of Hope. "Hope" is Rhode Island's one-word motto and it's plastered on everything from an oil company in West Warwick to an alpaca farm in Warren where, in the nineteenth century, the National Hope Bank stood at the corner of Water and Church Streets.

Rhode Island's hope thing goes back to 1664, when this one word and a simple image of a golden anchor were used for the official seal of what was then called the Colony of Rhode Island and Providence Plantations. (More about the plantations in a few pages.) Historians believe the choice was inspired by a passage in the Old Testament: "Hope we have as an anchor of the soul."

The faith that helped form Rhode Island wasn't the cruel kind found in neighboring Massachusetts, where being different could get you hanged as a witch. Progressive for its time, the Rhode Island colony was dedicated to absolute freedom of (and from) religion and the separation of church and state when it was founded in 1636. The colony's 1644 charter enshrined these values in law. (Apologies to Marylanders, who sometimes claim to be first with these freedoms. Their 1649 Toleration Act covered only Christians. Rhode Island granted freedom of conscience to all.)

At Rhode Island's founding, witch hunts and debtors' prisons were outlawed. Capital punishment was all but eliminated, and slavery was officially banned. (Tragically, this last law was not enforced.) In a recognition of their rights, the first Rhode Islanders insisted on purchasing—not seizing—land occupied by local tribes. In the other colonies all lands were regarded as the property of the British Crown, and those who received royal grants simply took what they wanted, if necessary waging war with Native tribes.

The most remarkable thing about life in early Rhode Island was its commitment to a kind of self-government that modeled American democracy. As founder Roger Williams declared that "the foundation of civil power lies in the people," the majority ruled, but the minority was protected. No wonder that at the time of the American Revolution, 10 percent of the entire country's Jews lived in the small city of Newport. There, like other colonists, they found the freedom, equality, responsibilities, and opportunities that the rest of the colonies would eventually embrace as core American values. The primacy of individual conscience was affirmed when the marble statehouse was topped with a heroic statue called *The Independent Man*.

I don't note the values that formed Rhode Island's political culture to brag about how we were the first true American progressives—although I could!—or to say that we are uniquely idealistic. I mention them because I think that the aspirations people announce when they set out to create a state or a nation have an effect. Cicero said ancient Rome promoted courage and fortitude. Its empire proved its people possessed both. Modern China's leaders have elevated the idea of "improving people's livelihood." In ten years the country's gross domestic product per capita almost tripled.

While aspirations and ideals can define certain parts of a community or country, they don't tell the whole story. Alongside every virtue resides the rest of human nature, including wickedness and vice. The Romans were brave, but also gruesomely brutal. China's leaders may be developing a middle class, but they still deny them human rights. Which brings us to Rhode Island as the land of hope that, according to the legendary newsman Jimmy Breslin, "the best thieves in the world come from." Breslin was referencing the mob bosses of Providence who, beginning in the 1950s, controlled much of organized crime in New England. Their presence, and the political corruption of the same era, served as a humbling reminder that high aspirations often collide with the sinister elements of human nature.

No person or place is perfect, and considering them in an all-or-nothing way suggests a certain immaturity. Children may cling to fantasies about the utter goodness, or even greatness, of their parents or their families or their communities. Their hometown teams can do no wrong while their rivals can do no right. But grown-ups know that while nearly all of us try to lead good and virtuous lives, nothing human is perfect. Individuals and institutions can fall victim to prejudice, excess ambition, greed, and avarice.

Long before *The Godfather* and its movie sequels and *The Sopranos* on cable, Rhode Islanders watched with fear and fascination as our small state became the setting for a criminal subculture that reached into many corners of life. As an Italian American, I felt a special kind of resentment for people in organized crime who were associated with my ethnic group, even as I understood why people found this type of crime fascinating. In the media it was a realm of high-stakes drama populated by colorful characters. If you set aside the criminality, this subculture represented life distilled to the kind of clarity most of us rarely experience. It was governed by rules, allegiances, and hierarchies. Violations and betrayals were punished.

Have you noticed that I haven't used the word—let's call it the "M word"—that so many people use when referring to mobsters with Italian last names? It's not because I refuse to see that in many places criminal enterprises led by Italian Americans have plagued parts of society. The reason is that for my entire life my father, whose clients included some of these people, argued that much of what people think about the M word is pure fiction. Much of this fiction was created by law enforcement officials to give themselves an advantage in court and to justify violating people's rights. Along the way this word was used as a slur that to this day is deployed against people with Italian last names.

Ask any Italian American and they will tell you about the times people have asked, "Is your family in the M?" If they don't ask questions, then they'll make statements about how much they love the *Godfather* movies or *The Sopranos*. When this happens, I feel like responding with a long riff on all the people with Irish, French, German, and British names who were gangsters in Rhode Island. I want to remind them that many of the Italians who emigrated to America were met with intense discrimination. (In much of the South, where dozens were lynched, many called Italians "Black Dagos.") With society denying them protection, let alone equality, some of the immigrants adopted criminal ways. Of course, I don't say these things. Instead I say, "Well, you know those are just shows, right?"

Because my father knew the full truth about the M word, it wasn't used in our home, and I don't use it to this day. But this doesn't mean I deny the existence of organized crime. In our state, mob activities exacted a toll on everyone. Extortion, loan-sharking, and thefts added a premium to the prices regular people paid for goods and services. The corruption of public officials, who gave mobsters no-show jobs, tax breaks, and lucrative contracts, added to everyone's tax bills and degraded public services. All of this damaged the state's reputation and its prospects for growth as industries considered the corruption and took their plans for new offices, service centers, and factories elsewhere.

In general, the police and prosecutors paid far more attention to the crooks than to the pols. This was in part because the crooks were more colorful—ours had nicknames like Joey Onions and Bobo—and brazen in their crimes. They were also a little less clever and therefore easier to catch. Also, media accounts of their arrests and trials, which were riveting in a car-crash kind of way, could turn cops and prosecutors into household names. The colorful elements of the Providence mob explain why the opening season of a long-running podcast called *Crimetown* was focused on the city. The most outlandish episode detailed the audacious robbery of a bank vault, where many mobsters hid their loot, that was housed inside the redbrick Hudson Fur Storage building on Cranston Street in the West End neighborhood of Providence.

The heist was carried out by eight men, who arrived at the fortresslike building in a van and a Chevy Monte Carlo. It was a bit after eight on a hot and humid August morning in 1975. One man stayed outside keeping watch while seven entered the building. Although the others wore masks, their leader, Robert "the Deuce" Dussault, showed up in sunglasses and a natty gray-checked suit and carried a briefcase to make himself look like a client.

Once inside, the Deuce flashed a pistol and told the owner, Samuel Levine, that if he pressed the button that would sound an alarm at police headquarters, "I'll blow your head off." A young clerk named Barbara Oliva asked, "Are those real bullets?" The Deuce replied, "What are you, a fucking comedian?" The Deuce put pillowcases over the heads of Levine and his employees and herded them into a restroom, where he kept watch over them. What he didn't know was that Barbara Oliva was able to watch him too, because the pillowcase that covered her face was so cheap and flimsy that she could see through the fabric. She got such a good look at Dussault that later she was able to sketch his face.

In the warehouse, Dussault's partners found that the giant door to the vault had been left open. They then set to work on dozens of safe-deposit boxes. Drills failed them, but crowbars worked on the hinges. Inside the metal boxes they found piles of cash, gold coins, silver bars, gems, guns, and jewelry. There was so much that they let the small bills and less valuable trinkets drop to the floor, making an ankle-deep pile. They spent ninety minutes filling duffel bags with loot later estimated to be worth as much as $30 million, the equivalent of $150 million today. The bags were so heavy that the Monte Carlo's bumper scraped the ground as they drove away.

Dussault, who loved Las Vegas, went there to live large. When things turned out the way they do in Vegas, he called his partners, demanding they send more cash. They got nervous about him talking too much and decided to kill him. Dussault's closest friend was sent to do the dirty work. Somehow, with his buddy holding a gun on him, the Deuce talked his way out of the hit. Then the police in Nevada arrested him for assaulting his sex worker girlfriend. A database check turned up the Rhode Island warrant. The cop who came to collect him tricked Dussault into confessing everything.

Barbara Oliva turned out to be the star witness at the trial. She was able to testify to what she had seen and also heard, including the fact that the men had called each other Harry as a way of avoiding using their own names. They said things like, "Harry, look at this!" and "Harry, come over here!" Three of the six accused thieves, including Dussault, were convicted. The others had alibis that won them acquittals. Among them was Gerald Tillinghast—note the Anglo-Saxon name—who had been handed a job as an environmental protection officer with the city of Providence. Although his lineage could be traced to one of Rhode Island's colonial founders and a major law firm called Tillinghast Licht, Gerald's branch of the family was much feared for its criminal tendencies.

A colorful tale of mobsters robbing mobsters, the vault-heist story riveted Rhode Islanders the way nighttime TV soap operas once captured the country's attention. The twists in the story included the strange detail—a coincidence?—of Tillinghast's having been hired as a waste management official, for which he had no qualifications, by the new mayor, named Vincent Cianci. Known to everyone as Buddy, Cianci had gained local fame as an Italian American who prosecuted organized crime cases. (This was before Rudy Giuliani followed the same pathway to become mayor of New York.) Cianci ran as the self-declared "anticorruption candidate." His link to the heist suggested that what Tillinghast once called the "two governments," by which he meant the one we all know and a shadowy "government of crime," sometimes worked together.

Another twist came when Dussault claimed the whole episode had been orchestrated from prison by the New England crime boss Raymond Patriarca. According to Dussault, Patriarca believed his crews were cheating him out of his share of their earnings. The heist was supposed to balance the ledger. Since most of what was taken was never found, this idea was embraced by many in law enforcement. However, no one would ever know for sure, not even my father, who was one of Raymond Patriarca's lawyers.

9

JUSTICE

I can guess what you are thinking now. *This guy Cicilline wants us to believe he hated the corruption in Rhode Island, but his own father represented the top mob guy. How can he square these two things?*

Well, the first thing I'd say is that my father was much more than a lawyer for some bad guys. In the 1960s he was a civil rights pioneer who pulled a group of schoolboys out of a conference in Washington when he learned the hotel there wouldn't welcome the two who were Black. He then organized a separate trip for the entire group. In DC he brought them to Speaker Sam Rayburn's private dining room, where they had breakfast with the state's two representatives.

As attorney for the city housing authority, my father pushed for equal housing for all. In his one run for public office, he championed integration of the public schools, economic development for crime-ridden neighborhoods, and more aid for seniors. These policies reflected his view that government could help correct injustices, whether they flow from deliberate prejudice or greed or arise simply because laws and programs haven't kept up with the times. Today, in education, for example, students need access to new technologies and the latest instruction in changing disciplines like the sciences if they are going to be ready for work or higher education. If we are to be an equal opportunity society, all kids—not just the ones born into wealth—should have access to these essentials.

In his one bid for public office, a run for state senate in 1968, my dad made his priorities clear by stressing education, economic development, and support for the Fair Housing Act, which barred racial discrimination by landlords and real estate sellers. He was an enthusiastic campaigner who got into the local paper for climbing a forty-foot ladder to give campaign literature to some roofers. His main opponent was an incumbent whose entourage included a bevy of young women dressed in matching orange blouses and straw boater hats. They urged voters in the largely Italian American district to take "la strada provada," which, in local slang, meant "the proven road." They did. The loss, and the experience of having a campaign car torched, helped my father decide he would try to do some good, and do well, in the practice of law.

Never a corporate kind of guy, my father opened an office and helped clients with whatever problems they brought, which ranged from immigration and housing issues to criminal defense work. He happened to do very well. Conscientious and dogged, my father has the kind of mind that helped him to see the big picture, like the standards that police and prosecutors had to meet so the accused got a fair trial, as well as the fine details that indicated where they might have cut corners. By demanding the other side play by the rules and prove charges beyond a reasonable doubt, he won case after case and developed a reputation as the best defense lawyer in the state. Still in practice at age eighty-three, he is so respected that other lawyers advertise that they once worked for him.

The second thing I'd say is that defense lawyers, by definition, represent some people who have actually committed crimes. Of course the finding of guilty or not guilty is for the judge or jury to make. A defense lawyer's job is to do his or her best because the whole system is premised on the presumption that the accused is always innocent until proven guilty, and the authorities must follow the rules as they try to make their case beyond a reasonable doubt. Under this system the government enjoys the enormous advantages that come with the control of police agencies and the state-sanctioned power to conduct investigations, carry out surveillance, and make deals that provide informants with dismissal of charges, leniency during sentencing, witness protection, and even cash.

The government's advantages remind me of a story a local lawyer named Peter DiBiase once told me. He was working at home one night when one of his children noticed the top page of an indictment that began with the words "UNITED STATES OF AMERICA V." and then the name of his client.

"Dad, does this mean that the whole United States is against you?" asked his son.

"Well, sort of, yeah," was Peter's reply.

Peter went on to explain that with the power of the United States lined up against his client, his job would be to present whatever evidence might refute the indictment and to make sure the government played by the rules that were set up to make the system work fairly. If the government brought you to trial on some charge and you faced the prospect of losing your freedom or, in a death penalty case, your life, you'd want someone to pour everything into your defense, wouldn't you?

The last thing I would say about my father the defense lawyer is that during his time in practice, he occasionally encountered law enforcement officers who were just as dishonest as the so-called bad guys he defended. In Rhode Island we have had judges who took bribes and looted trust funds and cops who dealt drugs, committed burglaries, and committed rape in a police station. One even killed three teenagers after one of them filed a police brutality complaint against him.

In the context of the courtroom, which he called "the best battleground in the world," my father's efforts served as a check on the abuses that could be committed by corrupt or just overeager police and prosecutors. He succeeded in case after case where judges and juries viewed the evidence and his challenges to the prosecutor's case and concluded that the prosecutor had not met their burden. Finally, in desperation, the feds began investigating my father. They surveilled his movements, rummaged through his trash, and interrogated people who knew him. With a judge's permission they planted eight listening devices in his offices. In violating the privacy of his relationship with his clients, the feds crossed a line that I had never known them to cross before. When this failed, they went a step further, sending a low-level mobster named Billy Smith to his office with a recording device hidden in his clothes.

In the office Smith's wire recorded a conversation with one of my father's clients, Frank "Bobo" Marrapese. Two years before, Bobo had been charged with buying 109 stolen La-Z-Boy recliners—not 108 or 110—and since they had been transported across state lines, this was a federal crime. You can't make this stuff up. Anyway, the recorder captured Bobo and Billy hatching a plan to commit perjury. My father wasn't in the room and didn't participate in the scheme. But after Bobo accepted a ten-year sentence as part of a plea agreement, the feds came back and charged him and my father with conspiracy to commit perjury. Bobo said the feds came to him with a sweet plea deal if he agreed to implicate my father and testify against him. Bobo refused.

When the government finally brought its case against my father, the jury failed to reach a unanimous decision, and the judge declared a mistrial. Another mistrial occurred when the government's star witness, Billy Smith, recanted his testimony. Although you'd think that would be the end of it, the prosecutors demanded a third shot, and the judge agreed to give it to them. At the third trial, the jury reached a unanimous decision after about eight hours of deliberations. (This included an hour spent listening to the tape of Bobo and Billy, whom the press called "an admitted liar and former cocaine dealer.")

We were notified the jury had finished its deliberations, but we had a little time before the judge would call the court to order. In this moment my father brought me and my brother John into the men's room, where he silently took his money and keys out of his pocket and the watch off his wrist. He gave them to my brother. This was something that made what was happening even more terrible. He could, I thought, be remanded to jail in the next hour. The thought froze me for a moment.

When we returned to the courtroom some of my father's colleagues and many of his former clients joined us to hear the verdict. The tension made some of our group shed tears. But then we heard the words "Not guilty" and we saw a huge smile appear on my father's face.

The judge praised the jury and said that the prosecution and defense teams had both done all that was possible. "It has been an ordeal for all concerned. It has been a difficult situation for prosecutors, particularly in view of the fact that one of the defendants in this case was a prominent and respected attorney." He

added that the case had been "particularly difficult for Mr. Cicilline because of his profession and because of the cloud that has
been hanging over his head. . . . Hopefully, Mr. Cicilline, now you
can return to your job as a lawyer without the heavy heart and
burden which the penance of this prosecution must have placed
upon you."

Although two of the prosecutors congratulated my father,
crossing the courtroom to shake his hand, and his faith in the
jury trial system had been affirmed, my father had still paid a
heavy price. His law practice had been shadowed by the federal
indictment and prosecutions, which surely kept many would-be
clients away. At age forty-two, with fifteen years in practice, my
father had been in his prime when the feds started going after
him. He was still quite young when the ordeal ended, but he had
aged more than he should have. He would never recover the five
prime years he'd devoted to defending himself from charges that
should never have been brought.

—————

What is the lesson of my father's experience? And what should
be learned from the fact that in a place founded on progressive
values, affirmed in the motto "Hope," crime and corruption were
also prevalent?

In the prosecution of Jack Cicilline, I saw how unconstrained
officials can weaponize the power of the government. Unable to
dominate him in the courtroom, these officials hoped to sideline
him with a conviction. Although they failed, the fact that they
could and would go on the offensive this way was profoundly
wrong. Compare this with the case that the feds used as the
means to go after my father. Bobo had received stolen property

in the form of all those La-Z-Boy recliners, and it was obvious he'd intended to sell them for a profit. He deserved prosecution.

But who had committed the more serious offense, a mobster participating in a scheme to rip off a furniture company or the federal authorities who decided to go after a lawyer they couldn't beat in court with extraordinary methods, including bugging his office? I would say that while Bobo committed a property crime that may have added a nickel to the price people paid for their La-Z-Boys, the feds broke the public trust in a way that did more significant harm. While we expect thieves to steal, we do not expect our public officials to abuse their offices.

In going after a lawyer in the way they did, pursuing three trials and failing miserably, the US attorney for Rhode Island damaged the reputation of the Justice Department and gave everyone who suspected that the system was corrupt a reason to think they were right. In a system where everything depends on trust, that quality is easy to lose and extremely hard to recover. Flash forward a few decades to the Trump era and consider how he tried to exploit public anxiety about whether government and elections and perhaps the "system" of society were somehow "rigged." Trump preached paranoia to his followers and told them to trust him and him alone. This led to the fatal conspiracy theories that caused people to reject public health advice for avoiding COVID-19 infection and to the January 6, 2021, attack on the US Capitol.

Back when it was happening, the charges brought against my father shook our whole family, but the effect was greatest on my mother. My parents' love story began with them eloping, while still in their teens, in defiance of those who would say that a Catholic boy and a Jewish girl had no business getting married.

Sixty-five years later, their love is still obvious to anyone they meet, and in my life I have never met two people whose devotion matches theirs. During the trials, my mother understood that my father's love of the law, which had been the bedrock of his career, was being threatened. She also saw the squeeze put on his earnings, which supported their family of seven. No wonder she was furious at what was being done to her husband.

In the aftermath, my father said little about his ordeal, choosing instead to focus on his clients as he rebuilt his practice. Much of what he did was for people with so little money that they paid practically nothing for his services. They were, in effect, subsidized by those, including mobsters, who paid in full. He also threw himself into pro bono work on behalf of death row inmates around the country. He did this work because he understood the flaws in investigations, forensics, and eyewitness testimony that often resulted in wrongful conviction. He also knew the biases in the system. Someone convicted of killing a white person is seventeen times more likely to be executed than someone convicted of killing a Black person. The bias in jury selection—white people are more likely to be selected than any other race—and favorable treatment of white defendants are well documented. Finally, he considered the death row inmates who had been found to be innocent before or after their executions and knew that there were so many flaws in the system that sometimes innocent people were convicted.

(One last word about Bobo Marrapese: After the La-Z-Boy case, authorities tried their best to put him away for good. In their first attempt they failed to convict him of the murder of Anthony "the Moron" Mirabella. With their next try prosecutors got Bobo convicted of murdering another mobster named Dickie Callei. Paroled after twenty years, he went right back into the crime business, operating a gambling ring. Police busted Bobo and about two dozen of his buddies. He wound up back in state prison. By this time Raymond Patriarca was long dead, and the mob era in Providence was over. When Bobo died, he was best known in the legal community for a case in which the Supreme Court had rejected his appeal of a larceny conviction. In that case Bobo's girl-friend had been the key witness. She had testified after he broke her arm and she peed in his soup. In denying Bobo's appeal the court noted that hell "hath no fury like a woman scorned.")

————————

Despite the conflict between the ideals of justice and the reali-ties he experienced, my father never lost faith in his profession, his community, or his fellow human beings. He witnessed lots of corruption and crimes and yet refused to become cynical about human nature or our capacity for good. For example, my father always treated the families of the people he defended as his responsibility. They had done nothing wrong but stood the chance of losing a spouse, a child, a sibling, or a parent to prison. He felt a responsibility to them as well as to the person he rep-resented. Their gratitude, whether he won or lost, was genuine. One client's wife, Angela, lived near my father's office and knew he worked late every night. One evening she saw the light on and brought him a plate of what she had prepared for her husband Raymond. She did it again. And again. For fifteen years. If Ray-mond called from his own job and asked, "What's for dinner?" her reply would be, "I don't know. I haven't talked to Jack yet."

Don't get me wrong. I know there is evil in this world. For all I know, Raymond had broken some law at some point. But when people turn to crime, violence, or corruption, it's more often than not because their life experiences led them to it. The solution to this problem lies in creating a combination of supports and constraints that prevents the wrongdoing in the first place. We're pretty good at imposing constraints, using the law, police, and prison system to both discourage and punish criminal behavior. Of course this part of the equation seems to affect street-level crime, while so-called white-collar offenses, including the betrayals practiced by public officials, go largely unpunished. Similarly, the rich and powerful are very well supported by public services and their own private efforts, while working people and the poor often lack the basics—good public schools, safe communities, health care, career education, etc.—that help people lead good lives.

In America we have always recognized both the importance of individual responsibility and initiative and the significant role community plays in creating happy people and societies. I think that too often we forget that some people begin life with advantages that make it seem as if they need little from society. It then becomes easy to say, for example, that if my kid in the wealthy East Side neighborhood in Providence can make it without help, then your kid from struggling Olneyville can too. For good measure people with this perspective will punctuate the argument with the example of an Olneyville kid who succeeded against all odds.

I know too many people from America's Olneyvilles to accept the bootstrap argument. I also don't accept the concurrent argument that says we should cut taxes on rich people and expect the benefit to trickle down to the rest of us. People who start off with the odds against them need more than encouraging messages. They need the rest of us to set the conditions that would allow them to thrive. How many of the criminals who made Rhode Island notorious would have chosen that dangerous and ultimately ignominious life if they had not been born with the odds against them? When Raymond Patriarca came into this world in 1908, anti-Italian prejudice was raging across the country. In the previous decade, Italians had been the victims of one of the worst mass lynchings in US history, which saw eleven of them killed and mutilated by a mob in New Orleans. When he was eight years old, the best-selling book in America, *The Passing of the Great Race*, declared Italians one of the inferior peoples who were diluting the American gene pool. In much of the South, Italians were buried in Black cemeteries. In much of the country, they were shut out of schools, labor unions, and the professions. They were employed in great numbers in mines, quarries, sweatshops, and steel mills.

In a story that has been repeated again and again, the shunned and unwelcomed find ways to first survive and then claim respect and wealth. Their shadow society makes the climb possible but also institutionalizes criminal activity. In Providence, which was one of those manufacturing-dependent cities that began to lose jobs in the 1960s, this corruption infiltrated politics. Eventually it seemed that only the pols, the mobsters, and what remained of the white Protestant elite wielded any power. Everyone else tried to avoid coming into conflict with these groups or departed.

As I finished undergraduate school at Brown University, my father was in the midst of his personal battle with the feds. The gap between the Rhode Island ideal and a reality that included all sorts of human failure neither discouraged me nor made me more cynical. I could see how the flaws in individuals and in the systems we create can lead to abuses and criminal behavior. But the same flawed individuals and systems gave my father the right to fight in the courts for the kind of fairness that even those who commit crimes deserve. Also, he never gave up.

During this time I thought often about how my mother and the five of us kids had gotten along without him because he was very rarely home for a weeknight dinner and could be absent on a Saturday or Sunday. We were a boisterous, attention-seeking bunch of kids, and I'm not sure how my mother managed these meals. At times it may have felt as if we were missing out on something. But at a fairly young age I learned what my father was doing and how much it mattered.

On most days he stopped in the office to pick up files or check on who had telephoned before spending almost all day— court generally opened at 9:00 a.m. and closed at 4:30 p.m.—in one courthouse or another. Late in the day he would go to the state prison, where he would meet with clients being held as they awaited trial. Then it was back to the office, where he would work into the night while eating what Angela had cooked that day.

My father didn't have a secret motivation for pouring his life into this work. He genuinely believed that too many people had been steamrollered by the legal system. However, I think he was more motivated by the plights of the people who became his clients. He found intense meaning in the work he did to make sure they were treated fairly. Law school had allowed him to do this according to his own conscience, and that seemed to me like a path I could follow too. I couldn't know where it would take me, but I knew that hope lay in that direction.

10

WHAT DO YOU STAND FOR?

Despite what had been done to him, or perhaps *because* of it, my father's example made me want to follow him into the law. As he would say, it wasn't the law that had abused him, it was a group of overzealous prosecutors who had let their personal feelings divert them from the path of justice. Fortunately, the jury corrected the prosecutors' actions, but only because my father was represented by very good counsel. It was a classic illustration of why real justice requires good defense lawyers. And becoming one seemed like a pretty good way to stand for this ideal.

I was accepted to Georgetown University Law Center, which, because of its location in Washington, receives more applicants than any law school in the country. (Yes, more than Yale and Harvard.) It was and is renowned for its "clinical" programs, which give students hands-on experience with real cases. The clinics work in the areas of civil rights, criminal defense, family law, and juvenile justice, and they even offer residents of the District of Columbia "street law" programs, where they learn about their rights and how the system works. Given what everyone knows about best-laid plans, it would be ridiculous for me to suggest that based on my father's example, I entered law school and always stayed on a path that would lead to my work as a defense lawyer and then to politics. I don't know anyone who picked a direction in college and never took—or at least contemplated—a detour or two. In my case, I tried out with one of the biggest law firms in New York, and while I was there indulged an interest that had long intrigued me: acting.

Before you get carried away with gay-musical-theater clichés, I should tell you, that wasn't me. I never owned an album of show tunes, and I was never much for singing and dancing. In fact, I remember quite well the moment when, as we were heading somewhere in the car, my mother interrupted my singing to say something like, "David, you have many, many talents, but singing is not one of them." She was right (I had sort of suspected it), so my stage-and-screen interest always focused on dramas. I admired serious actors who worked tirelessly to make their performances seem effortless. Watch Sidney Poitier or Meryl Streep and you forget their previous roles and what you know about them as people. They make you believe in the characters they play and make you care about the stories they reveal.

Never underestimate stories and the importance of knowing how to share them. Whether drawn from real events or fiction, they have an enormous impact on us as individuals and on our society. First shown in 1915, *The Birth of a Nation*, which valorized the Ku Klux Klan, did enormous harm to the cause of civil rights. Forty-eight years later, the stories in James Baldwin's book *The Fire Next Time* awakened many white people to Black America's experience and initiated a stream of books that changed minds. Most significant changes in law or legislation begin with the telling of stories, which, when heard, make us care. Rachel Carson told the story of wildlife killed by DDT in *Silent Spring*, which led to its ban and the rise of the entire environmental protection movement. Edith Windsor and Thea Spyer told their love story, and in time marriage equality followed. In law it's usually the side that uses facts to tell the most compelling story that wins.

In my own story, a gig as a summer associate in New York brought me inside one of the original white-shoe law firms. (The term hearkens back to the days when newly hired sons of the wealthy wore their pale summertime shoes to jobs that, barring some real disaster, they occupied for the rest of their lives.) The firm was called Dewey Ballantine. The Dewey had been Thomas Dewey, governor of New York and the GOP's candidate for president in 1944. Arthur Ballantine had been the first chief lawyer for the Internal Revenue Service and undersecretary of the United States Department of the Treasury. Among Dewey Ballantine's alumni were a Supreme Court justice, a US attorney general, and a US secretary of Health, Education, and Welfare.

Historically, white-shoe firms employed only white Anglo-Saxon Protestant men trained by the Ivy League. Although these practices ended before my time, this legal subculture remained a bastion of snobby reserve. Soon after I arrived, in a moment that made me think I didn't belong there, a Dewey partner took me aside to talk about my suit, which was from a hot young designer named Willi Smith. The suit was about as far as possible from the tailored look favored in the office, and, in retrospect, I'm a little shocked that my younger self didn't know this. The partner told me I was out of uniform and should wear only traditional gray or blue suits with white shirts. But I could, he added, express myself with my ties. At the time, fashion-forward WASP men were going crazy with pink and yellow paisleys. In the summer a trendsetter might even wear a tie with sailboats on it. But only on a Friday. If he was going to spend the weekend in Nantucket.

The work at big-money law firms was, to my mind, generally boring and impersonal. While they do worthy pro bono representation for ordinary people, giant legal shops that employ hundreds of attorneys (Dewey had about five hundred when I was there) exist to serve the wealthy and powerful who are eager to preserve what they have and, if possible, accrue more. Among Dewey's first clients were AT&T and John D. Rockefeller's Standard Oil. Decades later, the firm remained a resource for the country's largest corporations and richest individuals. From my perspective, one would have to be very interested in things like contracts or excited by transactions involving big sums to enjoy the legal work required by such clients. Since I found neither compelling or interesting, what I learned during my summer was that being a corporate lawyer at a giant firm wasn't for me.

My other summer fling led to a more difficult choice. On some evenings, after I left my job in Midtown, I went to the famous HB Studio in the West Village to take acting lessons. Established by actor/director Herbert Berghof and actress Uta Hagen, the studio served everyone from beginners to the most accomplished professionals. HB stressed the expression of emotions through action. Actors loved this method because it trained them both mentally and physically.

I liked how I was taught at the studio because it didn't require me to somehow dredge up memories and feelings of emotionally powerful moments from my own life to apply to a performance. (In truth I was a happy person from a stable family, so I wouldn't have had much to work with there.) However, moving around the stage and performing before an audience didn't faze me. It wasn't easy, but I could imagine that if I stayed in New York and dedicated myself to the craft, I would be good enough to find work, sometimes.

The "sometimes" was a problem. The more I learned about the life of an actor the more I became concerned about the difficulty they faced finding parts and how long they had to wait between roles. In the gaps people took temp jobs and waited tables. I had worked as a waiter through high school, college, and the work paid for my law school, so that didn't scare me. However, the prospect of all that downtime worried me. I may not be hyperactive, but I do like to be engaged and busy. And most of all, I prefer work that expresses what I stand for.

A lawyer who serves the rich and powerful can find a way to stand for something important in that work. Maybe she encourages her clients to be good and generous citizens. Maybe he nudges corporations toward ethical operations. And I have no doubt that in the right role, an actor can do enormous good. But for every revolutionary role that changes hearts and minds, the profession offers a thousand forgettable TV buddies. I was too influenced by my father's example of a busy life guided by values and service to take a chance on a long-shot career that, no matter how well it worked out, would involve far more waiting around than action and many more forgettable roles than memorable ones.

Having been given real options—corporate law, acting, or following my father's example—I found choosing easy. Despite the opportunities and rewards that were possible with the first two paths, they wouldn't let me put whatever talent and intelligence I possessed to work for people who needed them most. Families left out of the middle class, kids who couldn't dream of the advantages I had, and defendants facing the awesome power of the government interested me more than money or fame. I knew, of course, that I could make a good living at the law no matter where I focused. I wasn't exactly taking a vow of poverty when I turned toward defense work of the kind my father practiced in an office on Atwells Avenue in Providence. But what I valued more was the chance to do hard work that mattered to real people and could change their lives.

————

Turning away from corporate law was easy. Passing on an acting career was more difficult. But I grew more comfortable with my choice after I finished my law degree and went to work for the Public Defender Service for the District of Columbia (PDS). As most people know, the District of Columbia was founded to be a national capital separate from neighboring states and under the supervision of Congress. Its residents suffer under a system that denies them true representation in the body that governs them. Hence, since 2000, license plates issued by the district bear the slogan "Taxation without Representation."

One of the more peculiar things about the district is that its trial courts are a creature of the federal government. The judges are appointed by the president, and the prosecutors are federal prosecutors. All civil and criminal cases, including juvenile and family law cases, are processed in this system. One of the benefits of this arrangement is that the legal aid office that serves people who cannot afford to hire an attorney is funded by the Department of Justice. The department intends for the DC public defender's office to serve as a model for the country, and it provides a budget that gives poor clients excellent representation. As staff attorneys we were busy, but not so busy that we couldn't focus fully on each case. We had time to do our own investigations and the money to hire expert witnesses if we needed them. Other public defender offices are so chronically overwhelmed by the workload that new hires, fresh out of law school, are often handed serious felony cases right off the bat. And expert witnesses? Forget about it.

When I arrived at PDS, I discovered that just about everyone there had come from a top law school and many had been clerks for US Supreme Court justices. Charles Ogletree, who would become a legend in the profession, had recently left his position as chief of the trial lawyers. His successor, Michele Roberts, was tough as they come and keenly aware that the system, which had police working hand in hand with prosecutors to clear cases, was inherently tilted against defendants.

The prosecutor's power begins with their investigative tools, which include the ability to subpoena witnesses and the ability to offer deals to turn suspects into informants. Prosecutors also control who gets charged in a case and who does not. They alone can drop charges, add to them, or engage in plea bargaining. All of this is done in secret. And even with all these advantages, prosecutors too often break the rules by hiding facts that might exonerate someone who has been charged. There is also the well-established fact of racial bias, which begins with where police focus their resources and thus make arrests and ends with who gets a life sentence or the death penalty. Black youth make up 15 percent of the population under eighteen but 35 percent of those arrested. Once in the system they are four times more likely than white youths to be imprisoned. On the other end of the spectrum, Black adults, who represent 13 percent of the US population of adults, comprise 42 percent of the people on death row.

With defendants at such a disadvantage, we tried to outwork the other side as we prepared our cases and outperform them in the courtroom. Clients who were fortunate enough to have Michele Roberts handle their defense directly got someone who knew her way around the law and could take command of a courtroom. Like actors, great lawyers deliver performances that change hearts and minds. She was so good at this that at times jurors would say, "Amen!" when she made a point in her closing.

When we first met, Roberts was fresh off one of the most notorious criminal cases in the city's history. In a precursor to the more famous Central Park Five case in New York, seventeen men had been rounded up by police investigating a horrific murder. Twelve were charged. Two of those accepted deals and testified for the prosecution. Eight of the remaining ten were convicted even though prosecutors had no DNA, fingerprints, or eyewitnesses other than those who had made deals. Michele's client was one of the two found not guilty. Decades later it would be revealed that police and prosecutors had hidden evidence that just two men, including a serial rapist, might have done the crime. The two defendants who testified against the others recanted, saying that they'd caved to the pressure placed on them by detectives and lied on the stand.

None of what I note above takes away from the tragedy of the crime that the police sought to solve. But as the Central Park Five case would show, the more horrific the crime, the more everyone should guard against a rush to charge and convict. In New York all the convictions were vacated when new evidence was revealed. In Washington the men who were convicted were denied new trials. However, outside the court system the revelations and recantations led many in the community to insist that justice had not been done. Public opinion about judicial fairness matters. If people don't trust the process, they won't be willing to participate when police and prosecutors need their help. This is one reason why defense lawyers who keep the government on its toes are necessary.

In my stint at the public defender's office, where I began to work as an actual defense lawyer, I represented mainly young men and juveniles who were charged with drug crimes and faced severe penalties under laws developed as part of the so-called war on drugs. Richard Nixon rolled out this policy in 1971, just as his reelection campaign was getting underway. As his White House counsel John Ehrlichman would later explain, the campaign "had two enemies: the antiwar left and Black people. You understand what I'm saying? We knew we couldn't make it illegal to be either against the war or Black, but by getting the public to associate the hippies with marijuana and Blacks with heroin, and then criminalizing both heavily, we could disrupt those communities. We could arrest their leaders, raid their homes, break up their meetings, and vilify them night after night on the evening news. Did we know we were lying about the drugs? Of course we did."

Convicted of perjury, obstruction of justice, and conspiracy for his part in the Watergate scandal that ended Nixon's presidency, Ehrlichman didn't tell the truth about Nixon's drug war until he was interviewed by a journalist in 1994. In the years when he stayed silent, the war was escalated but also redirected. With vast numbers of college graduates and suburban kids smoking pot, law enforcement seemed to abandon interest in their illegal activity. They also ignored the white urban professionals—including many lawyers and doctors—who helped create a cocaine culture that was so big that when comedians joked about it on TV, all of America laughed because hey, everyone was exposed to it and hardly anyone got in trouble for it.

The picture was completely different in Black and Hispanic neighborhoods, where young men and teenagers were routinely stopped and searched by police looking for anything they could find that might indicate someone was a drug user or dealer. When the cheaper rock version of cocaine called crack became prevalent in the same neighborhoods, it was regarded as a national emergency. Laws were changed to make the penalties a hundred times worse for crimes related to crack than for those related to cocaine. As what historians call a "moral panic" arose, police, prosecutors, and judges in big cities redoubled their efforts to find and punish people suspected of drug involvement.

In Washington circa 1986, more than twenty years of economic struggle had produced a consistent decline in population and persistent poverty for people who didn't hold federal jobs or work in a business or profession that was related to the government. Much of the housing stock was substandard. The school system was subpar, and on many blocks despair had reached epidemic levels.

On visits to my clients' homes, which were always in rough neighborhoods, I found buildings that were crumbling due to landlord neglect. Appliances and fixtures didn't work or were missing entirely. Heating systems were either inadequate or so expensive to run that in the winter people wore their coats inside. But as bad as these apartments were, rents remained high. It is one of the paradoxes of housing markets that in most cities there's just a small difference between the rents in poor neighborhoods and the rents in middle-class areas. Back in the 1980s this meant that a bad apartment might save a tenant only fifty or a hundred dollars per month. In some cases renters took less desirable places because they really couldn't afford better. However, far too often people trying to change neighborhoods were turned down because of bad credit scores, spotty job histories, or other factors related to being low income. More often than you might expect, people were victims of landlord racism. This problem was famously revealed in New York, where Donald Trump's family business had a formal "no-colored" policy until the government forced it to change it. Even though housing discrimination is illegal, it is practiced informally to this day.

The defendant in one of my more challenging cases lived

in an apartment where the gaping hole in a window had been fixed with tape and cardboard and heat was supplied by the gas oven because the landlord hadn't fixed the furnace in the building. My client was a high school–age kid who had been caught selling marijuana that had been adulterated with phencyclidine, or PCP. Developed as an anesthetic, PCP was banned because of intense side effects that, it turned out, people looking to get high enjoyed. However, as with any drug made in illegal labs, its potency and purity varied widely, and people often took far more than they believed they were taking. The effects often included paranoia, delusions, rage, and violence. For a while many people subscribed to a reefer-madness myth that said PCP gave people superstrength. This was never true—it just made people numb to pain—but the myth added to the public alarm and the legal system's crackdown.

With judges trying to "fix" kids with punishment, the district was packing its two juvenile detention centers with four times the number of inmates they were built to house. Violent, rat-infested places, they were freezing cold in winter, broiling hot in summer, and incapable of providing basic education or health care. Too many young men who entered as juvenile offenders left as hardened criminals and then joined the 40 percent who were back in prison as adults before age twenty-five. For the rest of their lives, these men would be burdened with adult records that, unlike juvenile records, which are generally kept secret, made finding a job, getting an education, and even forming supportive connections with others that much harder.

Given the realities in communities where most of my clients lived and the way the system would make things worse for those convicted, my duty was to do everything possible to keep them out of jail. In Washington, where public defenders had the support they needed to fight hard, I was able to order independent analyses of the evidence and bring in experts to challenge prosecution witnesses. In one extraordinary instance I was able to aid my client with testimony provided by the psychologist Elizabeth Loftus, who was at the time one of the world's leading experts on memory and eyewitness testimony.

Loftus had shown through experiments that people often change their recollections of an event they witnessed based on information they learn afterward. For example, a police officer who has a brief scuffle with a suspect may, upon learning the guy once boxed competitively, recall a more serious fight than the one that actually occurred. When people do this, they aren't intentionally lying; rather their minds are influenced by information that changes how they feel about an experience.

Considering her fame and how many lawyers must seek her out, I was lucky that Professor Loftus wasn't too busy to fly to Washington from her West Coast home and that I had the budget to pay her fee and her travel expenses. Here I was at a juvenile trial with an expert who was able to show that the police were not being accurate in what they said they'd witnessed when they arrested my client. The story they told based on what they said they *could* recall had also changed over time. They couldn't prove that he had known the marijuana had PCP added to it, and they couldn't prove how much he had sold. My client was found not guilty.

———

The problem was that in the end the courts produce one of two results—guilty or not guilty—and all my juvenile clients deserved a third option that didn't exist. On one level or another they needed community support that should have included some combination of proper education, counseling, food and housing assistance, and, yes, law enforcement supervision. Some of these supports were available, but they were hard to access and inadequate in quality and availability. This required me to function as a social worker, helping clients get back into school or find part-time jobs. In some cases I may have helped keep some young men away from criminal activity in the short term, but given where they lived and the absence of real supports, I knew the odds were against them.

When I thought about it, I realized my juvenile clients in Washington, DC, had much in common with a younger Raymond Patriarca. The departed king of the New England mob had left school at age eight and gravitated toward the powerful men who controlled the neighborhood. He watched as they offered the supply to meet the city's demand for gambling, prostitution, and illegal booze smuggled from Canada and beyond. From this he learned that the people who discriminated against Italian immigrants were chummy when they wanted some illegal fun. As a teen he was charged with crimes that grew more violent with each arrest. My clients sold marijuana. Patriarca had sold bootlegged liquor during Prohibition. From age eight to age twenty-four, when he was first sent to adult prison, he had no contact with the regular world of school and honest work that would have shown him options outside a life of crime.

Better answers could come only from the branches of government outside the judiciary, where lawmakers and executives could change the world where my clients lived. Courts couldn't make the schools better or create decent housing where the flaws in the free-market economy made developers reluctant to invest. They couldn't create jobs, improve childcare, or help families obtain food. But on every level, from city halls to state capitals to Capitol Hill in Washington, officials did have the authority to spend public funds in ways that might help.

————

When my time at the public defender's office ended, I had to make a choice. The big New York firm where I had spent a summer offered me a job where I would make an enormous sum for a first-year associate. A position in a firm like that would come with great potential and if I made partner I would become, in a word, rich. When I discussed this with my mother, she tried to stay neutral, but I could tell she would be happier if I took the big firm's offer. The money was great. The firm was prestigious. And she had seen the stress of defense work as my father practiced it and knew I would do it the same way.

I thought about the work done at big firms where the cases were very complex and generally required teams of attorneys who, unless they were quite senior, also worked long hours. The difference was that the work was almost always impersonal. A lawyer could die in the midst of a case and be replaced by another member of the team, and the client might never know. In fact, the firm probably *preferred* that the client didn't know because that would mean the work had continued uninterrupted.

Because of my interest in criminal and civil rights law—and the thought that I might one day get into politics, where I could have a bigger impact—I went home to Rhode Island to practice in the same office with my father and my brother John. We each practiced independently, but since we handled the same kinds of cases, we consulted each other all the time. I loved the variety, as I represented people at every level in the system, from the state district courts all the way to the federal courts. My clients ranged from poor immigrants who were having trouble with government bureaucracy to people charged with murder, robbery, rape, and drug dealing.

I never entered the courtroom with any agenda other than to win and, if I didn't, to make certain that the prosecutors had made their case. This tenacity did irritate some people, including judges. The chief judge of the Rhode Island Family Court, Judge Jeremiah Jeremiah (that was really his name) heard many of the cases brought against my clients who were juveniles, and at one point he became a bit exasperated as I argued one client's innocence.

"Mr. Cicilline," he said, "haven't you ever represented someone who is guilty of anything?"

"Well, Your Honor," I replied, "I give those cases to my father or my brother."

The judge might have thought it was a pretty good joke, but in all seriousness, whether I was before a judge or a jury, I never indicated anything but the fullest confidence in my case. This attitude was something I'd learned from my father, who had explained, quite wisely, that judges and jurors look at defense lawyers wondering if they can discern a clue that suggests they believe their client is guilty. If they detect one, they'll use it as a shortcut to a conviction. Defendants deserved my efforts because despite what we think we know about the system, many people, even the defendants themselves, believe that someone charged with a crime is probably guilty. This is why I always ran through the law covering a charge moments after meeting a client. Too often they thought they were guilty when they weren't. A common example was people who had put up their arms to block a police officer's rough treatment. Charged with assaulting a police officer or resisting arrest, many assumed they were technically guilty when in fact they were not guilty because the law allows for self-defense, even when the police are involved.

⋆   ⋆   ⋆

On rare occasions my clients were people charged with white-collar crimes like embezzling. (In one of the most fascinating cases I ever saw, my father represented a man who had impersonated almost fifty different men and women in order to collect their unemployment benefits. He was a sports fanatic who hadn't been able to resist canceling an appointment at the welfare office to go to a big football game. The cancellation touched off an investigation that led to his unmasking.)

The law gave me an opportunity to learn about the lives of everyday Rhode Islanders. I heard about their hopes and fears, discovered what they felt about how the world worked, and learned how little most know about both the legal system and government in general. I don't expect people to be experts in these areas. Life is demanding, and if things are working the way they should, people can trust that the government is generally fair and honest. It's only when we meet the system personally, because we're involved in a legal matter or affected directly by the bureaucracy, that most of us need to know more.

Unfortunately, in Rhode Island in the 1980s the need to know was more acute than in many other places and at many other times. The state, and especially the city of Providence, was so riven by dysfunction and corruption that everyone was affected. And hope, the foundation of our community, was under threat.

11

THE REAL WORLD: RHODE ISLAND 1986

I think that most of us, especially when we are young, are very curious about what the world is all about. We know that what we see is almost always just the tip of the iceberg, and we long to glimpse the rest. Reality TV shows cater to this desire, which explains why they are so popular that the host of one, *The Apprentice*, rode the fame he gained playing the all-powerful "boss"—lots of viewers believed what they saw was true—all the way to the White House.

One of the first of the reality genre, *The Real World*, purported to show life as it really was through 24-7 filming of a group of people thrown together in a house equipped with surveillance cameras and microphones. Thanks to manipulative editors, what viewers saw were snippets of arguments, romance, competition, and upset stitched together to compress 168 hours of life into a compelling thirty-minute show. It was entertainment that did nothing to help anyone understand the real world at all.

Now consider the realness of the world that I jumped into in 1986 when I became a practicing lawyer in Providence. Because our clients came with serious problems that required a bond of trust, I was let inside people's lives in a way permitted by few professions outside of, say, religion and psychotherapy. The fear, grief, passions, and experiences that people rarely reveal were shared with me by people who were facing life-changing problems. I also got to see inside the *real world* of justice and politics, which turned out to have their own hidden truths.

As soon as I began criminal defense work, I discovered that people who were arrested often showed up in court with a remarkable number of bruises, black eyes, and sprained limbs. Too many than would seem plausible "bumped their heads getting out of a police car" or "fell inside the jail." On occasion my clients suffered far worse. One, who was nineteen years old when I met him, had gotten into a fight outside a nightclub. It was closing time, so dozens of people were on the sidewalk when the police arrived. They focused immediately on my client, Trent Manning, who they reported was wielding some sort of weapon. Here's what was written in the police report:

> Manning then came at Officer Tefft with the pointed weapon at arm's length, pointed directly at Officer Tefft's chest. At this time, Officer Tefft fired one round, striking the suspect in the midsection, causing Manning to cease his life-threatening actions.

Trent spent an entire month in the hospital recovering from the shooting. He left with a colostomy bag, expecting that he would need it for the rest of his life. The police reported that the "weapon" he had flashed was a screwdriver with a broken handle, which they found at the scene. Trent was charged with three counts of assault. Two were allegedly with "a deadly weapon."

Although Trent said he hadn't had anything in his hand outside the club and that he'd been at least twenty feet away from the officer who shot him, we didn't have to depend on his word alone. Eight of the other people who had also left the club at closing time and watched what happened agreed to testify in support of Trent. But the witnesses and the extreme force used by the police weren't enough. I will say this case was different from most because the prosecutor actually asked a grand jury to indict the officer, but the jury declined.

Grand juries act in secret but are generally so cooperative with prosecutors that every defense lawyer you meet would agree with the cliché that district attorneys can "indict a ham sandwich" if they present even a middling case. In this instance you have to think the prosecutor went through the motions to satisfy the public but didn't try very hard. Add the tie-goes-to-the-runner advantage that most people give to the police out of respect for law enforcement. Jurors also have a fear when it comes to their communities and safety even when they live where there's virtually zero crime. Invariably someone on the jury will say, "If we don't support the police officer, no one's going to keep us safe. And we're going to be in more danger." It's also true that most people who serve on grand juries are not, you know, people who are worried about police brutality, because it's mostly white people who have the time and interest in doing it. You can tell them, "We only want to discipline the bad apples in the department," but they are still going to rule in the officer's favor most of the time.

Among the many sad things in the tale of Trent Manning is the fact that thanks to petty crimes, Trent had been in the "system" since he was fourteen. In all that time he hadn't received the kind of educational, vocational, and rehabilitation services that we know can prevent many troubled kids from becoming troubled adults. Conviction on drug charges sent him to prison for a long time, but when he called me recently from California, he said he had settled into a stable, law-abiding life.

When I was a full-time defense lawyer, nearly every client was treated professionally by Rhode Island police officers and jailers. However, on too many occasions I encountered a client with a black eye, a gashed forehead, or a story of being some-how abused on the way to being charged with a crime. On many occasions the crimes they were charged with had nothing to do with what they had come into contact with the police for in the first place. Instead they were charged with something like disor-derly conduct or resisting arrest—care to define these offenses?—and either arrested or given a summons. (If you are up on your civil rights history, you know that after the Civil War this kind of trumped-up charge was used to inflict mass incarceration on Black southerners, many of whom were put in prison work gangs sent to the very plantations where they had been enslaved.)

In contemporary Rhode Island I was able to fight on behalf of abused clients by filing lawsuits. In the beginning I brought most of these cases in federal court, and I won judgments or reached beneficial settlements about half the time. This doesn't mean that federal judges were especially receptive to our com-plaints. In fact, some were quite hostile, which meant that I even-tually started using state venues more often. No matter the court, or the clients, I came to see a pattern, especially in Providence, where most of the trouble occurred. During the Cianci years, the officers were often hired because of their political connections. In Providence this meant connections to the mayor or one of his allies. Once on the job officers were backed up by a thuggish police chief named Urbano Prignano Jr., who, as Cianci's friend, had skipped the ranks of lieutenant and captain to become chief. A crude man with an explosive temper, he established a culture in which the officers acted in a way that prompted some outsiders to call the department the King's Army.

(Proof that Cianci's dirty hands controlled the police had emerged during his first tenure as mayor when he pressured Police Chief Robert Ricci to add five people to the department even though they had been rejected by the police selection board. Three were put on the force. With the two rejected applicants threatening lawsuits, Ricci dreaded testifying to what really went on during the hiring and promotion process that led to these five hirings. Politics had even begun to influence police work, with investigations being launched into Cianci's foes. All this was confirmed by officers, including the personnel director, after Ricci died by suicide.)

Under Prignano, the Providence police developed a reputation for using more force than was necessary and relentlessly targeting minority communities. At headquarters evidence including gold, silver, and cocaine went missing. And the political aspects of the job were evident in the way officers were pressured to sell tickets to Cianci's political fundraisers. It was widely rumored that promotions were based on "donations" made to the mayor or others.

Of all the complaints I brought against the Providence police, the one that stands out the most involved a client named George McKenna and an officer named Peter Flynn. McKenna was not a Boy Scout, but neither was he a real criminal. He was a guy who often drank too much and had caused a ruckus that the police were called to handle. In this instance patrolman Flynn responded, and things got rough right away.

Were you to search the local newspaper's archive for Flynn, you'd discover he had trouble with lots of citizens. In one case a disabled sixty-three-year-old woman accused him of shoving her inside a courthouse and knocking her unconscious. Before that he had also been accused of using excessive force, and antigay slurs, while responding to a noise complaint about a party. Before that he was the subject of a complaint from a man who said Flynn hit him and slammed his face into the ground while making an arrest. Flynn alleged the man had thrown coffee at him. Before *that*, Flynn, responding to a possible abduction, fired two shots at the driver of a car, causing him to crash. It wasn't the car supposedly involved in the abduction, which it turned out had never actually happened.

After Flynn knocked McKenna around, he charged him with resisting arrest. We dealt with that issue first, going to trial in criminal court, where I wanted to make sure everyone saw Flynn's temper. When he took the stand, I relied on a trick my father had taught me, asking him questions in a very calm way until he seemed to think we were in some sort of conversation. He then responded to me by asking a question of his own.

"Officer Flynn," I replied, turning stern. "Perhaps you've forgotten. This is a court of law. I ask the questions. You answer them."

As the words came out of my mouth, Flynn's face began to turn red, and the veins on his neck bulged. He began to get up, as if he was going to leap out of the box and strangle me. George McKenna was acquitted. And when we brought our claim of misconduct against Flynn, the department settled. George received a few thousand dollars, but that was not the important thing. The important thing was that we stood up against an officer who had apparently thought he could get away with abusing a man whose troubles with drinking were widely known. But a drinking problem doesn't erase anyone's rights as a citizen.

Peter Flynn went on to further scandals, including an incident in 2000 when he grabbed a newspaper photographer's camera and ripped the film out of it. In 2001 he would be found guilty of assaulting a parking lot attendant over—if you can believe it—the towing of another officer's car because he'd refused to pay six dollars to park.

Eventually Flynn would be pushed out of the police department, but before that could happen, we had our own little brush with conflict. It happened when my car was hit by the one behind me as I stopped at an intersection. Flynn was the responder. He said, "Oh, let me see how I can put you at fault in this." My response was, "Officer Flynn, as good a liar as you are, even you can't put me at fault for this." I'm sure that once again, he wanted to punch me.

————————

As one of the Providence officers involved in incidents where I brought complaints, Flynn serves as an example of how political corruption at the top, in this case the corruption of Mayor Cianci, filters down to street-level problems that could, in the extreme, lead to people getting abused, roughed up, and shot by officers who feel politically protected. But what Flynn and other rank-and-file patrolmen did was minor compared with the astounding behavior of a uniformed officer named James Hassett who was on the scene when the mayor summoned an old political associate named Raymond DeLeo to his home on Power Street.

Cianci's house sat across the street from the most historic mansion in the state. Built in 1786 for one of the founders of Brown University, the John Brown House was a landmark that anchored one of the more prestigious neighborhoods in the city. Cianci's home was built at the start of the twentieth century as a large and elegant horse stable with a high roof. When it was converted into a home, the builders added a rather incongruous clock tower/steeple and outfitted the interior with lots of dark wood and gold-colored light fixtures.

DeLeo arrived after 8:00 p.m. on a Sunday night in March 1983. Hassett answered the door and let the visitor in. Cianci, who was nearby shouting into a phone, called out, "Frisk him!" While DeLeo demanded to know what was going on, Hassett pushed him against a wall and patted him down. He then led DeLeo to a chair near the fireplace in a room where Cianci's lawyer and the city's public works director filled out the group of five. When Cianci appeared, he went straight to DeLeo, said, "You've been screwing my wife!" and slapped him. He taunted DeLeo, saying, "You strike me back, you're gonna get a bullet to your head." On the other side of DeLeo's chair, Hassett put his hand atop the pistol that was holstered at his side.

Over the course of about two hours, Cianci would continue to assault DeLeo with his hands and fists. He kicked him, spit on him, poked a lit cigarette in his eye, and brandished a fireplace log as a weapon. At one point he hurled a heavy glass ashtray at DeLeo, who caught it before it could hit him. In between the assaults Cianci demanded that DeLeo sign an affidavit admitting the affair and a promise to pay the mayor $500,000. DeLeo noticed that Cianci's eyes were bloodshot and his nose was running. He wondered if Cianci was on drugs.

The violence ended with the arrival of a Cianci associate, Herbert DeSimone, who had been called by the mayor's attorney. A prominent Republican who had been attorney general from 1967 to 1971, DeSimone had played college football, and the first thing he did was wrap his arms around Cianci and get him out of the room. At DeSimone's urging, Cianci let DeLeo go, but he wasn't through threatening him. At 2:00 a.m. he called DeLeo and said, "Get the five hundred thousand dollars or you're gonna be dead."

I learned what happened at Cianci's house on that March night in the same way that everyone in the state learned it. The story came spilling out first in the press and then in documents supporting charges of assault with a deadly weapon, conspiracy, extortion, kidnapping, and ordinary assault. (It's noteworthy that on the day after the charges were announced, police put disabling boot clamps on the wheels of cars owned by several prosecutors.) Two years after the assault, Cianci, who had puffed up his chest and promised to go to trial, meekly pleaded guilty of assault with a deadly weapon. This earned him a five-year suspended sentence (why he was not sent to prison I'll never know) and forced him to resign.

Elected at age thirty-three, Cianci had run the city for nine years. In that time he'd transformed himself from the young Republican who'd promised to end the corruption of a century of Irish/Democrat rule into the walking emblem of corrupt and abusive politics. In that time people had grown accustomed to corruption in the handling of city jobs, contracts, and services. In many cases those who weren't political insiders, meaning those who hadn't provided something of value to the mayor and his people, would not be treated the same. Sidewalk repairs, to use one example, were done by favorite companies and only in response to requests from citizens deemed worthy by the mayor's people.

How did Cianci's crew know who merited sidewalk repair and who didn't? You'd be surprised by how easy it is for a mayor to keep tabs on folks if he can call on an army of people who depend on city hall for their jobs or who rely on sweetheart arrangements with the city to keep their businesses going. It all works a little bit like the informant systems that arise in authoritarian states where everyone whispers about everyone else and the government keeps track.

In Providence, one result of the Cianci way was that you could walk down a city block and see that new sidewalks had been installed in front of some houses but not others. Worthy, qualified applicants were passed over for city jobs while positions were given to those who had no relevant education or experience. Dozens of people took paychecks but rarely showed up for work.

Despite all the corruption, during Cianci's time Providence began to climb out of the economic hole it had found itself in when factory and textile jobs left for the South in the 1960s and 1970s. The city had not been alone in its suffering. All across the Northeast and the Midwest, factories closed as owners sought lower wages elsewhere. Sprawling complexes of redbrick mill buildings were vacated, and once-vibrant downtown business districts shriveled. Revitalization became the watchword as communities sought to reinvent themselves by developing shoreline districts, improving downtrodden neighborhoods, and luring new kinds of industries. In the Boston area, big technology firms that relied on the minds produced at Harvard and MIT poured money into new facilities. Portland, Maine, put its hopes in tourism. In Western Massachusetts, villages and towns cultivated the arts.

In our city a civic center built with federal, state, and local funds by Cianci's predecessor opened in 1972 and became home to a minor-league hockey franchise and college basketball. It drew people downtown for big concerts and circuses and became a magnet for new businesses. Historic houses that had declined in value attracted newcomers with the money to update them. New theater companies became immensely popular, adding to a virtuous cycle. In 1980, the *New York Times* announced to the world that "poor, shabby Providence . . . is blossoming."

As the *Times* noted, students who came to study at our Ivy League university, Brown, had begun to stick around after graduation to work in the growing health-care sector or try their hands at business or some artistic endeavor. In Providence, where we'd never had the wrecking-ball kind of urban renewal, they found grand old buildings that, while vacant, retained both their beauty and their sturdiness. Sandblasting and new interiors were enough to put the boarded-up, eighteen-story Biltmore Hotel, first opened in 1922, back in business.

Superficially, Providence was a renaissance city, as other publications, in addition to the *Times*, would recognize in print. (*Town & Country* lavished twelve pages on the city under the banner headline "Providence Regained.") In most of these accounts, Cianci would take credit for things that were not his doing. Rarely did anyone cast doubt on his claims or include the type of caveat that would make the picture seem more realistic to those of us who lived in the city. Only the *Times* noted the glaring problem with our rebirth: it came with virtually no new jobs. This was because with just a little investigating, executives who might bring jobs to Providence would discover that city government favored its friends and might not offer fair and impartial treatment when it came to taxes, regulations, permitting, and other key concerns. Providence was not an honest place to do business.

As companies went elsewhere to create the jobs that made middle-class communities hum, they confirmed the anxiety some of us felt about our city in its renaissance. However most visitors were impressed by the renovated houses, new entertainment venues, and growing list of great restaurants, which provided our relatively small community with big-city pleasures.

The good news was ballyhooed by the mayor, who genuinely excelled at the showman/cheerleading aspect of his job. People loved it when Cianci hosted Henry Kissinger, President Gerald Ford, Frank Sinatra, and others who, when they came to Rhode Island, took the opportunity to meet with one of the country's youngest big-city mayors. Gradually Cianci became a magnet for attention, playing a role that was distinctly different from that of the hard-drinking and sometimes depressed man whom people saw in rare unguarded moments. This uncomfortable side would start to show after he spent an evening dashing from one event to another. No awards ceremony, banquet, or family reunion was too small. This was before the selfie era, so Cianci often brought a photographer with him. Autographed pictures were later sent to everyone who had shaken Cianci's hand. People began to think that he was a celebrity, and they liked the glad-handing show he put on. Only the late-night regulars at certain bars saw the more surly and profane version of Cianci.

When mayors rally citizens with optimism, the good feelings can give people enough hope and faith in the future to invest their time and money where they live. The effect of this effort could be seen in population figures. After a long, slow decline that had begun in 1950, we had stopped losing people and begun to gain a little. Nothing is more important to city life than population growth and the signal it sends. Hispanic residents, both American born and born abroad, made up most of our gains, followed by immigrants from other countries. The wealthier people who came to Brown and stayed or were lured by the glowing press were a relatively small group that created a kind of bubble in which they interacted mainly with similar people in the shinier places.

As the Cianci years marched on, the poor neighborhoods of

Providence and the people who lived in them saw no real change in their circumstances. City services like schools, recreation, and public works were delivered haphazardly, with the people who needed them the most often getting short shrift while the King's Army policed them like an occupying force. Meanwhile those with political connections enjoyed a kind of supercitizen status that meant their calls were always answered and they went to the head of the line with their requests for anything from a building permit—*permit issued!*—to an application for a business license or first priority when city snowplows cleared the streets.

12

BUDDY RETURNS

After Mayor Cianci became a convicted felon and resigned in disgrace, City Council President Joseph Paolino suddenly found himself mayor of the second-biggest city in New England. He was just twenty-eight years old. With the aid of a brief incumbency, he won a special election and then reelection in 1986. In all he would serve for almost seven years. In that time the state of Rhode Island began to build a park along a downtown bend of the Woonasquatucket River and gathered up $100 million in bonds to build a big new convention center.

State and federal governments fund projects in big cities because people living ten, twenty, or even fifty miles away may be affected when a city rises, or for that matter falls.

Joe Paolino was young and energetic and assembled a strong team. He got some credit for the improvements in city life created by the big state projects. He would also get some reflected glory as a long-planned effort to uncover the Providence River, which had been obscured by pavement for decades, was begun. Funded almost entirely by the federal government, the $190 million project would eventually include a dozen new pedestrian bridges and miles of riverfront walkways. Parts of the city separated by the construction of highways would be reunited, and new businesses would sprout along the riverfront.

But as Paolino encouraged the renewal of the city it remained difficult to correct the problems Cianci had left behind. There were few departments or city functions that were not burdened by the former mayor's practice of doing favors for his supporters and giving others short shrift. Friends and their relatives got jobs whether they were qualified or not. Spending was focused on either making the mayor look good or cultivating political support. One place where this happened was in the fire department.

Ever ready to literally risk their lives doing very dangerous work and happy to let neighborhood kids clamber onto their shiny trucks, firefighters are even more beloved than police officers. Unfortunately for the police, they're the ones who write tickets, inevitably annoying just about everyone who lives in any city. Add the public relations value of rescuing cats from trees, and firefighters are the ones who get the plates of homemade sweets during the holidays and cheers when they pass in a parade.

Mayors tread lightly in their dealings with firefighters because of their popularity and the bonds that promote unity in their ranks. Cianci didn't just tread lightly. He gave them everything they could ask for, including a sweetheart deal that gave retirees increases in their pensions every year. This arrangement meant their pay would double every seven years, and since many firefighters retired with full pensions in their fifties, some would collect these enhanced payments for more years than they'd spent on duty. This was a consequence of the mayor's neglecting his responsibility to the taxpayers in favor of his own political interests.

But wait, there's more. In Providence firefighters and police officers who couldn't work due to on-the-job injuries received disability pay and, when eligible, retirement benefits. They were *also* permitted to withdraw all they had contributed to their pension fund. No government workers in the state had such a generous benefit and, though we searched, we couldn't find anyone in the country who did. According to actuarial consultants the pension withdrawals alone cost the city more than $5 million a year.

In addition to the big-ticket items, the firefighters got special treatment when it came to employee contributions to health care—they were exempt—and they had the work life benefit that comes with the city that employs a larger number of firefighters than comparable cities. The extra firefighters were hired when the Cianci administration included them in the last contracted negotiation before the mayor lost to Paolino. With sixty more men and women added to the rolls, at a cost of $6 million per year, the rank-and-file grew to number 539.

Compared with others in the region serving similar populations with similar building stock, the Providence department was clearly outsized. The population of Springfield, Massachusetts, for example, was just 2 percent smaller than the population of Providence, but its fire department employed 20 percent fewer people. With this manpower (and womanpower) it covered a city that sprawled across 50 percent more territory. Hartford and Bridgeport, Connecticut, also covered more territory with fewer firefighters and nothing indicated that they were less protected than Providence.

Why did Cianci do so much for the firefighters? I have no doubt that one factor was his reluctance to engage in a protracted contract negotiation with the city's favorite employees who wouldn't hesitate to complain publicly. However, he also reaped political gains by giving them so much. Beginning with hiring practices run out of city hall, Cianci worked hard to win the political loyalty of all those men and women and their families. Come election time, many would feel it was in their interest to vote for the person who made them so comfortable.

By the time Paolino took office, Cianci's mismanagement, symbolized by the firefighters' contract, had put the city in financial peril. Faced with the rat's nest of problems at city hall, Paolino focused mainly on economic development, which is what political leaders tend to do when things are a mess. The hope, in all cases, is that new businesses and their employees will pump new economic life into the city and thereby increase tax revenues. Money, goes the theory, fixes everything else.

Paolino recruited American Express to open a service center that would employee two hundred people at middle-income wages. It worked a little bit, as the new economic activity combined with better management to improve the city's fiscal position. Paolino even made progress on collecting unpaid taxes that the Cianci team had shown little interest in collecting. The mayor could have stuck with the job and done more, but like so many in politics who have some success at a tender age and lots of ambition, he decided he would try to jump to a higher office. On second thought, maybe he knew what was coming.

———————

Paolino might have wanted to build on his work, but during his second term in office rumors that Cianci was considering a comeback turned into reports that he was preparing to run. Then a political group created by Cianci's former chief of staff Patrick Conley announced it had conducted a poll that found that 23 percent of the city's voters would happily overlook Cianci's crimes and put him back in office. As Conley put it, they would support Cianci "even if he robbed a bank at gunpoint."

As appalling as Conley's words were, you might think the poll results were not such good news for his man. However, with his charm and enough effort, Cianci could build on a 23-percent base to the point where he might win over 40 percent. At least that's what his boosters said. In a three-candidate race, something quite common with mayoral elections, this would give the guy his old job back.

It's hard to believe that so many people would give such a bad guy so much responsibility, but in fact there will always be those who love someone who confirms their negative stereotypes about politicians. For them, a vote cast for Cianci would represent flashing a big middle finger at the whole political system. This prospect was especially appealing to the city's Italian American voters, who still harbored resentment toward the powerful old Yankee families who had lorded it over everyone else for generations. Others might have been insiders when Cianci ruled and longed to get back on the gravy train. Finally, there were those who paid so little attention to politics that they would support Cianci simply because they considered him a local celebrity or he had shown up at their kid's ball game. (Cianci was an inveterate wedding crasher and was so eager to appear at local events that everyone joked that he would show up at the opening of an envelope.) In the time since he'd left office in the 1980s, he had reinforced his appeal by hosting a local radio talk show.

Before Cianci became synonymous with the criminal element in American politics, there had been Boston's James Michael Curley, a longtime and very corrupt pol who ran for mayor in 1946 while under federal indictment. Thanks to the intense loyalty of Irish Bostonians who hated the city's old elite, he won election with just 45 percent of the vote. The love dimmed after he was convicted and went to federal prison. In the next election he lost to John Hynes, who, like Curley, was the son of Irish immigrants. Hynes then dragged Boston politics into an honest era, defeating Curley twice more along the way.

As he'd reigned over a city with three times the population and vastly more wealth, Curley's corruption was by some measures more impressive, but Cianci's was likely more intimate. In fact, Providence was small enough that whenever anyone dealt with the city on any matter, the mayor or one of his surrogates would have a say in what happened. On rare occasions your status as a political donor or supporter might not matter. But typically a would-be vendor with the right connections would be coached to go for a series of small contracts that could be authorized without competitive bidding. Others would be left to sink or swim on their own.

In his comeback run, Cianci got the three-candidate race he wanted as the Democrats nominated a young city councilor named Andrew Annaldo and the Republicans offered up a seventy-three-year-old blue blood named Frederick Lippitt who was the son of a United States senator and grandson of Rhode Island's thirty-third governor. Lippitt loved Providence with a passion but was a stiff and clumsy campaigner. Annaldo was a young man with lots of ideas. Neither one had a real chance in debates against the glib and charismatic former mayor. Nevertheless, Cianci's own polls estimated that 58 percent of the electorate wouldn't vote for him under any circumstances.

On Election Day the voters showed they were even more disgusted with Cianci than he knew. Sixty-five percent voted against him. However, Lippitt and Annaldo were so closely matched that they split the anti-Cianci vote. Neither got more than his

35 percent. In a truly spectacular display of how a fervent minority can best a listless majority, a former convict returned to the mayor's office thanks to a 317-vote margin over Lippitt.

In the aftermath of the election our local paper, the *Providence Journal*, calculated that Cianci's campaign had spent a whopping $36.13 for each of the votes he received. His nearest competitor, Fred Lippitt, had spent even more and done so thanks to his own wealth, which permitted him to lend his campaign $500,000. Cianci's financial condition, at least as far as his tax returns indicated, precluded big personal investments in politics. After promising to release his 1989 returns, as had the other candidates, Cianci slipped out of the pledge by asking tax authorities for a filing extension. When that expired weeks before the election, he asked for another extension, claiming he had been unable to gather all the information he needed. Finally, *after* he won the race, he made good on his pledge, revealing a doozy of a record.

According to his tax forms, Cianci had had no income at all in 1989 and instead suffered losses in excess of $230,000 (more than $500,000 in current dollars). The losses had been racked up by two restaurants he owned called Trapper John's and Flyers. Located near the state's largest hospital, the first place was decorated to recall the TV show *M*A*S*H*, in which Trapper John was a character. It opened in 1989 and closed in 1990. Flyers closed soon after. In 1993 the Hooters chain, known for the revealing outfits its servers are required to wear, saved him from foreclosure by leasing the building for one of its own restaurants.

Cianci's finances were made all the worse thanks to some very bad choices about expenses. He'd borrowed $200,000 to buy a yacht and spent almost $75,000 on two cars, a Lincoln and a Mercedes. Add $715,000 in mortgages on his home, and he couldn't possibly escape the hole he was in on the basis of the

$1,575 he would earn each week as mayor. Could savings he'd accumulated in the past help? Of course. He had also made modest investments in real estate, which could generate income. But any public official with nearly $1 million in known personal debts and an annual salary of $81,898 would merit close watching.

————————

While Cianci brought his circus back to city hall, my public political life was confined to serving as cohost for a fundraising breakfast that my father, brother, and I hosted for the Democrat who ran for governor of Rhode Island in 1990. Bruce Sundlun had been a bomber pilot in World War II. On his thirteenth mission from a base in England, his B-17 Flying Fortress, named *Damn Yankee*, was hit by flak. One of its four engines was destroyed, and the bomb bay doors were stuck open. As Bruce tried to return to the base, he was caught by a squadron of German fighters that forced him to make a crash landing. Somehow he managed to avoid the Belgian town below, landing instead in a turnip field. No civilians were killed, but four of the ten crewmen died. Five others were captured, but Bruce escaped to fight with the French Resistance and eventually rejoined the American forces.

In his postwar life Sundlun flew as high as he had in the Air Force. He partnered with a couple of Hollywood stars and two famous generals to create the first executive jet leasing company. He was a founding director of the federal government's quasi-public satellite communications operation, COMSAT, and he ran several big companies, including a chain of TV stations. He was seventy years old when he ran in 1990 and was elected. In two terms he would run perhaps the cleanest administration the state had ever seen and apply his imagination and skill to the development of the waterfront in Providence and a list of projects that

would create a tourism boom. These included complete reconstruction of the state's main commercial airport.

We were happy to help Sundlun, and the breakfast raised
about $5,000 for his campaign. Of course, when the local press
reported on the event, it made a big deal out of the fact that the
Cicillines "have represented many organized crime figures."
We didn't much care, since our practices were booming in part
because we were known for taking the tough cases. The implica-
tion for Sundlun was that he was somehow tainted by his association with us. When he won with almost 75 percent of the vote,
the largest share ever gained by a candidate for governor, the figures belied any suggestion that we had hurt him.

Watching Sundlun as governor gave me some faith that a
good person could rise to the top of Rhode Island politics and
that government could be run honestly. I started to ponder how
I might participate one day but didn't dwell much on this idea. I
was much too busy representing a full roster of clients. Because
of my reputation, a surprising number of them had been charged
with terrible crimes and needed expert help. Their cases became
media sensations. Among them were:

Dawn Magee, a twenty-seven-year-old mother of three
whose eldest child, a nine-year-old girl, was the state's
key witness to her stabbing of her husband. She was
charged with murder but eventually pleaded guilty to
manslaughter. Her brother-in-law, the victim's brother,
testified on her behalf.

Pov Pech, a seventeen-year-old Cambodian boy who
fired a gun at students outside Providence's Central High
School. First charged with conspiracy and assault with

intent to murder, Pov had been imprisoned as a child by Pol Pot's brutal regime. He'd sought refuge in America only to be bullied by racists. He had intended only to scare his tormentors. Prosecutors confirmed the background of the case, and we agreed to have him plead guilty to lesser charges. When the plea bargain was announced in court, one of the jurors said, "Thank God."

The younger of two brothers who, at ages thirteen and sixteen, were charged with stabbing and raping a woman they had tricked into letting them into her home. The assailants had used drugs, and the younger one was under the influence of the elder one with psychosis. I worked to minimize the sentence for my young client. Both pleaded guilty and were sentenced to thirty-three years in prison. My client did eventually get released, and last I heard, he was living a law-abiding life.

When another seventeen-year-old came to me because he was charged with delivering heroin to an undercover officer, the police refused to reveal how they had observed this happening. I argued that it would be impossible to defend my client without that information. The judge agreed. The case was dismissed.

Frank Arache and Wanda DeJesus, who were convicted of drug crimes after police raided an apartment in Providence. When we argued that the police had planted evidence connecting our clients to the drugs, a federal judge listened. After a weekend in which he was troubled by what he called "second thoughts," a federal judge vacated the convictions, freeing our clients.

In all these cases my job called for making sure the system worked fairly. Overall, I think it did and that I produced results that were just not only for my clients but for everyone involved. I certainly understood that some people would disagree with my view and thought that by representing people accused of doing terrible things I was doing something terrible myself. This issue hit close to home one weekend when I was at my Jewish grandmother's apartment for dinner and she wondered aloud "just who would represent" some young people who had been caught desecrating a Jewish cemetery.

"Well, Nana," I said, "you just served kasha to one of their attorneys."

My grandmother understood, of course, and the subject was quickly changed. Soon after, though, I got a handmade booklet from my mother, who had gone to the library and looked up dozens of quotes, passages from literature, and sayings about children betraying their mothers.

13

INTO POLITICS. AND YES, I'M "OPENLY" GAY

The excitement of the 1990 elections—the utterly honest Sundlun became governor while the utterly dishonest Cianci returned as Providence's mayor—made me think the time might be right for me too. After law school I had come home with politics in mind, and at age thirty I felt I was ready. (Who doesn't think, at that age, that they're ready for anything?)

When I looked at the state government, it seemed the state senate, with fifty members, offered a chance to get something done while avoiding getting lost in the lower house, the house of representatives, which had twice as many seats. (Together the legislative bodies were called the General Assembly.)

In retrospect, as I decided to run for senate, I should have thought more about where I might actually be needed. In 1992 I lived in the Third Senate District, which is on the East Side of Providence. Home to Brown University and much of the Rhode Island School of Design, it's a diverse community of historic houses and many parks and includes both middle-class and wealthy areas. District Three is also a Democratic Party stronghold that was, at the time, well represented by someone whom the voters had no reason to throw out.

Rhoda Perry had herself been a first-time candidate in 1990 when she swept a four-person primary and won the regular election to replace a retiring senator. Her life's work had involved bringing health care to working-class Rhode Islanders in places like Woonsocket. She was also devoted to protecting the environment, women's rights, and LGBTQ equality. I'd estimate that at least 90 percent of her constituents were with her on these issues. This included me. Nevertheless, I wanted to represent my district and believed (or convinced myself) that I could do better.

In the 1992 campaign, Rhoda used my family connections to some of Rhode Island's leading Democrats to define me as an establishment guy who would play along with the leaders of the legislature. In fact, I hated the system in place at the time because it vested enormous authority in the legislative leaders, allowing them to control the agenda, the staff, and all the resources of the General Assembly. Without their support, an individual senator or house member could do very little.

I wanted to attack the concentrated power of the leaders, but once Rhoda defined me as a creature of the establishment, it was hard to get rid of the label. Still, as a neophyte, I thought I was doing well as the primary approached. Everyone I met said they were definitely going to vote for me, and I spared no effort, spending about 50 percent more than both Perry and a third candidate named Stephen Broomfield. We were all liberal Democrats, and when the press asked me how I would distinguish myself from the others, I said, "I really believe I can make a difference and get more done." I then quickly added something about corruption and how "you have to either stop complaining about it or make an effort to do something about it."

On Election Day, Rhoda won handily with 60 percent of the vote. I got 24 percent, and Broomfield got 16 percent. The lessons I learned were that my ego was indeed the problem and that whatever good intentions I may have had, I'd failed to temper my ambition with enough humility. If a senator's job involves serving the people of a district and representing their values, and it does, then Rhoda Perry *should* have won. And if I wanted to get into politics with the purpose of serving others as well as my own ambition, then I should find the right spot, one where I might be needed.

————

The right spot would be a house seat in the state assembly. Fortunately, the person who represented my district, Linda Kushner, decided not to run in order to seek a higher office. (Actually, she accepted the duty of representing the party against United States Senator John Chaffee. One of the last of the moderate Republicans, Chaffee was pro-choice, pro-environment, and one of the few in the GOP to support gun control laws. Most people thought Linda didn't stand a chance against him. They would be right.)

With the path clear, I campaigned as someone who both understood and represented the liberal values that predominated in the district. My party's vast advantage in registrations meant I needed only to win a two-person primary, which I did. In the regular election I would run unopposed and win a seat I would occupy at the start of 1995.

Though it could easily fill more than forty hours per week, the job was officially part-time, with legislative sessions rarely scheduled outside of six months per year. Since Yankee thrift and the concerns of the taxpayers held the pay to $10,000 per year, only independently wealthy people could serve without holding another job. As an attorney I had some flexibility in my work hours and colleagues who made the transition to having the two jobs easier. Both were fascinating. In the assembly I could work on issues that affected Rhode Island's one million people. In my law practice I entered realms I would never have seen otherwise, including some that were shocking.

One of the more notorious cases involved a foster child's allegation of abuse at the rural home of a family known for taking care of dozens of children in crisis. As the world would discover, the family of Walter and Frances Burt was actually a kind of criminal cult that committed crime upon crime upon crime. The 158 charges brought against various family members would include defrauding the foster care system, multiple arsons, multiple instances of abuse, neglect, and assault, various thefts, and even training foster kids to commit crimes. The family was led by a cross-wearing matriarch who was convicted of kidnapping, extortion, racketeering, sexual assault, arson, and welfare fraud. Our offices did most of the defense work, and I don't think anyone could have done better. But the evidence against our clients was insurmountable. Despite our efforts, nine defendants received long sentences and a suspended sentence for one who'd turned state's witness. They were all despicable people, but the system required they be represented, and we did it well. Eventually the whole thing became a TV movie.

In other cases my legal work intersected with my legislative work in ways that informed both. One example arose when I received a letter from a Black citizen who had appeared in handcuffs before a court official who in another state might be called a magistrate but in Rhode Island was called a master. It was the archaic practice for everyone in the courtroom to address the presiding official as "Master," which meant that Black men and women were routinely humiliated by being forced to stand in handcuffs, and sometimes leg shackles, and utter the word *master*, like slaves, when they spoke. (At the time, all these officials were white men.)

Rhode Island has its own awful history when it comes to slavery. Newport was a hub for the slave trade, and consequently the state was a hotbed of conflict between abolitionists and slavers. The famous Brown family (of Brown University) was split. Abolitionist Moses feuded with slave-trading brother John. Among the ships John sent to Africa was one named, without irony or shame, *Hope*. (Yeah, even that word can bite you sometimes.) Although some Rhode Islanders, like many in the North, would have preferred to ignore this past, we had a duty to face it, and I thought one way to contribute to this process would be to end this "master" thing. And to my surprise, so did a majority in the legislature. The title was changed to magistrate and one problem, albeit a small one, was fixed.

In another case where my practice of law aligned with lawmaking, the court appointed me to represent a state prisoner who had committed one of the worst crimes imaginable and was trying to starve himself to death. Convicted of raping a fourteen-year-old girl, Stephen G. Senecal had concluded his life had no value and stopped eating in order to end his own life. The state asked the court for permission to keep him alive by forcing a feeding tube through his nose and into his stomach against his will. Lawmakers had refused to allow assisted suicide in the state and would soon affirm that position. But in this case my client wasn't asking for help in dying but merely trying to escape the state's effort to force him to live by feeding him through the tube.

Senecal's crime was horrendous, but that didn't mean that as a matter of law, and the Constitution, the case wasn't important. The Supreme Court had found that mentally competent people have the right to refuse medical treatments, and the insertion of the tube in Senecal's body would constitute medical treatment. (Great Britain had recognized a prisoner's right to starve to death when Senecal went to court.) However, in many states prison authorities had argued, successfully, that the state interest in preserving life and maintaining order in prisons outweighed a prisoner's right to control what happened to his body. None of the previous cases had been decided in a convincing way, which meant the judge who heard this one had his chance to do it. Judge Richard Israel, a deeply intellectual and thoughtful jurist, wrote a brilliant decision in my client's favor. The state supreme court reversed him, citing a long-standing common-law tradition that regards suicide as a crime. Though there had been comment from the bench about how Senecal owed the state the suffering he would experience by fulfilling his complete sentence and how suicide would therefore cheat the people, this point was not made in the decision. Months later Senecal would succeed in determining his own fate by hanging himself.

In the assembly I would deal with issues related to the Senecal case, like the question of physician-assisted suicide. I think we can create safe ways for terminally ill people to end their own lives with the aid of their doctors and that they deserve the right to do this. Gallup says nearly 75 percent of the American public believe this too. However, in Rhode Island, where the Catholic Church can exert great influence, its position that life must always be preserved held sway.

The Church remained very active on everything related to abortion and equality for LGBTQ people. In every case I supported individual autonomy, equal rights, and keeping the government out of our lives. In each case conservatives, whose political philosophy aligned with my positions, ditched their principles to join with Church-minded lawmakers to maintain faith-based laws that elevated theology over the conscience of the individual. Given that our state had been founded by Roger Williams as a refuge for those seeking the "liberty of conscience," voting against reproductive freedom, the right to die, and LGBTQ equality was a very un–Rhode Island thing to do.

Although I really enjoyed my work, disappointment was a regular feature of life for me in the state assembly, where, despite our status as a democracy, what the majority of the people actually wanted did not necessarily determine what lawmakers did. This was true even when it came to concerns like deaths related to firearms. Although the majority of the people wanted sensible laws to prevent gun violence, too many lawmakers believed that progun fanatics would punish them for voting for those laws. This meant that some commonsense ideas, like restricting access to guns for those with convictions in cases of domestic abuse and limiting the number of reasons people could cite for obtaining permits to carry concealed guns, were defeated.

I also ran into a surprising wall of opposition when I tried to remove the word *plantations* from the official state name. I thought that in the same way that the word *master* should be changed to *magistrate*, we could let go of the word *plantations* out of respect for citizens whose ancestors had been enslaved on plantations. But though the assembly thought nothing of adjusting the court system, many members suddenly saw many reasons to resist changing the official state name.

First the objectors talked about the expense of changing signs and stationery and everything else emblazoned with the state seal. I amended my proposal to exempt historically significant inscriptions that would be expensive to fix and with a little research found that all the other changes might cost about as much as a midsize car. In other words, the state could afford it.

Next came arguments about the sanctity of our heritage and how the word *plantation* could be applied to farms without slaves and besides, Rhode Island didn't really have slaves. It's true that *plantation* can have a neutral meaning, as it did when the colony was named the Colony of Rhode Island and Providence Plantations. (*Colony* was changed to *State* when it joined the Union.) We also banned slavery long before the Civil War. However, for generations thousands of men, women, and children were enslaved in our state, and for a time we had a greater number of slaves per capita than other New England states. Our unique landscape, which permitted farming on larger tracts, meant that some slaves really did work on properties called plantations.

None of the above should need to be debated in our time, when it's clear that people associate plantations with slavery, and we should respect our fellow citizens enough to spare them the indignity of being confronted with the word and all that it implies if we can. Besides, no one ever used the long formal name. Nevertheless, in shades of what was to come when southern states would grapple with the fate of Confederate monuments, many white Rhode Islanders resisted the change I suggested. The state's largest paper editorialized against it, using an argument that perpetuated the myth of New England as a slave-free region.

With the true style of a self-interested politician, our Republican governor punted, saying he wouldn't take a stand on the change unless the assembly got behind it in a big way. I couldn't move the assembly, so the idea just languished. In twenty years' time, however, the people of Rhode Island would prove themselves to be better than their representatives two decades ago, when they approved a referendum making the change.

The word *languish* could be applied to many good ideas brought to the assembly in my time there. Back then, the leaders were more powerful in some ways than the governor but were elected on the basis of a few thousand votes cast by the people in their districts every two years. They controlled what bills came to the floor for a vote, and if they were against your legislation, there were no alternative pathways. This reality made me decide that no matter the strength of his hold on certain voters, I would challenge Cianci for the job of mayor of the city of Providence.

The task of challenging Cianci would not be easy. For one thing, downtown Providence was in the midst of a kind of renaissance that had gained national attention. Starting in the 1990s, a weekend art installation called WaterFire, which featured beautiful fires arranged in the water along the restored riverfront, brought thousands of visitors. In the same period gentrification and state-backed developments led many to declare Providence a shining example of renewal. Naturally Cianci took credit for it all, but as the political scientists who wrote *Providence: The Renaissance City* put it, "Buddy Cianci, for all of his deal making and ebullient spirit, is *not* the story of the Providence renaissance."

The sparkle of certain downtown blocks and Cianci's attention seeking distracted many from the facts of life for people who lived in the city. From 1990 to 1999, median housing prices across the country rose more than 25 percent. In Providence they *dropped* by 10 percent. In the meantime all the tax breaks given to commercial developers burdened homeowners with higher taxes. Much of this money was required to pay wages, pensions, and benefits for city workers and others with whom Cianci made sweetheart deals that guaranteed him votes and campaign support.

Add Cianci's corruption, and he seemed like little more than a self-serving Republican autocrat who considered the city his personal playground and was willing to let most of the citizens suffer so the favored could be served. I wanted to offer people an alternative vision of government—one that was positive, constructive, fair, and effective—and get the chance to prove it could work. I didn't have any doubts about this. Nor did I have doubts about what was going on at city hall during the second reign of Cianci. Indeed, his financial troubles meant he had reason to be *more* corrupt than he had been the first time around.

I had strong ties to the Democratic Party, which would help me in the race. I had strong family support and whatever advantages might come from being younger and more attuned to the needs of a city that was becoming more diverse by the day. Looking at my candidacy from the outside, some might find my work as a defense attorney a negative, but I knew it wouldn't be. There may have also been some who considered my status as a gay man a problem. Remember, in 2000 no major American city had ever elected what was then termed an "openly" gay person mayor, and only a couple of openly LGBTQ people had been elected to Congress.

My own experience with this issue began when Rhode Island's leading political columnist, M. Charles "Charlie" Bakst, interviewed me in 1992 as people were mentioning me as a future congressional candidate. (I wouldn't run.) At the end of the interview, he said, "Oh, I have one last question for you. Are you gay?"

I said, "Yeah."

Charlie was a good person, and I expected that if he was going to write about me being gay, he would handle it just like anything else in my background. He'd say something like, "Cicilline grew up in Providence and Narragansett. He played high school football. He's gay. He went to Brown and Georgetown." What I didn't expect was for him to call the next day to say, "The editor will not include in the article that you're gay."

By the time Charlie called, I was feeling pretty good about his pending column. I mean, on the one hand it's ridiculous that my sexual orientation mattered. Heterosexual people aren't identified as "openly heterosexual" in the media. But I understood that in the context of LGBTQ struggles for equality, it was something that should be noted. When Charlie told me it had been cut from the article, I decided to call the editor. It was probably the first time anyone, anywhere, had called a media gatekeeper and asked, "Why aren't you publishing the fact that I'm gay?"

His explanation was odd. He said something like, "Well, it's just like if someone were running for office who has a handi-capped child. We wouldn't include that without explicit permis-sion." He also said that if it was raised by an opponent as some sort of attack, they would cover it. Now I began thinking that this editor thought there was something shameful about disabilities *and* something shameful about being gay.

"You know," I said, "you are asking me to give you special permission because you're homophobic. And you think being gay is something to be ashamed of." Things went downhill from there. We shouted at each other and hung up with things still unresolved.

When I next heard from Charlie, he was upset because the editor was still keeping the bit about me being gay out of his piece. I called the editor back. I said, "How about you respect the integrity of the journalist in this case? Publish what he wrote."

When they did publish Charlie Bakst's matter-of-fact refer-ence to my status as a gay person, nothing noteworthy happened. And it was wonderful. It was wonderful because for all my adult life I had simply lived as I was. I had gone out with men and had a couple of serious relationships with men, and no one had reacted in a way any different from how they would have reacted were I a straight man dating women.

I knew my experience had been quite easy because my family and friends are incredibly loving and supportive people. In the nineties lots of LGBTQ people couldn't say the same. (In fact, many lack this support today.) We were then and are now the only minority that doesn't have any legal protection against discrimination. And thanks to the intolerance that had been institutionalized in some religions and normalized in many parts of society, being LGBTQ could be dangerous. Long before the torture and murder of Matthew Shepard made anti-LGBTQ violence impossible to ignore, our community experienced the constant threat of assault and murder at the hands of people who often got away with it based on a legal argument called the "homosexual panic" defense. This argument, based on the assumption that LGBTQ people were, by their very existence, threatening, was used right up to the 1980s.

I offer all this background to explain why being identified as a gay politician was both a big deal and not a big deal. Being gay had never been an issue for me as a person. I don't think I ever even sat down with anyone in my family and said, "Hey, by the way, I'm gay." They just saw me grow from a teenager who dated women into a man who found happiness dating men. I knew who I was. When I spoke with my family before Charlie's article came out, to let them know about the column, they were a little confused about why I'd even raised the subject. They loved me, they said. That was it.

The love I received from my family was consistent with the values that had prevailed as I was growing up. We were a Jewish/

Italian/Catholic clan that knew all about prejudice and injustice and how acceptance and love are the best responses to them. Our house had been filled with people from all races, ethnic groups, religions, and sexual orientations. We respected people whose politics were different from ours and whose experiences gave them a different point of view.

I knew that in the world outside my friends and family, our open way of dealing with people wasn't always the norm. Meanness, cruelty, violence, and intolerance are easy to find. But while these qualities may be everywhere when you read the news, they do not govern our lives. In my experience, most people want to be kind, generous, caring, and fair. They want to live in communities that reflect these values. And they want representatives and leaders who feel the same way.

Why don't we always get the good leaders we need? Well, first of all, there are many people who seek leadership positions without any of the idealism that would keep their egos in check. Second, there are some who bring that idealism to politics and gradually lose it once they are in power. Hence all the sayings we know about the corrupting effects of power. Finally, we must acknowledge that some people gain office, try their hardest, and are unable to move a system where their efforts to do the most good for the greatest number of people are never supported.

The answer to the problem of power is not for people with ideals to walk away because the system is corrupt or unmovable. The answer for people with ideals is to keep trying, which is why I began planning to run for mayor in the summer of 2001 and in February 2002 found myself inside the redbrick building where I'd attended elementary school in the Providence neighborhood called Silver Lake, to announce I was running for mayor. Inside Webster Avenue Elementary I could almost hear the noise of my

classmates and the voices of my teachers from the days when I
was a student there. One of the many memories that snapped
into focus came to me from third grade, when I'd had an enormous crush on my teacher, Maureen Raia, who was very pretty.
I never had a problem in that class until my father questioned a
grade that appeared on my report card. It was an A-plus and he
thought that plus was a very bad idea. "You answer every question right and it's an A," he told my teacher. To go higher with
the grade would just inflate a boy's ego. She stood her ground,
explaining that since an A could be awarded for getting 90 percent or more of the answers right, a score of 100 percent deserved
better. Looking back on it now, I wonder if my father might
have also thought Miss Raia was quite pretty and just wanted an
excuse to go see her.

Beyond my chalk-scented nostalgia, the school reminded me
of our city's constant renewal. As immigration brought new life
to Silver Lake, the school had educated diverse groups of children, helping them become successful citizens. By 2001, Hispanic
shops and restaurants were joining the Italian restaurants on the
business streets, and some services at churches were being offered
in Spanish. I was thrilled to know that yet more new energy was
arriving on the old thoroughfares with names like Tripoli Street
and What Cheer Avenue. I also hoped the newcomers would find
their curiosity piqued by places like What Cheer, which echoes an
old English greeting. Legend has it that in their first contact with
the Narragansetts, the English said, "What cheer, *netop* [friend]?"
The only other official use of *What Cheer* I know can be found in
Iowa, where a tiny city of 697 bears the name. It was suggested
at the community's founding by a settler from, you guessed it,
Providence, Rhode Island.

Whether they learned our city's history or not, serving the

children of Providence would be one of my first priorities, along with ending corruption, improving public safety, and spreading the benefits of the city's progress to all. In the Cianci years, our schools had fallen so low that all but one of the forty-three were rated "low-performing" by the state. I said I would work for changes that would include a longer school day—it was then the shortest in the state—upgrades to facilities, and accountability for everyone. I promised to focus on improving education, and I would get parents, teachers, and administrators working together.

In my fifteen-minute talk I didn't mention the name of the incumbent once. When I took questions, I also resisted saying his name, even when someone reminded me that Cianci had a 63 percent approval rating in a recent poll. Here I relented, but only to make my main point. "I'm not running *against* Buddy Cianci," I stressed. "I'm running *for* the city of Providence."

14

UNDER THE DOME

You gotta give the feds credit for one thing: they sure know how to name their big operations. The one that ensnared Mayor Cianci was called Operation Plunder Dome. A play on the title of the dystopian movie *Mad Max beyond Thunderdome*, Operation Plunder Dome captured in three words the way the mayor ran things beneath the mansard dome of Providence City Hall.

Built in the late 1870s, our city hall is a premier example of Second Empire municipal architecture. Set on one end of a large open plaza, the five-story granite building occupies all of a small block. It is exuberantly decorated with columns and elaborate stone molding and features sets of circular, arched, and rectangular windows, sweeping steps that bring you inside an atrium, and three floors of balconies reached by an ornamented flying stairway. An arched skylight illuminates the marble floors, granite columns, and wood paneling. The showpiece is a council chamber with a thirty-six-foot ceiling.

That Cianci's craven, corrupt administration operated in such an uplifting and historic place makes his record all the more appalling. When JFK spoke from the steps of city hall in 1960, he argued against politicians like Cianci who endanger democracy with both immorality and incompetence. We could advance democracy, he said, by "building a strong society committed to progress." Though Kennedy drew a bigger crowd—forty thousand according to police—the most important address ever given at city hall was President Teddy Roosevelt's 1902 speech "The Control of Corporations." Roosevelt was just beginning his effort to deal with the monopolies that ruled the economy, seizing enormous power in a way similar to what we see with today's tech companies. Our "great prosperity," he argued, was accompanied by "a measure of evil." He then said that "regulation of these great corporations" was necessary to curb that evil. As the *New York Times* reported the next day, the crowd responded with "cheer after cheer."

In 2001 the main "evil" that would have been recognized by the citizens of Providence emanated from within city hall, revealing that some people will not be humbled by inspiring civic architecture or informed by a heritage that includes Roger Williams's commitment to democracy, morality, tolerance, and equality. As freestanding offences, Cianci's crimes were remarkable. But the breadth of the wrongdoing, the audacity of the perpetrators, and the number of people involved were impressive in a rather shocking way.

The first sign of the scandal to come—and the first time anyone heard of Plunder Dome—came when the FBI raided five city offices and carted away boxes of documents. Soon the tax board chairman and vice-chairman would plead guilty to federal charges of corruption and soliciting brides. Next the deputy tax assessor, Rosemary Glancy, went to trial. The government made public a trove of videotapes that showed officials conspiring to lower taxes for property owners who gave them bribes—some exceeded $20,000—and crediting the mayor with teaching them how to do it. In one a city official recalled how Cianci had taught him, "Never talk on the phone, never get a check, but cash when you're one-on-one." Unfortunately for the corrupt officials, their one-on-one crimes were surreptitiously recorded by hidden cameras.

At Glancy's trial jurors heard how she had been required to pledge allegiance to Cianci before she received a raise and how she'd held a political fundraiser for him to help her police officer brother get a promotion. In one of the videotapes, she was in a small group discussing a tax cut obtained by a bribe and how more payoffs were coming. "Stai zitto," she said, using the Italian phrase for "Shut up." She added, with a laugh, "I'm Irish. Stai zitto." In the same tape Glancy could be heard advising the man giving the bribes to keep building inspectors away lest they note how he had improved his property and raised its value.

"She conducted a dishonest-services seminar," the federal prosecutor told the jury. "Soup to nuts, A to Z: How to Cheat Providence Taxpayers."

After Glancy was found guilty, reporters dashed straight across Kennedy Plaza to city hall, where word of what had happened was already spreading. The jury had pronounced her guilty on all seven charges, including conspiracy to commit extortion, conspiracy to commit mail fraud, two counts of attempted extortion, and three counts of mail fraud. The mayor was prepared to answer the reporters with a snappy rejoinder. "Do you think if I knew for one minute what they were doing, I would have tolerated that?" he asked. "You think I'm running Stealing 101 here?"

If you have nothing to hide, it's not a good idea to answer pointed questions with questions of your own. It makes you look as if you're prevaricating. Of course Cianci was lying because, as so many people had discovered firsthand, the city was run like a criminal enterprise. In sentencing Glancy, Federal Judge Ronald

R. Lagueux said as much, declaring that in city hall "nothing gets done unless money changes hands." The corruption, he added, "started at the top."

As Operation Plunder Dome continued to produce indictments, more city officials prepared to either make deals and flip on the others or go to trial. Through it all Cianci's hold on the political system was so strong, or at least people thought it was, that few could imagine underlings flipping on him and fewer still thought he would be taken into custody himself. Then came the ninety-seven-page grand jury indictment that charged Cianci with thirty crimes related to corruption in both politics and government. Among the juicier bits noted in the indictment were the following allegations:

- Tow truck companies had paid Cianci $250,000 in campaign donations to be on a list of approved companies police called to tow vehicles. (By the way, one of the first things I would do when I became mayor was abolish the list so that all tow companies could share the business. The ones on the list promptly sued me and the city. They lost.)
- A Cianci associate had been given sweetheart deals that resulted in his earning $2.2 million for leasing property to the school system. The associate had then paid kickbacks to Cianci.
- Cianci had accepted a $10,000 bribe to erase an overdue tax bill of $500,000.
- Cianci had held up permits sought by the University Club and used city officials to pressure the club for a free membership (after it had previously snubbed him), which he'd accepted, before arranging for the permits to be issued.

Altogether the indictment indicated that Cianci and two codefendants named on April 2, 2011, had taken more than $1.5 million in bribes and campaign donations given in exchange for favorable treatment from the city at the expense of taxpayers. The news brought a caravan of TV trucks to the plaza where the courthouse faced city hall. Cianci could look out his second-floor window and see the horde of reporters getting larger by the hour as crews from Boston, Hartford, and the national networks joined the locals.

When he at last spoke to the press, he did his best to sound confident. "I assure you that I'm not guilty of these charges," he said before waving a copy of the indictment and adding, "I'm not afraid of this. Ninety-seven times zero is zero." After showing his confidence, Cianci turned defiant, saying, "I'm going to fight this as far as I can. I'm going to go all the way to the Supreme Court, to The Hague, wherever they want to go." After promising to defend himself "until the day I die," the mayor then pivoted to promise that he would not falter in his duties as mayor. "I'll continue to lead the city to new heights," he pledged, "while my lawyer prepares for trial."

————————

You might think that a multicount indictment and so many convictions of people in his administration would have prompted Cianci to step down. When he did not, I thought that a bunch of people might begin testing a potential run for the mayor's office. No one did. They had their reasons. First was the possibility that Cianci would win at trial and thus make himself politically bulletproof. Second was the intimidation factor.

In adult circles, people sometimes summon the courage to confront someone by joking, "What's the worst thing he could do, beat me up?" Anyone who remembered how Cianci had beaten Raymond DeLeo would have to answer, "Maybe." While he might not assault a person who challenged him politically, Cianci would almost certainly deploy building inspectors, tax assessors, fire marshals, even traffic cops to harass them. The same would go for those who might endorse or donate to a challenger.

As Cianci's reputation scared away would-be challengers, he hired a Boston-based attorney named Richard Egbert who had previously defended him against a civil suit. An extremely aggressive lawyer known for humiliating witnesses, Egbert would handle the real defense work. Cianci, in his typical carnival fashion, also enlisted attorney Alan Dershowitz in an apparent attempt to rattle any judges who might hear a case against him. An avid publicity seeker, Dershowitz was notorious for many reasons, including ferocious attacks on Rhode Island's judiciary. In seeking his aid, Cianci signaled to judges and prosecutors that they should expect to have a rough time of it.

I obviously didn't care about Cianci's violent streak. He was twenty years my senior, and my football days were not *that* far behind me. Also, I had no business interests that could be affected by his goon squad. Fortunately, as I quietly contacted potential campaign donors and important potential endorsers, I found many believed they couldn't be touched by the Cianci machine either or cared so deeply about what was happening to their city that they were willing to take a risk.

From the start of the Plunder Dome scandal to the moment I announced I would challenge Cianci, I expected that he would be indicted and/or that some prominent person would announce a run. When neither happened, I did one last scan of my strengths and vulnerabilities. The strengths included backing from family and friends, a solid base of people who had supported me in state assembly races, and connections to both the Italian and Jewish communities. The things that others might consider negatives included my being gay and my being a criminal defense attorney. In my opinion, neither of those things was a negative.

I knew that Cianci didn't think my being gay was a liability because as soon as I declared, he criticized me for being slow to come out of the proverbial closet as a gay man, implying that I was somehow ashamed of who I was. The truth, as everyone who knew me understood, is that I was never *in* the closet to begin with. I had always been open about my sexual orientation, even if I didn't make some sort of announcement about it. In my view I was no more required to do that than a straight person would be required to announce, "Hey, I'm heterosexual." But if anyone asked, I didn't hesitate in my reply. And I always thought that in asking the question, people revealed far more about themselves than I did as I replied.

Cianci also signaled his awareness of the importance of the gay vote in the city by naming a liaison to the gay community, granting benefits to same-sex partners of city workers, and supporting gay pride celebrations by requiring the fire department to drive one of its trucks in the annual gay pride parade. This was a turnabout from the days when he was best known in the gay community for his abusive behavior toward an assistant to the actress Carol Channing. The incident had happened at the 3,100-seat Providence Performing Arts Center. Cianci, who made a habit of taking a break from drinking at the Biltmore Hotel to visit backstage, brought some of his pals to meet Channing. When her assistant noticed Cianci was smoking, he asked him to put out his cigarette. In the squabble that ensued, Cianci called the man "a fucking faggot," and Channing then refused to accept a key to the city. Later in the evening, a Providence police officer was seen searching the assistant's room for evidence that might be used against him if needed.

The Channing episode made it into the local press, which explains in another way Cianci's effort to court gay Providence. Whatever he did, it was with the purpose of getting positive media attention, as when he went to a gay club and asked a local reporter to sit with him at a table where he drank, watched a drag performer called Lady Chablis, and shook hands with every patron who came within reach. When I was asked about this little show, I said Cianci "spent more time in gay bars than me."

In the beginning of the campaign, as Cianci made his play for the gay vote, it seemed he didn't consider me much of a threat. He tried to make something out of the fact that my car at the time was a Rolls-Royce when, in fact, it was a very old car that I had accepted as payment from a once-wealthy but now down-on-his-luck client. (This client was Felix de Weldon, the world-famous artist who had created the Iwo Jima sculpture displayed near Arlington, Virginia.) Cianci also mocked me for stressing that I would be mayor for all the city's twenty-five neighborhoods because I believed he had neglected most of them.

In a data survey issued by bestneighborhood.org Providence scores an 80 out of 100 for ethnic and racial diversity. This makes our community far more diverse than the old-time Italian and Irish politicians realized. Interactive maps that track diversity block by block show that even within neighborhoods there are very few spots where you won't find people of different backgrounds living close to each other. This is true even in Federal Hill, where the Italian style—restaurants, shops, cafés—is as much about drawing tourists as making residents feel comfortable. The most recent data indicates that almost 15 percent of the neighborhood's residents are Black and about 33 percent are Hispanic.

Hispanic residents of Providence, especially those in the large and growing Dominican community, considered Cianci little better than many of the politicians who ran things in their country of origin. There the victors collected the spoils and distributed them to their friends and supporters. In Cianci's case this meant donors, campaign big shots, and close friends got the city jobs and contracts along with tax breaks and kid-glove treatment from the city. For those who had lived in the Dominican Republic, where, as our State Department says, corruption is "endemic," Cianci seemed like a normal politician and proof that America doesn't live up to its claims to be a place of equality, democracy, and the rule of law.

When I welcomed the neglected people of Providence to be part of my campaign, they warily considered whether I might be just another challenger whom Cianci would defeat by getting his city workers and other loyalists to the polls. But over repeated visits, people in the community began to sense my commitment to doing the work of beating the Cianci machine. I opened my campaign headquarters in a storefront on Elmwood Avenue, the main business street in the Dominican community, and spent hour upon hour talking with whoever walked in. I also knocked on the door of the home of every voter in Providence. Some even twice. Gradually we won endorsements from Latino political organizations and prominent leaders. We also sparked a bit of hope in those who saw my commitment and let themselves imagine that the old regime could be toppled.

When I speak of "we," I am referencing a team that included some high-profile polling and media advisers—Mandy Grunwald, Mike Donilon, and Diane Feldman—but also many friends and family members. Most of all, I'm thinking about my closest Rhode Island allies and a campaign manager who for most of US history would have been too young to vote for me. Christopher Bizzacco was a brilliant twenty-year-old who took a leave from his studies at Brown to put in eighteen-hour days running the campaign. Though he had absorbed a great deal growing up in a family that was politically involved, Chris's main asset was a temperament that was perfect for the job. Patient, focused, and unflappable, he could coordinate with unions in one moment, mediate a personality conflict in the next, and then make sure we worked on a schedule for me to address every important community organization. He did this on a diet heavy on Dunkin' Donuts coffee and doughnuts, which may have been what gave him the idea that I should get to local Dunkin' Donut shops at 5:00 a.m. and post myself beside the ordering intercom at the drive-through so I could talk to people fueling up on the way to work. I did it.

At every moment we campaigned as if this was a race we could win, even though half the people we talked to said Cianci was unbeatable. Then the mayor and two of his senior city hall cronies went on trial for running the local government like a criminal enterprise, and he began to seem mortal.

For three weeks the jury listened as more than sixty witnesses described pay-to-play city contracts, bribery, extortion, no-show jobs, the sale of tax breaks, and petty vendettas. However, in most cases prosecutors lacked direct evidence in the form of a surveillance tape or documents that Cianci's underlings had been doing his bidding. Many witnesses testified that this was the case, but time and again the issue came down to one bad guy's testimony that another bad guy was really responsible for the crimes in question.

With local, regional, and national TV news reporters on

hand, much of the country tuned in to see if Cianci would take the stand on his own behalf. Given his roguish charisma and many public claims of innocence, people were curious to see what would happen. Thanks to some extraordinary lawyering and his good fortune in having his trial conducted by a judge who held prosecutors to a high standard, most of the charges Cianci faced were dismissed as the trial wore on. However, by the end he was still on the hook for being part of a criminally corrupt enterprise under so-called RICO (Racketeer Influenced and Corrupt Organizations) laws.

RICO statutes were passed to make it easier for authorities to prosecute people at the highest levels of criminal organizations. Where previously the top people might be insulated by their underlings, under RICO laws the bosses could be held accountable. Over time the definition of *enterprise* would be expanded to include not just the criminal gangs first targeted by the laws but also governments, nonprofits, and businesses. The infamous financier Michael Milken, for example, was charged under RICO laws as a racketeer who had infiltrated a brokerage firm.

In the Cianci trial, prosecutors had to overcome the methods Cianci had used to separate himself from the bribery and extortion. The best evidence offered to link Cianci to specific crimes came from a former city tax official whom Cianci's lawyer savaged on cross-examination. But still the connection was obscure, and no one could know if the jurors had been able to follow the prosecution's case. In the end things went so well, at least from Cianci's perspective, that he decided not to risk taking the stand. With this choice he avoided an onslaught of new witnesses whom prosecutors planned to call to rebut his inevitable claim that he was an upstanding citizen and mayor. Among them were people who would testify to payoffs they'd made to him and threats of violence he'd made that could not be prosecuted because the stat-ute of limitations had run out but that could be presented in court if he took the stand and claimed innocence.

In the end Cianci's buddies were convicted on multiple counts, but he was found guilty on just one: RICO conspiracy. When the verdict was read, the color drained from Cianci's face, and the near certainty of prison must have entered his mind. Free as he awaited sentencing, he considered that the filing dead-line for the coming election was two days away. He could stay in the mayor's race even if he had to conduct his campaign from a cell. But how would the judge weighing his sentence be affected by such a brash move? Cianci decided he'd rather not find out. He was sentenced to five years and four months in federal prison. He would serve them at the sprawling federal prison complex at Fort Dix in New Jersey.

———————

Between 1975 and 2002, Cianci had been mayor for a total of twenty years. But for his first conviction, he might have held the office for that entire period. But even with that break, the man's corrupt hold on the city, combined with a certain evil charisma, had made him a constant presence in our local press, our political conversations, and even our minds. The vacuum created by his conviction was so powerful that within forty-eight hours, I had eighteen opponents in the race for mayor.

Some of the candidates were unknowns who, perhaps in fits of exuberance, filed the paperwork required for those who intended to gather the five hundred signatures that would get their names on the ballot. Eight failed to get the requisite signa-tures and dropped out. Two, who held seats in the state assem-bly, met the signature threshold but decided they preferred their current offices and scratched themselves from the mayor's race. This left three independents, one Green Party candidate, one Republican, and five Democrats, including me. The overwhelming advantage the party had in registration meant that the winner of the Democratic primary would be the odds-on favorite to capture city hall in November.

My early announcement, which I'd followed with steady campaigning, had given me a head start. Among the others running, the most formidable was Joseph Paolino, who had been mayor between the two Cianci regimes. There was no question he was the front-runner. Behind Paolino was a state senator named David Igliozzi who came from a family very active in party politics.

None of the four I would face in the primary were bad guys. All were improvements on Cianci, who had been the municipal version of a petty dictator. Cianci seemed to understand that he was this kind of figure. He would even speak in admiring terms about a right-wing dictator and kleptocrat who would be familiar to my Dominican friends. Rafael Trujillo's thirty-one-year reign had been powered by a cult of personality and maintained by murder. (In one weeklong crackdown his army massacred more than twelve thousand ethnic Haitians.) In a conversation reported by the journalist Mike Stanton, Cianci told a story about Trujillo's agents coming to New York to kill a critic. Then he said, "We need more of that around here."

Though hardly so monstrous, our little kleptocrat dictator demonstrated that the United States is far from immune to the insidious charms of a corrupt and violent man. Some are ready to fall in line if they think they'll gain from it. Others will tolerate the abuses because they don't affect them too directly and they find it all somewhat amusing. I never found it amusing. In fact, I found Mayor Cianci a dangerous creature, and I hated the fact that whenever people anywhere talked about our city, his name came up.

In 2002 I didn't think my election opponents matched my commitment to helping Providence recover and thrive after the Cianci scandal, and I believed I understood the city's people better—their diversity, their desires, their concerns, and their ambitions.

Even though the feds had revealed years of corruption, and Cianci and his coconspirators had been convicted, many older voters couldn't believe the city was ready to abandon its criminal political culture. I knew better because I had made it a point to base my campaign at a headquarters on the South Side, where the shops, bodegas, cafés, and even pizza joints were run by recent immigrants and their children. Here were thousands of people whom the old system had never served. They were ready to respond to someone representing a bridge to the future, and I showed up speaking nearly fluent Spanish and ready to recognize that the future belonged to all of us, including them.

15

BEYOND BEANBAG

Politics ain't beanbag is a Gilded Age expression people still use to explain the rough parts of campaigning. The full quote, uttered by a fictional Irish immigrant in Chicago, is, "Sure, politics ain't bean-bag. 'Tis a man's game, an' women, childer, cripples an' prohybitionists'd do well to keep out iv it."

Until recently the list of those who were expected to "keep out iv it" included "openly" gay men. In 2002 my rivals knew the bigotry that would have once helped them was no longer so powerful. But as Brown University professor of political science Darrell West observed, it would not stop my opponents from "campaigning openly on family values." This didn't keep Joseph Paolino from trying to exploit it in a very clever way. Three weeks before voters went to the polls, a new group supposedly devoted to equality for LGBTQ people was formed one morning and held a press conference that afternoon to endorse Paolino as the better candidate for gay voters.

It turned out that the new group had just four members and no agenda other than to back my opponent. The man-bites-dog element of the press conference—gay voters endorsing Mr. Family Values over me—was irresistible for the press and briefly made it a big deal. But as it all blew over, I concluded that the little staged episode had been intended to remind a homophobic minority that I was gay and therefore somehow scary. Fortunately, the four-man group didn't put a dent in my own support, and I faced just one more issue that belonged in the "ain't beanbag" category.

After the gay endorsement stunt, another opposing candidate, David Igliozzi, distributed a flyer that told voters that because of my work as a defense lawyer I would be "the number 1 advocate for less jail time for criminals." Distributed in the two whitest areas of the city, the message assumed that recipients had no idea how the legal system worked and might believe that as mayor I would somehow favor criminals over the city as a whole *and* that I would have some way of influencing the judges who sentenced people convicted of crimes. Of course there might be a few hundred voters just uninformed enough to believe this claim and fearful enough to cast votes based on it. In a four-person race, that number could determine the outcome.

When we weren't distracted by ridiculous questions about my credibility in the gay community or my desire to see violent criminals run amok, my campaign focused on the ways that I would practice politics and run the city. The first thing I stressed was that I would not mix the two, as Cianci had. For example, where he'd sought campaign contributions from city workers, I refused to accept donations from anyone employed by taxpayers. And I made it clear that no one would be able to buy access to me, or city contracts or services, with a campaign contribution.

But as much as I thought it was important to assure people that I would end corruption, voters seem to care more that everyone in the city, and every neighborhood and block, would be treated the same. They wanted to know that a broken sidewalk in the richest neighborhood wouldn't be fixed any faster than one on a poorer corner and that I understood that the sparkling down-town that tourists loved to visit wasn't all that mattered. Indeed, while the state and city had lavished money and attention on the center of the city and the area around the state capitol, poverty had increased among the people who called the city home.

I knew that people were affected by the city's problems even if they didn't articulate their concerns like policy wonks. My cam-paign was built around finding ways to have one-on-one conver-sations with as many voters as possible, and I managed to connect with thousands of people this way. When they said they were having trouble finding a new apartment, I knew they were talk-ing about the city's failure to support good, affordable housing. When I heard they were afraid to go out at night, I knew they were referring to a spike in crime made worse by the problem that many police officers had been demoralized by Cianci's cor-ruption. When they said they were worried about their kids and exhausted by the challenges of work and family, I understood that our schools needed work and that the city's failure to provide after-school programs was stressing people out.

As I kept my promise to walk every one of Providence's twenty-five neighborhoods, my list of problems grew. Parks out-side the richer neighborhoods were a mess. Dead city-owned trees were removed when they stood in front of a Cianci donor's home, but others were left to rot. Then there were the rats. Called brown rats or Norway rats, these one-pound critters occupy every continent except Antarctica and can carry a number of dis-eases. Well-run cities fight rats with everything from poison to heavy-duty trash cans that choke their food supply. Poorly run cities, like Providence under Cianci, neglect rat control, which means the rodent population explodes and people start finding them in their gardens, their kitchens, and their children's rooms.

Rats became a key issue, and I told voters all it would take was a citywide effort to deprive them of food by using ratproof waste containers, which the city could provide, and, where needed, to exterminate them.

I also had plans for improving the schools and the parks and creating after-school programs to take the pressure off families. Improving public safety would involve a long-term endeavor led by honest, competent professionals. A similar approach would be required to deal with the city's fiscal problems, which were substantial.

By Election Day all that was left was the most basic task: getting more votes than the other guys. This meant making sure that people who supported me were able to get to the polls, and for this task we deployed more than a hundred people, who snapped up every van available to rent within a hundred miles. With teams working the phones, we contacted voters who needed transportation and dispatched drivers to provide it. Often the callers and the drivers were neighborhood people known to the voters. If a mother said she couldn't leave young children, we brought them along and watched them while she went into the polling place. If a driver spotted a likely voter along the way, a quick stop might put another person in the van and another vote in our column.

Our entire campaign plan had been based on the fact that Providence was becoming a *majority*-minority city, but this shift in demography did not guarantee a shift in political power. This is something the national Republican Party has understood for years, and it has often prevailed by doubling down on its visceral appeals to white voters and ignoring or even insulting the rest. To capitalize on population trends, we needed to inspire and motivate minority voters, many of whom felt apathetic about politics. We did this with allies I trusted, and by showing up, over and over again, until we gained trust. It worked, as polling places in the minority wards of the South Side registered double the usual traffic and almost all the votes cast were for me. Add the strong vote I got from my General Assembly constituents on the East Side and a majority in almost every other ward, and the outcome was better than the polls had predicted. We got 53 percent of the total, compared with 34 percent for the next-highest-ranking vote getter, Paolino.

I was with my family when the election results came in, but I went to our campaign headquarters within minutes. "¡Lo tenemos! We've got it!" shouted people in the crowd that had spilled onto the street, where drivers honked their car horns. With people starting to clog the busy street, we moved the celebration to Roger Williams Park, where excited Spanish mingled with equally excited English as people absorbed the fact that a new coalition—Latino, Black, white, Jewish, Italian, gay, you name it—would get a chance to serve the city. Merengue music filled the air and people danced near the lit carousel.

We still faced the general election, but in a city where Democrats outnumber Republicans two to one, the result was a foregone conclusion. In fact, we would win 84 percent of the vote. The local press would hail the outcome as proof that things were changing in Providence. This was true, but not everyone understood what that change meant. Even before I took office, I received requests from people who wanted the kinds of favors that had been the former mayor's currency. Some people asked for jobs they would never be qualified to perform. Others wanted to jump the line to get special attention for their problems. I may have made a few enemies as I said no to these requests.

————

As usual, the city welcomed its new mayor at an inauguration ceremony on the same city hall steps. It snowed while I got my chance to address a crowd from those steps, and many noted the way the flakes that piled up gave everything a clean look. With the mayor of Santo Domingo, a special guest, seated nearby, I spoke proudly of our diversity and the spirit that had ended "a generation of cronyism and mediocrity."

The problem had not been with the people, I stressed, but with elected officials. "When government is worthy of neither the people it serves nor the people who work within it, it corrodes the heart of democracy. Cynicism may make for shrewd politics, but it makes for ineffective government and a disengaged citizenry."

While Cianci loyalists who had come to gawk retreated indoors, two thousand people stayed to hear all of my thirty-minute speech, even as the wind began to turn the snow into freezing pellets and the temperature dropped. They heard me promise to begin after-school and weekend programs for students and communities across the city. I praised the thousands of city workers who were devoted to their jobs and assured them they would have the support of an administration that would elevate "old-fashioned principles of right and wrong." Finally I noted three decades of fiscal irresponsibility and pledged to get the city's finances in order.

The message I heard in return from the people was consistent. They said they had heard my promises but were a little worried about what would come next.

Over and over again they said, "We're with you. We really are. We just hope you can do it." As I finally turned to leave, my campaign consultant Mandy Grunwald pointed to the people who stayed and said, "Never forget the people who elected you. There they are."

16

QUEEN FOR (ONLY) A DAY

Providence had gotten used to being entertained. My predecessor had trained people to expect their mayor to bring a little fun and excitement to the city. He had done it with little stunts and outrageous comments and relentless attention seeking. When the circus came to town, he played the ringmaster for a special performance. He turned a downtown bar into his performance space, where at any moment he might join the resident cabaret singer in a duet or crack mean jokes like Don Rickles. All that separated him from a Vegas lounge act was that he didn't say, "I'm here all week, folks." He didn't have to say it because everyone knew.

More ordinary mayors presented personas that could inspire hope or ambition and project competence as they competed with other mayors in seeking big federal grants or wooing companies with plans to create jobs in a new facility. But while performance has been a part of leadership throughout recorded history, it has never been as important as it is now. Outside of the smallest villages and towns, people rarely meet political leaders face-to-face and have little chance to get to know them in a real way. We make do with impressions gleaned from the media or formed in a moment when we might see and hear them from a distance.

Although I agree that when a politician meets a crowd they are "on" in a way they might not be at home, I won't do anything that conflicts with my basic character. I won't play the insult comic the way Cianci did or indulge in sly race-baiting the way the first President Bush did with his Willie Horton ad. But I will choose to show people different sides of myself at different times, depending on the moment. And I know that it's important to be as open as I can so I don't seem one-dimensional. I mean, there's more to me than the guy who talks about corruption and promises ethical government.

Two months after I took office, the Providence Newspaper Guild held its annual follies at a semi-campy banquet hall called Venus de Milo. The charity event had begun in 1974 as a goodwill gesture following a bruising guild strike. Bigger and better every year, it featured local media folks, politicians, and other boldface names. The best poked fun at themselves with a skit, song parody, or stream of jokes. With a crowd of over 1,200 made receptive by plenty of alcohol, you almost had to try to fail.

Each year the show featured a secret special guest who appeared in the last skit of the night. Since I was the new kid on the block, the guild asked me to be the surprise special guest. I waited out of sight while other performers ran through skits about, among other things, the federal conviction of our former mayor and a speaker of the house having sex in the capitol basement. The song parodies included a version of "I Feel Pretty" from the losing Democrat in the recent gubernatorial election and "Leader of the Pack," about the speaker of the House.

When I planned my act, I'd had a wealth of material to choose from, including my Italian and Jewish heritage, my short stature, and my previous life as a defense lawyer whose clients included some infamous characters. But the thing that others probably considered out-of-bounds was my sexual orientation, so of course I went there.

After I was introduced, the sound system erupted with "It's Raining Men" by the Weather Girls, and I was brought onto the stage in a sedan chair carried by two young men who obviously spent a lot of time in the gym. They were shirtless. I wore a full-length white fox fur, which I had borrowed from my best friend, Harriet Quinn.

The laughter and applause only grew louder as the chair was set on the stage, I got on my feet, and everyone could see more clearly who was underneath the coat. The bearers took away the chair, but two returned to help me with my act. I introduced them as "my qualified staffers Lars and Enrique, who are in charge of domestic affairs." After I explained that the coat had been made of "free-range foxes who died a natural death," I launched into a speech about all the changes I was making at city hall. I said I had removed the bar where my predecessor entertained special guests, but I didn't think anyone would miss it because I had heard that my visitors said they had been treated like royalty. Then I added, "Well, what they actually said was that it was like having tea with the queen."

For a split second the room was quiet and then I heard loud laughter and applause. With the ice broken, Lars and Enrique assisted me with the props that I used to demonstrate how I was getting rid of the old and bringing in the elegant new. We set a little table with bright linen and a candelabra that would have made Liberace proud. Everything that could be made more beautiful would be, I explained, even the police dogs. With that a beautiful (and beautifully behaved) white French poodle, clipped so she looked like a canine pom-pom, scampered to me from offstage and brought the house down.

So I was willing to play queen for a day, but that would be it. Today this kind of camp performance would be considered a put-down of men who may fit long-standing stereotypes, and it is something I would never do because everyone has a right to be fully respected and to be who they are. This is why twenty years later, with marriage equality the law of the land and "openly gay" people everywhere, I would definitely not repeat my Venus de Milo act.

Attitudes about homosexuality have flipped, with 60 percent of Americans now telling pollsters they accept LGBTQ people for who they are. (In 2003, 60 percent expressed the opposite view.) This doesn't mean we don't face discrimination, some of it enshrined in state laws, or that we are safe from hate crimes and homophobic or transphobic violence. What it does mean is that the days when people needed someone like me to put them at ease because *Oh my God! there's an LGBTQ person in the room* are over. Only troglodytes would be ignorant of our presence across society and require a bunch of safety signaling to calm their bigoted hearts. But in 2003 it was necessary for me to perform the way I did, if only to take control of the issue and deny others the chance to even suggest that I wasn't comfortable with myself.

17

DEMOCRACY DELIVERS

Having fulfilled my follies duty, I let go of any concerns about being accepted and plunged into the pile of problems that my predecessor left behind. Although they varied widely, taken together, the failures of the Cianci administration had robbed many of their faith in our civic life. People who lacked connections or the means to donate to the mayor's campaigns—in other words most people—had been given second-class treatment. For too many who knew only this kind of local government, the experience had led to a cynical conclusion: American politicians don't live up to their ideals.

If Providence was to become a better place, I needed to show people that a democratically elected city government could deliver and was preferrable to the autocratic and criminal cult of personality that had dominated the city for most of thirty years.

The only way to reach the big goal was by taking on all the issues, great and small, and deal with them in a transparent, effective way. I started by hiring the best people I could find, starting with Chief of Staff Mike Mello. A smart, politically savvy, completely honest bulldog, Mello was the top aide in the state treasurer's office and a city council person in Bristol. He had worked for Congressman Patrick Kennedy. This experience at every level of government, combined with his winning way with people, made him perfect for the job.

It was a very tough job from the very start. In almost every city office, including the mayor's office, we faced an enormous struggle just finding accurate information on where things stood. Although computers sat on many desks in city hall, they held almost no data. They were used mainly as glorified typewriters. In most cases even the letters written on the computers were not saved. Incoming correspondence seemed to have been stuffed with files at random. Some city departments, like Public Works, didn't have any computers at all. Records there were paper-and-pencil things, full of erasures.

The one exception to the data black hole was at the public safety complex, where it turned out someone had set up a system that recorded every call that was made to and from the building. We discovered the hardware locked in a closet and, once we saw how it was wired into the phone system, understood that it was capable of sweeping up and storing every word of every call. In Rhode Island it was (and still is) illegal to record calls without consent. This meant that with every incoming and outgoing call, whoever had installed the system may have committed a felony.

Once the discovery was made, we could easily imagine the other crimes that might be enabled by the system. Blackmail was the most obvious one, but recordings could also be leveraged to make all sorts of coercive threats. And since the system could record calls made by prisoners in the building's lockup, law enforcement could violate their rights with the information they could glean from their conversations with lawyers. Knowing how the recordings could be used led us to conclude that top officials had had the most to gain from its installation, but they all denied responsibility. However, the fact that the phones in the offices of the police chief and top fire officials were *not* bugged fed our suspicions. The police chief had previously been caught in a scheme to record officers at roll call via a device hidden in a clock. He was also an expert in electronic surveillance.

Our investigation into the public safety bugging system led us to the city's Department of Communications, which had arranged for the hardware purchase. There we were shocked to find eighty-five employees doing... well, it was hard to tell, but some of them had been busy shredding cell phone records and making mysterious purchases. (How could anyone spend $14,000 at Staples in one go?) We fired several of the communications managers and referred the whole thing—from the installation of the phone monitoring system to the suspect purchases—to the state attorney general's office.

The attorney general discovered that the recording technology was an off-the-shelf thing called Total Recall that had been ordered less than a year before at a cost of roughly $1 million and had been logged into the city's books as public safety equipment. The most unexpected finding was that no one had ever accessed the system to listen to calls. No one could say why the system had been installed and switched on but then never used. Chalk it up to cold feet, incompetence, or forgetfulness, the fact was that no chargeable offense had been committed but nearly a million dollars in taxpayer money had been wasted.

Beyond the tech problems were people problems that we had to sort out. A small number of Cianci holdovers still wanted to operate on the basis of favors and needed to be retrained or replaced. Similarly, a few members of the city council would need time to get accustomed to a new way of doing business. Under the old way, residents got trees trimmed, sidewalks fixed, and streets plowed by calling their city council members. (Plowing was done so informally that the only way you could tell where the trucks had been sent was by following the tire tracks in the snow.) We changed that by establishing routines, schedules, and policies that distributed services fairly and hired people based on merit. When we did away with this patronage system, some people on the council could not understand it. One even said to me, "Why would you even run for city council if you can't do things for your family and friends?"

A somewhat similar but more surprising reaction arose among city workers who complained about my no-political-donations-from-city-workers policy. In the past the mayor would organize political fundraising dinners and parties by distributing tickets to workers, who were expected to buy some themselves and sell the rest. The cash came back to the mayor's campaign, where officials kept track of which workers had raised the most dough.

I thought that my policy was a win for city workers, who would be relieved of buying and selling tickets, and a win for the citizens of Providence, who could have faith that the government was being operated in an aboveboard way. The people of Providence got it and liked it. Many of the workers objected to my approach because they had enjoyed the previous mayor's parties and banquets. The events, which allowed them to get close to the mayor and his top aides, had created a sense of belonging, and to them this feeling was worth the annoyance of fundraising. Indeed, some people considered our approach insulting. "Are you too good for our money?" they wondered.

When we heard this, we explained that our approach was intended not as an insult but as a sign of respect for the service they rendered to the people of Providence, which had nothing to do with politics. To fill the social void, we created regular events we called "friendraisers," parties city workers could attend for free. Some were held in downtown hotels. On summer evenings we gathered in a city park. City workers were also always welcome at our political events, where they could mingle and talk with whomever they met. They just couldn't give money to my campaigns.

———

As we dealt with the overall culture of the city workforce, we also hired new leaders who shook up the ranks and made changes that the people of the city could see. One of my first appointments was the new chief of police, Dean Esserman, who had developed a national reputation for turning around troubled police departments, including the four-thousand-officer Metro-North Railroad Police Department in greater New York City and the New Haven and Stamford, Connecticut, police departments. He had started his career working in New York for William Bratton, who was renowned for using data and street-level policing to bring down crime.

Esserman had an unusual background for a cop. He had been raised in a Jewish family in Manhattan, and his childhood home had been a haven for writers and artists whom his physician father treated for free. Many of his summers were spent in extremely poor communities abroad, helping his father on medical missions. He thought about studying medicine but was bitten by the police bug after training to be an emergency medical technician and volunteering for a Central Park rescue squad.

In Providence, Esserman found a city in the grip of a violent crime wave—our rate was double the national average—where trust in the police was exceedingly low. The spike had begun halfway through the second reign of Cianci and occurred while the rest of the state saw a steady decline. Drive-by shootings and other gun crimes were occurring at an alarming rate, and police were warning that Providence, like other cities, was dangerously awash in firearms. (This was the time when the number of guns in our country began to grow more rapidly even as the number of people owning them declined sharply.)

The solution, as Esserman saw it, was to build closer ties between the police and the people they served. Within a year violent crime was down 20 percent. By 2006 the decline would be almost 40 percent. At the same time morale in the department improved as officers saw that recognition and promotions were offered on the basis of merit, not connections or cash.

———————

As mayor I made it a point to circulate in neighborhoods to listen to what folks had to say. This outreach was something I had in common with Mayor Cianci, who had been renowned for spending his evenings and weekends bouncing from event to event. The difference was that Cianci had traveled the city, vodka glass in hand, in a luxury black sedan driven by a police officer and visited to cast a celebrity spell. I considered myself to be on a never-ending fact-finding tour, and, given that I don't care much for alcohol, I was always sober.

The issues people raised with me ranged from complaints about how the police were suddenly enforcing laws that Cianci's cops hadn't, like those concerning underage drinking, to reports of persistent quality-of-life crime. The bar owner who said "the other guy woulda taken care of" his liquor law violation didn't get any sympathy from me. However, the senior citizens who told me they were being terrorized by local teens who threw rocks at them made me eager to help them.

After hearing about their problem, I went to some of the homes where the seniors thought the rock throwers might live. At one house I had to navigate my way around a surly pit bull chained to a stake in the front lawn. At another I was greeted by a woman who was disappointed that the man in the suit (me) wasn't there to tell her she had won the Publishers Clearing House sweepstakes. At both homes I introduced myself and explained that before I became mayor, I had been a defense lawyer and that I had seen too many young people traumatized after minor offenses led them into the juvenile justice system. I didn't say that the neighbors thought their kids were the culprits. Instead I asked them to help spread the word that the harassment had to stop. I later heard from the seniors that it had.

Other improvements came when we were able to identify corrupt practices within city government and simply replace them with normal procedures. A case in point: liquor licenses.

Licenses to sell liquor at bars, restaurants, and stores are regulated because alcohol is a kind of controlled substance governed by laws that establish age limits for purchases. Depending on the state and municipality, liquor sales may be subject to other laws and even special tax arrangements. In New Hampshire, for example, hard liquor is available only in state-operated stores that generate $160 million annually for the state government. On the other hand, California laws make hard liquor available at supermarkets and drugstores.

I didn't give much thought to liquor licenses until a local restaurateur asked to see me about a problem. He was an older fellow, and, as he explained it, he had two successful places and wanted to open a third restaurant but was having trouble buying a license. It's not that he wasn't willing to pay. He said he had paid $70,000 to acquire his two current permits from restaurant owners who had closed their businesses and sold the licenses as if they owned them. Now there weren't any available for less than $50,000, which he couldn't afford.

It's almost impossible to describe the look that came over my visitor's face as I explained how the system was *supposed* to work. The number of restaurant liquor licenses wasn't capped by a city ordinance. All he had to do was apply and pay a fee of a couple hundred dollars. If his place met certain technical requirements for new restaurants, which were related to floor plans, menus, etc., getting the license should be almost automatic.

The fact that a market for licenses had arisen at all indicated to us that under the old mayor, the city had created a system that improperly limited the availability of licenses, guaranteeing they would have inflated value. My guess is that a cross-check of license holders and the mayor's campaign fundraising would have revealed lots of donations flowing from restaurateurs to the campaigns. Although he threatened to sue the city to get back his $70,000 and more, the man who had demanded to talk to me about his license problems never followed through. I hope it was because he saw the changes we were bringing to the city.

In our first year, my administration kept discovering ways, big and small, that our predecessor had rigged the bureaucracy so that it would add to his personal and political power. Faced with a budget crisis but fearing the voters would punish him if the city's books looked out of whack, Cianci devised a clever scheme to make the city's finances better, at least in the short term.

The plot involved hiking valuations, and thereby tax assessments, on big downtown buildings, some of which paid annual taxes in the millions. By picking out a few dozen properties and suddenly tripling their taxes, the Cianci administration was able to put millions of dollars into the city's coffers because the law required real estate owners to pay the taxes levied in full. Only then could they begin the appeals process that would lead to the courthouse. It was obvious that the assessment wouldn't withstand legal challenges, and huge refunds would have to be paid. It was, therefore, a typical Cianci scheme. Make things look good in the run-up to election and then either devise another scam in the next term or let your successor deal with it.

The state supreme court took such a dim view of what Cianci had done that it called the scheme "municipal thuggery." In his decision for just one of many plaintiffs, Judge Francis Flaherty also lambasted former city officials for their efforts to deny property owners due process. "The mythical and legendary law firm of Hinder, Stall and Delay could not hold a candle to the efforts of the City of Providence to retard the wheels of justice from grinding to their inevitable destination in this and kindred matters," he added.

Although the city was required to refund many millions of dollars, with interest, and pay more for the plaintiff's legal fees, the tax fiasco was small compared with the trouble in our pension systems. As we discovered upon my taking office, Cianci had not limited his foolishness to sweetheart contracts with public employees to secure votes. Once the contracts were signed, he had also neglected to fully fund the city's contributions to the pensions established by these agreements. With overly generous cost-of-living increases built in, the agreements forced higher costs on the system every year. By 2003 many retired firefighters younger than sixty were collecting pensions in excess of $100,000 per year. They also remained on city benefits, which covered family members too. Some used the educational benefits provided in the contract to get free college degrees and commence new careers. Several used this get-paid-to-attend-school-free setup to become lawyers.

The size of this problem—an anticipated $600 million shortfall in the coming decade—was stunning and would require years of effort to address. The firefighters' contract, which covered other benefits in addition to pensions, was the most challenging.

Amiable as they were with the general public, the firefighters were ferocious negotiators with me. When they didn't like my responses to their demands, they organized teams of picketers who seemed to follow me wherever I went, for years. After he was released from prison, the former mayor occasionally tried to exploit the protests. When hundreds showed up to protest being required to contribute to their health insurance (they had never paid anything), Cianci arrived to cheers and joined the chanting against me.

The firefighters' union leadership was bugged by a lot of things we did, including my hiring of George Farrell as the chief of the department. Farrell came up through the ranks and was a person of great integrity. He ran the department in the no-nonsense way taxpayers would expect. He showed up every day even when he was undergoing harsh chemotherapy for cancer. He took on the issues of overtime and worked to make acceptance to the fire academy merit based, which ended privileges previously given to those with connections. Every time we instituted this kind of change, we'd detect a certain pushback. Sometimes, responses to calls were slowed, especially if it seemed that no lives were at stake. "We would have been here sooner," they would say, "but the mayor won't get us any more rescues." (*Rescues* was the term we used for ambulances. And the city had enough of them.)

We never would have faced such animus if Cianci had been a

straight shooter, and I often found myself wondering how things would have been different if he had simply done his job. All the energy he had poured into complicated schemes drained time and attention from actual government work. As a result we had dilapidated schools and parks, inadequate services, and decades of a do-nothing approach to jobs. The problems in these areas weren't insurmountable. However, they did require the kind of effort that's hard to sustain when you're preoccupied with corrupt schemes. Cianci's crew had been so distracted that they hadn't even known how bad things were.

Our school system faced all the challenges found in urban districts across the country. Eighty percent of the students came from low-income families, one-quarter of our students changed addresses annually, and more than 20 percent needed bilingual instruction. Nearly all of our school buildings were overdue for major renovations. Roofs leaked, floors sagged, and heating and water systems were in disrepair. In all, Providence needed more than $500 million in school construction and repairs. Fortunately, a little-used state program would pay more than 90 percent of the costs of approved projects. We jumped in and gradually began transforming the places where roughly 28,000 kids went to school.

Nothing illustrated our city's uniquely bad approach to caring for children better than our Head Start program. In other places Head Start preschool, which is generally offered free, had proven to be the single most effective means of helping kids, especially those in poorer communities, develop into children ready to learn in school. This happens because the program stimulates brain development at a critical time in a child's life. The effect lasts long enough that it leads to higher achievement in elementary grades and all that means as a child moves on in education.

As I discovered when I became mayor, the program's regional office in Boston had opened an investigation into Head Start in Providence because it had been turned into a patronage machine for my predecessor and his allies. Instead of hiring qualified teachers and childcare workers, it had put the mayor's lower-skilled supporters, who weren't qualified for these jobs, into Head Start positions. The program also leased substandard facilities from favored landlords. With almost all the money coming from the federal government, the gravy train didn't require fuel from local taxpayers. And since the kids, more than a thousand each year, came from families most in need and least likely to rock the boat, this went on for many years.

As we raced to fix what was wrong with Head Start, bringing in qualified people to operate centers in appropriate spaces, the gravity of what Mayor Cianci had done took up space in my mind. This scheme, which had robbed kids of what they needed to get ready for school and life beyond, was one of the most damaging things he ever did because it hurt children and corroded public trust in our city government. Nothing does more harm to our prospects for making life better by pulling together than a selfish public official who deprives kids for political gain.

Snowstorms are big tests for officials in every cold-weather state. In a famous illustration of this fact, Chicago mayor Michael Bilandic, who had inherited the power of the Daley Machine, was driven out of office by the city's failed response to a two-day snowfall that paralyzed the city. (His rival in the Democratic primary, Jane Byrne, used a single TV ad, which showed her standing in an impassable street amid huge drifts, to cruise to victory.)

In the case of the storm that hit Providence on December 13, 2007, it wasn't the amount of snow—ten inches—or the wind and cold. The problem was the rate at which the snow fell, beginning at the most inconvenient time. Forecasts had predicted a mid-afternoon start for the storm, but the first flurries fell at around 10:00 a.m., and, as the storm pulled moisture and warmth from coastal waters, the snow began to come at a rate of two inches per hour. At noon workplaces across the region began to close and people tried to commute to their homes. The result was traffic so heavy that plows and salt and sand trucks couldn't maneuver. Snow packed by tires turned to ice, which sent cars skidding and crashing. The main streets and highways looked like parking lots filled with cars, trucks, and yes, school buses.

The school buses departed in early afternoon because on the evening prior to the storm, our superintendent, in consultation with us at city hall, had announced that schools would be open for a full day. This was one of the three options he'd had, each of which came with a risk. Cancel school for the day and you force parents to scramble for childcare. A half-day closure creates the same problem. But if you proceed with a full day of instruction, there's a chance that children will be sent home in treacherous conditions, which will make lots of people very worried.

Having made the decision, we had no option but to hope for the best and, ultimately, accept the outrage that came with something much worse. With families growing more anxious by the minute, buses got stuck in massive snarls of traffic that also trapped our seventy-plus snowplows and salter/sanders. Hours passed while the local press—radio, TV, newspaper websites—offered constant updates. Fights broke out at collision sites. Drivers, some of whom feared running out of gas to keep themselves warm, abandoned their vehicles and tried to walk to shelter. Their immovable cars made the jams even worse.

While I announced parking bans to aid the plowing effort and urged everyone to stay home, city hall was deluged with calls from parents, some of whom became quite angry and hysterical. Efforts to get kids home were hampered by the fact that a new school choice program required longer routes, as students no longer necessarily attended schools in their neighborhoods. (This also meant they couldn't walk home.) At 6:00 p.m. the district reported the good news that nearly ninety buses had completed their routes. The bad news was that sixty buses carrying roughly a thousand students were still somewhere on the city streets. The police then started taking kids off buses and delivering them to their homes. The last child was finally returned to his family at 10:30 p.m.

The school bus debacle was one of the toughest moments in my time as mayor. I accepted my share of the blame, and my administration cooperated with a committee that investigated what happened and concluded that the schools had not planned for the kind of emergency that arose and, when it did, had suffered from communication breakdowns that left no one in charge. (The superintendent had gone home for the day at five thirty because he believed everything was under control.) The committee recommended the district develop real guidelines for snow closures, identify shelter options along bus routes, and establish systems for emergency communications. We did these things.

Although most other problems in city government were readily identified and resolved with some concentrated effort, the issue of the firefighters' contract, especially their special health-care benefit, defied my best efforts for seven and a half years. During that time I grew frustrated, and some of the firefighters came to think I was disrespecting them. Nothing could have been further from the truth, but they still felt angry.

Certain the public was with them, and against me, the

firefighters began showing up to picket whenever I attended an event. Their protests were generally annoying and often disruptive. In 2007 I couldn't even be included on a list of cochairs for Hillary Clinton's campaign because Democrats back unions.

When the national economic crisis started in 2008, the firefighters were required to chip in an average of one hundred dollars per month for health care. They also accepted a 5 percent cut in personnel and very modest pay raises. In the end the city would save $16 million per year. This was an important start on getting control of the extra burden the firefighters' contract put on the taxpayers. My one regret was that it took far too long for us to reach an agreement and I've always wondered how I might have resolved this matter more quietly. I didn't like being the object of their pickets or the subject of their complaints to the public. And I sure didn't like the stubborn style they brought to the bargaining process. But I never imagined in a million years I would be in a fight with a union for seven years, trying to balance the interests of taxpayers and the necessity of taking care of firefighters. This is an example of why being a mayor is a hard job.

————

With much left to do to keep improving the city, especially on jobs and housing, I expected to seek a third term. Then Patrick Kennedy announced he would not seek reelection to Congress. Senator Ted Kennedy's son Patrick had come to Rhode Island for college and never left. He won a seat in the statehouse at age twenty-one and six years later won one of the state's two seats in the United States Congress. In his public service he was best known as a health-care advocate who pushed for mental health treatment to be covered on a par with other kinds of care. Much of his motivation for this work came from his own struggles with addiction, including a stint in rehab for OxyContin addiction, which presaged the national crisis caused by prescription drugs falsely marketed as nonaddictive.

With his state and federal positions combined, Kennedy had served twenty years as a legislator, which, if you are doing it right, is demanding and often frustrating work. And though he had been supported by many, his struggles with sobriety had pointed him in a new direction. He wanted to launch some advocacy and research projects on addiction and mental health and had already begun putting them together.

Kennedy's decision signaled to every Democrat in the state that a rare chance was at hand. Add all that I knew could be done for America's cities with the right kind of federal support, and it seemed there would be no better time to take a shot. If I won, I would go to Washington to represent Rhode Island and to help the federal government become a better partner to America's cities. This was of real importance because the country was becoming steadily more urbanized and I knew what worked in cities and what didn't.

On February 14, 2010, I announced my run for the seat and argued that my experience made me well prepared to work in Washington on behalf of the same causes that I addressed as mayor. I was opposed in the Democratic primary by three other candidates, including our state party chairman, a young state representative, and a businessman-lawyer who billed himself as a "conservative Democrat."

I won the primary and in the general election defeated a Republican state representative named John J. Loughlin II, whose key promise—to destroy the newly created health-care program called Obamacare—seemed notably off-key in Rhode Island, where Obama was very popular and people generally welcomed the overhaul in our health-care system.

PART III

LOONEYVILLE

In which we discover things are much worse than we could possibly have imagined.

18

IT'S MUCH WORSE UNDER *THIS* DOME

"There are people we are electing who will destroy this country if we aren't careful."

—John Boehner, former Republican Speaker of the House

If you are a lucky freshman representative, you arrive in Washington with your party in the majority, enjoying control of the House, and setting the agenda. You climb the steps to the Capitol, stand in awe beneath the enormous dome, and imagine how you, or at the very least your party, might achieve the kind of greatness represented by the likenesses in National Statuary Hall.

Suffice it to say, I was not lucky.

With President Obama reaching the halfway point in his first term, the national Democratic Party had suffered the usual midterm election setback and then some. In what the president called "a shellacking," the GOP gained sixty-three House seats. Add newcomers who replaced retiring members and there were eighty-seven new Republican faces. As Republican John Boehner took the Speaker's gavel from Democrat Nancy Pelosi, he counseled humility. The Tea Party freshmen ignored him as they joined veteran Representative Mike Pence, who was himself dreaming of the presidency, at a rally where they cried, "No compromise!"

The incoming GOPers had much in common. Among the eighty-five were seventy-four white males. One-quarter of them were millionaires, with seven reporting fortunes *in excess of $20 million*. Not one of them was Jewish, which meant that Eric Cantor of Virginia remained the lone Jew in the Republican caucus. Not one was part of the LGBTQ community.

My side of the freshman class numbered just nine—we called ourselves the Noble Nine—but we represented the diversity of America very well. Among us were three Black women, one Black man, an Asian American woman, a Pakistani American man, and three white men. As one of these last three, I contributed my Jewishness and sexual orientation to the mix.

I know that even my talking about how diverse we were might irritate some people, but with people with so many different perspectives we could refine our ideas to make them better. Besides, the country itself is getting more diverse at a faster rate than ever before. And that is a good thing.

The only problem with this was the hysterical reaction of white nationalists who let themselves feel insecure about the future. They were represented in Congress by the likes of Steve King, a Republican from Iowa, whose racism and extreme anti-immigrant rhetoric presaged Donald Trump. Among his lies were claims that murderous immigrants were causing a "slow-motion Holocaust" for white America. Yes, he really said this, and of course Fox News and other right-wing outlets featured him regularly.

Though the worst, King was not alone. There were so many Republicans in the House who expressed similar views that they could have formed a white nationalist caucus. Alongside these extremists were members of the GOP who would, if they could, end separation of church and state and make us a Christian nation. These colleagues actually believed in the existence of a "war on Christmas" (a ratings-grabbing fantasy cooked up by Fox News).

In most cases they viewed gains made by others, like marriage equality for people like me, as threats against them. Of course nothing was being taken away from them except the sense of superiority they might have felt holding special rights and privileges—like marriage—others were denied.

Racial and religious nationalists were barely visible in the Northeast, and their language was a coded dialect unfamiliar to most outsiders. At that time, I didn't immediately recognize their champions in Congress, nor did I understand that they represented a danger to democracy. Besides, in 2011 I was busy trying to understand my new job and settle in on Capitol Hill. I hired key staff and leaned on our leadership team to get up to speed on votes and committee work. I also tried to set myself up for a life split between Washington, one of America's most expensive cities, and my district in Rhode Island. This explained why some members crowded into apartments set up like college dormitories and a few even slept in their offices, using the facilities at the House gym for showering.

I didn't have to worry about finding a place immediately because Patrick Kennedy had allowed me to stay in his apartment, which was close to the Capitol. If you have visited the neighborhoods in and around Capitol Hill, you've seen block after block of pretty, exquisitely restored townhomes, most of which were built in the nineteenth century. The location meant even the tiniest houses sold for $1 million or more and about half the homes had been divided into apartments for all the workers who wanted to be close to congressional offices.

You might think a Kennedy would have a sunny home where he could recharge in comfort after a long day of lawmaking. Wrong. The key he had given me opened the door to a cramped basement space where the windows were below ground level and you could feel the vibrations made by the traffic on the street. Although I was grateful to have a landing spot when I arrived, it was not the kind of homey place that would feel like a refuge after a long workday. Fortunately, Washington is a good place for renters, and I was able to eventually settle in a comfortable place.

The important parts of my job had to do with policy. I focused first on issues related to the committees I was assigned to—Foreign Affairs and Small Business. Foreign Affairs is a much-coveted committee and I was thrilled to get it. I had a strong interest in a seat on the Judiciary Committee. However, with small businesses still in crisis in my district due to the Great Recession, I knew there were things I could do to help with a spot on a committee that focused on their needs.

Unfortunately, as the minority party, we had limited power to help, and no one had to tell the Noble Nine, as freshmen in the minority, to be humble. Still, it came as almost a shock when, at the first meeting of the entire Democratic caucus, we heard our colleagues say tearful goodbyes to defeated members. Some of them had been swept into office on Barack Obama's coattails and represented districts that were historically Republican. In Ohio, for example, John Boccieri had won a seat that had been held by the GOP for the previous thirty-six years. The guy he'd snatched it from took it back in 2010.

The departure of more veteran lawmakers was harder to accept. Jim Oberstar of Minnesota and Ike Skelton of Missouri, for example, had each served more than thirty years. They were among the few who had been in Congress during times when it was much easier to get things done.

In our caucus meeting we also absorbed the fact that Nancy Pelosi, who had made history as the first woman to become Speaker, had lost her position after using every bit of her political capital winning the battle for President Obama's landmark health-care program, created by the Affordable Care Act. She would often say she had no regrets about her devotion to the vote, which had allowed the other side to make her a target of Tea Party rage. This tactic had been so effective that a handful of congressional Democrats had voted against her when it came time to choose our minority leader. They had done it so they could go home and tell their constituents they weren't "Pelosi Democrats" and perhaps make themselves more appealing to conservatives in their districts.

The way some in our caucus distanced themselves from Obamacare was emblematic of a problem I would see time and again. While we Democrats worked hard to address the country's problems, the GOP promoted just one policy—tax cuts for the rich—and otherwise devoted themselves to blocking us with hysterical cries of "Socialism." When we succeeded, we moved on to the next challenge and neglected to claim credit. In the meantime, if there was something in our success that voters came to like, our opponents would glom on to it and promote it as their own. In the case of the Affordable Care Act, they seized upon one key element, the requirement that insurers cover preexisting conditions, as if it had been their idea.

Obamacare was our party's greatest achievement since the 1960s. In time it would halve the number of people without health insurance and end most of the cruel insurance industry practices that bankrupted people in their moments of need. The problem was that these benefits were to be phased in over the course of four years, which meant that no one felt them in 2010. Instead people were treated to the GOP's sky-is-falling campaign to repeal it.

After the farewell party/caucus meeting, we few freshmen Democrats went to our offices, which were rather lonely places. Mine was on the first floor of a century-old building named for Speaker Joseph Gurney Cannon (1903–1911), which was the oldest of the House office buildings. (Before its construction most members worked at desks in the chamber.)

My experience in the Rhode Island legislature helped me understand how the House of Representatives worked. But to my disappointment the United States Congress often seemed a more dysfunctional and partisan place, one where even when people made inspiring arguments on important issues they had to assume their words meant nothing to those on the other side.

To be fair, in Rhode Island the Republicans were so outnumbered that they had to work in a bipartisan way to get anything accomplished. Still, I often saw people change their minds, and their votes, after hearing a colleague speak. And when we did speak, the chamber was usually filled with attentive representatives. In contrast, the United States House Chamber was almost always nearly empty during speeches as people stood to offer their arguments for the unblinking eye of the C-SPAN cameras. Snippets of these talks might be used on TV news programs back home, and sometimes members had the feed playing in their offices (usually on mute). But a distressingly significant portion of what was said evaporated into the ether since everyone seemed locked into unchangeable positions.

The inflexibility commonly called gridlock had developed with the hyperpartisanship of Newt Gingrich, amplified by Fox News and its imitators. By 2010, a significant number of GOP representatives, especially younger ones, had never lived in an environment free of this extremism. As Speaker Boehner discovered when newcomers called him "enemy" and "liberal collaborator," compromise in the name of getting stuff done had become all but impossible.

As Boehner would later write, he was alarmed by so-called Tea Party Republicans who were lost in the misinformation and rage they absorbed from right-wing media. He called them "knuckleheads" and "the crazies" from "Looneyville." They truly believed nonsense like the disproven "birther" conspiracy theory about how Obama was not legally president because he had been born outside the US. Boehner so despaired of the poisoned information environment that he visited his friend who ran Fox News, Roger Ailes, to ask him to stop spreading disinformation. He was dismayed to discover that Ailes, a former political consultant for the GOP, had been "swept into conspiracies and paranoia and [had become] an almost unrecognizable figure."

In a nod to a common right-wing fantasy about federal forces poised to round up citizens, Boehner would say Ailes "had black helicopters flying all around his head that morning. It was every conspiracy theory you ever heard, and I'm throwing cold water on all this bullshit." Remember, Ailes was the man who had constructed and still operated the most influential media outlet in red America.

The bunker mentality was reflected in Congress, where I often heard people speak on the House floor or in committee hearings and wondered if they really were the best their home districts might send to Washington. The 2010 class included the likes of Arizona's Paul Gosar and Alabama's Mo Brooks. Mo Brooks presented himself as a defender of his race in what he called "a war on whites" led by Barack Obama. When pressed on this claim, he said, "If you look at current federal law, there is only one skin color that you can lawfully discriminate against. That's Caucasians—whites." He also included traditional Republicans among the enemies of white people because in their efforts to appeal to Black and Hispanic voters they necessarily "discriminated" against whites. Bizarre as this logic was, it apparently pleased the folks back home, who kept reelecting him.

Gerrymandering had created many districts where a member with extreme views could be sure of reelection simply because he wore the right party label. Paul Gosar's district was carved to avoid every city of any size, including Flagstaff, so he could rely on rural voters, who were reliable Republicans. This meant that he could do and say things that were so out there that he caused the *Washington Post* to ask, "Who is this guy?" when he picked a fight with Pope Francis. It was the fall of 2015 and the pope, who was popular all over the world, had accepted Republican Speaker of the House John Boehner's invitation to become the first pontiff ever to address a joint session of Congress. Everyone expected Francis to stand up for immigrants, to call for action to slow climate change, and to criticize the excesses of capitalism.

The pope's job is to present his moral views, and if he doesn't make you a little uncomfortable, he's not doing it right. The stuff about immigrants, the climate, and capitalism, not to mention his opposition to the death penalty, would discomfit many Republicans. However, the pope was also certain to speak against abortion in a forceful way that would bother many Democrats. All these views aligned with those of previous pontiffs, even if their priorities had made them seem more conservative or traditional.

Mature people, Catholic or not, respected the pope's office enough to sit and listen when given the chance. This was why

Boehner had invited Francis in the first place. But Gosar, whose prior claim to fame involved a fight to strip a tortoise of its protections as an endangered species, was not a mature person. On the eve of this historic event, he said the pope should fight climate change "on his own time," as if there's a moment when he's not the pontiff. Gosar said he would respect Francis if he spoke up for persecuted Christians, "but when the pope chooses to act and talk like a leftist politician, then he can expect to be treated like one."

As Francis spoke it was easy to imagine Boehner's gratitude. Although long committed to conservative ideals, the Speaker had always tried to listen to others and was open to compromise. However, his party was rapidly abandoning him in favor of what the pope called "fundamentalism" and "individual delusion or ideological extremism." Indeed, GOP newcomers were so intent on showing their antieverything cred that they refused to approve even the mundane bills that kept the government functioning. Fortunately, when Boehner was faced with a crisis caused by the sandbox crowd, like their effort to block a routine increase in the national debt, Nancy Pelosi rallied enough Democrats to save the day. In practicing normal politics for the good of the country, Pelosi would come to Boehner's aid many times.

Having heard Boehner was being pressured to step down, it was reported that Pelosi had even hatched a plan to save his speakership. (Democrats would join Republicans to support him.) But Boehner had had enough of the extremists. He announced his retirement on the day after Francis spoke. In meeting with reporters that day, he revealed that the pope had used a private moment on the Speaker's balcony to grasp his arm and say, "Please pray for me" and then more insistently repeated, "Please pray for me."

————

When historians later considered Boehner's time as Speaker, they identified the parliamentary move, little recognized at the time, that signaled his time as the GOP's leader in the House was ending. The key player was a member of Congress who was in just his second term and who had rarely attracted much attention before he filed a motion to declare the Speaker's chair "vacant." At the time *National Journal*, an establishment source of unbiased reporting, said the motion had "almost no chance to succeed." Those of us who had watched the GOP move steadily toward extremism weren't so sure.

Officially referred to as a "motion to vacate the chair," the tactic that was deployed against Boehner is so extreme it hadn't been tried since 1910, when Democrats tried and failed to oust Republican Speaker Joseph Cannon, who was widely regarded as a tyrant. When raised, such a motion calls for the Speaker to be removed from his position and then replaced.

Two months before the pope's visit, Representative Mark Meadows of North Carolina filed a motion to vacate against Boehner. Although he didn't push to have the House take it up immediately, it was widely understood that Meadows had some support from the rank and file. In fact he was acting on behalf of the forty-member Freedom Caucus, and the motion was intended to send an embarrassing signal as the House began a six-week break. Boehner was out of step.

As everyone left town, Meadows was praised by an organization called FreedomWorks. Funded by deep-pocketed donors, FreedomWorks put big money behind the "grassroots" Tea Party movement and was known for signaling who among those running for office was in and who was out when it came to major donors. When asked about Meadows's filing, his colleague Devin Nunes of California suggested the following: "My guess is he's probably in trouble in his district, so he needs a way to raise money."

Like everyone on the Republican side, Nunes was trying to figure out how to respond to extremists like Meadows, whom he'd once called "lemmings with suicide vests." First elected to Congress at the age of thirty, long before the Tea Party arose, Nunes was in such a safe seat that he could reasonably expect to retire from it. His fellow Californian, Kevin McCarthy, took a different tack. After Boehner put McCarthy on his leadership team, McCarthy took the Tea Party freshmen under his wing and arranged for them to have weekly meetings with the Speaker. McCarthy then allowed the newcomers to use the sessions to berate Boehner from start to finish.

McCarthy's brood considered the chain-smoking, backslapping Boehner the personification of what was wrong with Washington. The Speaker was serious about his role and Congress's responsibility to meet the country's needs thorough policies and lawmaking. The radicals didn't study the issues like health care or climate change, or reflect on solutions, because they didn't think these activities were part of the job. For them, serving in Congress was a matter of attitude, expressed by their flashing air quotes when they used the word *govern* and by stunts they staged to attract the attention of Fox News cameras.

If the extremists had an agenda, it began and ended with rolling back Obamacare and then eliminating or vastly reducing everything else done by the government, except perhaps defense. When Boehner admitted that he liked working with Obama and counted the Democratic leader of the Senate, Harry Reid, as a friend, the Speaker became in their minds a traitor to conservatism. With him gone they consolidated their power in the Freedom Caucus. This caucus gave strength to what Representative Mick Mulvaney of South Carolina once called "just a bunch of pissed-off guys" who lacked cohesion. They chose the most pugnacious person in Congress, Representative Jim Jordan of Ohio, as their leader. Among the founding members were Meadows, Mulvaney, and Justin Amash of Michigan. Soon they would have enough members that should they vote in a bloc, they could defeat anything their own party put to a vote.

————————

Perhaps the vilest thinking I ever heard voiced on Capitol Hill came from House Republicans who told me, in so many words, that the lives of LGBTQ people were not worth protecting. The context involved the Equality Act, which I sponsored to protect people from discrimination on the bases of sex, sexual orientation, or gender identity in employment, public accommodations, education, federally funded programs, housing, credit, and jury service. At a Judiciary Committee hearing held to review the bill, I heard a gusher of nonsense from Republicans who tried to outdo each other as they expressed their prejudice. The worst came from Debbie Lesko of Arizona, who complained that the legislation meant the federal government was giving special status "to men who want to dress like women." She proposed calling my bill the "Forfeiting Women's Rights Act."

Lesko claimed, falsely, that the bill would "outlaw private facilities for women and girls" and put women in physical "danger" (she really meant rape) from transgender people whom she ignorantly described as "men wanting to dress as women." She said doctors would be "forced to perform sex change operations on adolescents" and that women's sports would cease to exist altogether. It's hard to know where to start with all the ignorance she spewed, but she was wrong about everything she said, including the idea that transgender people are people who want to dress a certain way. Transgender women and men feel they change not their clothes, but their entire gender identity. Some choose to change their bodies with reassignment surgery. Some do not. And everyone in the LGBTQ community deserves to be freed from the discrimination now widely practiced against us.

————————

The cynical bigotry, and pandering to hate, made it easy for me to tell Lesko, at a public hearing, that she needed to educate herself before making claims that were just not true. "Some people really don't understand who transgender people are," I said, "and yet they still want to offer their dangerous opinions." During a break she got out of her seat and walked halfway across the hearing room to confront me.

"I don't appreciate what you said to me. I know what I'm talking about."

"No, you absolutely do not know what you're talking about," I replied. "You either don't understand the bill or you are making false claims about it on purpose. You don't know anything about the LGBTQ community, and what you said is deeply offensive. It's also dangerous for transgender kids to have somebody like you, a member of Congress, say these things."

Unfortunately, transgender or gender-nonconforming people face real dangers just because of who they are. On average, about fifty people a year are murdered in America just for being part of this community. Add the suffering experienced by those who are rejected by family, peers, employers, business operators, and others and you've got many Americans who deserve not mockery but equal rights.

One of Lesko's ideological soulmates, Vicky Hartzler of Missouri, also demonstrated her callous disregard for LGBTQ lives. Like Lesko, Hartzler has an obsession—maybe an illness—when it comes to LGBTQ people. This made her someone I was never eager to ask to talk. But I heard that she was seeking signatures for a letter that urged then-president Trump to reduce the scope of duties for the US special envoy for LGBTQ persons or perhaps eliminate the position altogether. She was also arguing, falsely, that the envoy was promoting marriage equality and other policies to bring equality to LGBTQ people. Given how often and how loudly Hartzler talked about the right to life of fetuses, I thought she ought to have the same concern for living, breathing human beings.

I think it's not enough for members of Congress to debate issues in speeches. Conversation must also be part of our debate, so I scheduled an appointment and went to Hartzler's office. I brought with me an inches-thick file of reports on the lethal repression of, and unspeakable violence against, LGBTQ people worldwide. It could have been labeled "The Atrocities File."

I said, "Vicky, you know, the envoy is not charged with going out and promoting marriage equality. He is out there working to protect human rights, the right to be free from murder, torture, and unlawful detention. You ought to be aware that what you want to do is prevent America from standing against the most horrific violence ever."

I received no real response. Hartzler took my file. Said something bland about it being good that I'd stopped by and ushered me out. I don't know if she ever sent her letter. However, when the House later considered the Global Respect Act, which required that people who had committed gross human rights violations against LGBTQ people be denied visa, she was among the nay votes.

The lying done by Republicans is a consistent feature of their politics, and they do it at every turn. One recent egregious example involved the false allegation that Attorney General Merrick Garland had sent a memo to officials across the country in which he supposedly called outspoken parents "terrorists" and called on law enforcement officers to deal with them accordingly.

The real issue behind the lies involved threats of violence against school board members, teachers, and school officials from people who were outraged over another false concern—critical race theory in public schools. This too was a lie. Critical race theory is a form of analysis discussed in some law schools. No example of it being taught in a public school has ever been documented. In this way the outrage was like that over the nonexistent problem of widespread voter fraud. However, both myths were promoted in right-wing media, most particularly Fox News, which mentioned the theory more than fifteen hundred times in one four-month span. A feedback loop had developed, with politicians taking up the cause so they could appear on Fox News and amplify the anger, which caused protests at school boards and inflamed the criminally minded to make threats.

True to form, at a Judiciary Committee hearing on a different concern, Republican Jim Jordan of Ohio began railing about Garland, who, as everyone in DC knows, is among the most careful, nonpolitical attorneys general to ever hold the office. I weighed the values of responding (it's not a good idea to react to all the crazy stuff Jordan does) and decided to vent a little truth. Here's what I said, verbatim:

> Mr. Chairman, before I begin my remarks on the bill before us, I want to let folks who might be watching this hearing in on a little secret: what the Republicans

have just claimed is simply not true. The memorandum that they're referring to, in fact, doesn't label parents as terrorists. Here's a surprise. The word *parent* is not even in the document.

It's a made-up story that somehow Merrick Garland has labeled parents as terrorists. It is not true. And in fact, what the memorandum says is that individuals have threatened violence or threats of violence against schools, administrators, parents, and teachers, and of course that's what we should all want to investigate.

Everyone has a right to work in a school setting without the fear of violence. That's all this was. So this notion that somehow Merrick Garland has labeled parents as terrorists is not true.

I can recall my statement here because I went to the archive of hearing videos, found the one featuring this statement, and had it transcribed. As I did this, I discovered that the real topic we were supposed to discuss had been the subject of another GOP lying campaign. The topic was funding the police, and the GOP had said it was the Democrats' official policy to "defund the police," which had been, for a time, a slogan shouted by protesters against police brutality. Defunding the police would lead to anarchy, and this idea has been rejected by literally 99 percent of House Democrats. Instead we had provided $350 billion in the American Rescue Plan to state and local governments and specifically said they could use it for police. The Senate had approved this spending, and the Biden administration had then distributed it. How many Republicans had voted for this? None. As I said at the hearing:

Every single Republican on this committee and every single Republican in the Congress of the United States voted no for this funding for police departments in direct response to the increasing crime because of COVID.

We wrote it specifically for the purpose police departments are using it, and it's funding they need but which every single one who made one of these big, loud speeches today voted against.

What I said about police funding and the Garland memo would never reach the people who view Fox and accept its lies. But I wanted to say the truth out loud and at least require Jordan and the others to hear it.

Those of us who live in reality, and care about the truth, are challenged by the sheer volume of the outrageousness and the question of how to react. A delayed response generally requires too much work and repeating the offensive statements, which only amplifies them. I favor engaging lies with the truth when it can be done in the moment. A good example of this arose when John McCain ran for President and immediately corrected voters who raised all sorts of conspiracy theories about Barack Obama. "No," he said, "he's a decent person, a person that you don't need to be scared of as president of the United States."

McCain demonstrated his own decency back in 2008, when most of the disinformation in politics came from people on the fringes. Fourteen years later, the algorithm that had allowed the Tea Party to push the GOP to extremes has continued to the point of producing Donald Trump and then a host of congressional imitators who practice politics as trolling with no real concerns other than grabbing attention by shocking people. The 2020 election brought to the House of Representatives two women who embody this trend. Marjorie Taylor Greene of Georgia emerged from the conspiracy theory realms of the internet with a campaign that included a photo op with a fifth-generation Klansman and a Facebook post showing her holding an automatic rifle beside photos of Democratic women. Greene is often mentioned in the same breath as gun-toting Lauren Boebert of Colorado, who brags about packing a pistol inside the Capitol complex. She and Greene both heckled President Biden for the length of his first State of the Union speech, even during the moment when he spoke of his son Beau's death from cancer.

In another time Boebert and Greene would have been dismissed by their own party and the press. In this era they are frequently invited to appear on Fox News and at high-level right-wing conferences and fundraisers. Powered by donations from the rabid right, where people respond to inflammatory lies by opening their checkbooks, Greene raised $6.2 million during her first year in office, and Boebert netted $3.6 million, which was less than Greene but more than any other House member in her state.

My only direct dealings with either of these women came after a debate over Greene's disruptive habit of calling for the House to adjourn. So-called motions to adjourn trigger an automatic vote. There's no debate allowed. Members must quit whatever else they may be doing and vote to either close shop for the day or keep the House in session. When I looked for a way to stop this abuse of the rules, I realized the House could simply restrict the right to make such motions to members of Congress serving on committees. Greene had been stripped of her committee assignments after she endorsed calls for violence against her colleagues. Angry that I was trying to block her adjournment stunt, she answered a question from a reporter with the following:

Do you mean Representative Mussolini? Not only did Democrats unilaterally strip away my committees, now they want to remove any powers I have to represent my district. The Democrats run the House of Hypocrites with tyrannical control.

Reckless historical references to tyrants are becoming commonplace for the GOP. Before Greene attacked me, her freshman colleague Mary Miller of Illinois observed COVID-related school policies and said, "Hitler was right on one thing. He said, 'Whoever has the youth, has the future.'" Another Republican in Congress, Warren Davidson of Ohio, responded to public health initiatives against the COVID-19 virus with a social media post showing a Nazi document and the message, This has been done before. #DoNotComply.

Davidson and Miller met with criticism from Jews in their districts. In my conflict with Greene I handled it with a Twitter post that read:

> I'm an Italian and a Jew. Mussolini was a fascist dictator in league with Adolf Hitler, who murdered six million Jews. Marjorie Taylor Greene can get lost.

On the day I posted this, the Italian ambassador to the United States called me to thank me. "You have to understand that the invocation of that name calls back a very dark period of Italian history. It's very important that you correct her because her statement has already been widely reported in Italy." What the reports said was that one member of Congress had lambasted another as a Mussolini. Greene's status as someone on the lunatic fringe wasn't part of the news accounts, so for all Italians knew, she was a powerful American politician, end of story. When my response was then reported, it put everything in context.

Here most people know that Marjorie Taylor Greene is a publicity hound whom no one should take seriously. Those who aren't convinced just aren't paying attention, since she makes outrageous and stupid pronouncements all the time. One recent one, which was reported widely, involved her saying that Nancy Pelosi had ordered the Capitol police to treat people like "the gazpacho." Though she had confused a chilled soup with the Nazi terrorists called the gestapo, it isn't enough to make fun of her ignorance. Behind the stupidity lurks the mind of someone who is willing to spew any sort of venom in order to raise her profile, enrage her followers, and make the fundraising checks pour into her campaign.

———————

As John Boehner fled, the new GOP orthodoxy pulled the party of Lincoln away from supporting civil rights and toward opposition to just about anything that would advance or protect Black Americans. When not overtly racist, sexist, or homophobic, most of the GOP nevertheless opposed protections for minorities who had long suffered discrimination. They refused to approve voting rights bills of the sort that had long enjoyed overwhelming bipartisan support, and they made appeals for protections by LGBTQ people into vicious culture war skirmishes.

I wanted to think that the Republican Party, which has an essential role in our country's political life, could withstand the pressure from the extremists. The evidence suggested otherwise. Time and again, when the old guard of the GOP tried to do something normal, members of the Freedom Caucus rose to stop them. Take, for example, the House Republicans' effort to repeal

Obamacare. Defeated time and again by losses in the Senate and presidential vetoes, they finally got a clear opportunity in Donald Trump, who said he would "repeal and replace" Obamacare when he became president. But when the Freedom Caucus saw the legislation, they liked the "repeal" part but hated the replacement. With their leaders Mark Meadows and Jim Jordan calling the shots, they formed a secret pact and, when the time came, joined us in keeping Obamacare alive mostly because they had nothing to replace it.

Ultimately, what the Freedom Caucus did was good for the country because the best estimates showed the legislation they helped to defeat would have taken health insurance away from twenty-four million people. However, the caucus also diminished the mainstream party's appeal to right-wing voters, who were coming to dominate the turnout in primary elections. Those voters were adamant about killing Obamacare and didn't care about the fine details of the GOP's failure to put it to death. All they knew was that the party establishment had failed. These base voters were the ones who had been activated in the Tea Party backlash against Obama's policies and the change signaled by the presence of a Black family in the White House.

As it developed, many experts noted the racial aspect of the Tea Party movement and the fact that a small number of participants were truly hateful racists. But as a whole these folks, as numerous studies showed, were not bile-spewing bigots but rather were misinformed about issues related to race. Many thought that the problems and claims of Black and brown Americans were getting too much attention while poor and working white Americans were being ignored. This idea was muddled by long-standing false assumptions about how white people somehow miss out on federal aid programs—they don't—and by similarly ill-informed ideas about politically red rural regions losing out to those in blue big cities. In fact, on a per capita basis, rural and red communities get far more federal dollars than blue ones.

Although the facts weren't with the Tea Party point of view, Republicans and business activists who exploited the anxiety and anger many felt during the Great Recession captured the loyalties of millions. In the beginning the Tea Party's targets included Wall Street, subprime mortgage lenders, and big banks, which were seen as the main culprits in the economic meltdown. However, the politicians and business groups saw nothing to gain in attacking the very institutions that paid their bills, so focus was soon trained exclusively on the government, Democrats in general, and Obama specifically.

The Tea Party was good at tapping into the anger of the American people. More should have been done for everyday Americans who suffered during the Great Recession. But to blame Democrats and focus on Obamacare was boneheaded. Indeed the health program would do more to improve the lives and protect the bank accounts of Tea Party people than anything Washington had done since Lyndon Johnson's Great Society. Attacking it may have served health-care corporations and politicians who wanted to undermine Obama. However, as they joined this effort and identified with the political right, the movement's rank and file became pawns. In states whose governors refused to implement parts of Obamacare, they were denied its benefits. In the meantime the Republicans they'd elected to Congress arrived determined to dismantle as much of the government as possible and to block any effort to solve the nation's problems through any means other than tax cuts.

Like most zealots, the new extremists in Congress were more upset by comrades (other Republicans) who let them down than by their natural opponents (Democrats). When they identified Republicans who were willing to compromise or work with Democrats, they supported fire-breathing primary challengers to burn them out of office. The prime example was Representative Eric Cantor of Virginia, who was beaten by challenger David Brat even though he'd outspent Brat by forty to one. Cantor was, at the time, the majority leader in the House of Representatives. In the 115 years since the position had been created, no majority leader had ever lost a primary, but such was the power of the Tea Party wing that Cantor lost by 10 percentage points.

Cantor's defeat shook like-minded Republicans. Nineteen of them retired before the 2016 election, while others scrambled to change their ways. The net result was a steady march to the extreme right, away from the kind of Republicanism represented by the last of the GOP's mainstream presidential candidates—John McCain and Mitt Romney. McCain and Romney were hardly liberal, but they were reasonable and decent men who rejected the politics-as-warfare model. They also lost, because people believed that Obama truly did represent the hope and change that were themes in his 2008 campaign and were satisfied enough with his performance that they believed he deserved reelection.

As much as the Tea Party and Freedom Caucus folks insisted that he had been a disaster, Obama got credit for addressing the economic crisis that started in the Bush years, and his health-care program had begun an immediate and steep decline in the number of people without health insurance. Americans were especially happy about the provisions that expanded coverage and protected them from being dropped from their plans, and they didn't want to let these benefits go.

On Capitol Hill we Democrats had worked hard to preserve Obamacare and felt good about our success. However, those of us in safer seats in blue districts couldn't know that rather than dissipate, the energy of the Tea Party movement had been spun into something new and more dangerous. Political and media operators who recognized the power of the anger in this movement cast about for ways to keep participants engaged even though they had failed in their original mission.

With internet-based propagandists leading the way, the extreme right coalesced under a new kind of populism that, unlike previous brands of American populism, ignored big business but homed in on Washington and the Democratic Party. With more than 60 percent of Tea Party members saying that antiwhite sentiment was as troubling as anti-Black bigotry, the extreme right became impatient with any talk of anti-Black racism. If anything, they thought that *they* were victims because such discussions were painful for *them*. (Eventually laws would be proposed to shield white students from the discomfort they might feel during academic discussions of race.)

The new populism was also vehemently opposed to America's long-standing policy of welcoming immigrants and asylum seekers. This had happened before, as frightened Americans opposed immigrants who were Jewish, Italian, and Irish to name just a few groups. However, the value of immigration had been proven so many times. I thought our nation had grown past knee-jerk xenophobia. As I saw the fear in the eyes of those who wanted to reject the newcomers—who this time came from Asia, Africa, the Middle East, and the Southern Hemisphere—I wanted to tell them, "You've run just about everything for centuries. It's time to share. There's enough for everyone."

19

MINORITY RULE

The GOP battle over "purity" was *the* compelling drama on Capitol Hill during the time when they held the majority in the House but the Senate and the White House were in Democratic hands. The Republicans had no chance for success in their effort to kill Obamacare, for example, but they could also block us if we tried to pass any meaningful legislation. So instead of serious problems like climate change, attention was focused on political nonsense.

Little appreciated at the time was the fact that on the extreme right, paralysis was considered a victory. Their whole project involved destroying the parts of the political system where compromise got things done for the majority of the American people, whose views landed near the middle of the partisan spectrum. While blaming us for the inaction, they would game the system established in the Constitution to grab power when they could and wield it as a ruthless minority.

The point I should reiterate here is that the government established in the Constitution is not a pure democracy. As the founders stitched together our republic, they structured the Electoral College and the Senate in ways that favored sparsely settled rural states and penalized populous ones. The problems this created were obvious, and as the country left behind its agrarian roots, the risk that the Electoral College might elect a president who had garnered substantially fewer votes than his or her opponent grew. The esteemed historian James MacGregor Burns likened the system to Russian roulette and warned that "one of these days we are going to blow our brains out."

In 1968 we came close to the calamity Burns feared as the racist George Wallace threw the presidential election into unprecedented turmoil. In 1969 a constitutional amendment that eliminated the college was passed by the House in an over-whelming bipartisan vote, as both Republicans and Democrats recognized the danger in the Electoral College. The amendment enjoyed a groundswell of support, even from prominent con-servatives like Irving Kristol of New York University and Paul Weaver of Harvard, who declared it an idea whose "time has come." With surveys showing the amendment would garner the requisite approval by thirty-eight states, the goal was within reach. America was on the brink of genuine democracy. But then the Senate took up the amendment, and it was derailed by, you guessed it, a filibuster.

The filibuster that preserved the Electoral College was deployed by three segregationist senators from the rural South. They were determined to block the possibility that the votes cast for president by Black citizens in the North would equal those cast by their white constituents. Their argument would sound famil-iar today. Electing a president by popular vote would encourage voter fraud, they claimed without evidence. On the other side were the amendment's main sponsors, Democrat Birch Bayh of Indiana and Tennessee Republican Howard Baker, who fell five votes short of the sixty-seven required to break the filibuster.

Thanks to three racist senators, in the twenty-first century we've already seen two presidents elected with a minority of the votes. Since 1996, Republican senators have never represented a majority of the people, but they have ruled the Senate more than half the time. In 2014 they took control while representing just 46 percent of the people. Indeed, Democrats running for Senate got twenty million more votes than their GOP opponents.

As the GOP exercised minority rule in the Senate, race was a key element of their power. As political scientists discovered, the overwhelming support of white voters in rural states ensured the party's Senate majority. These voters were Fox-watching conservatives who were steeped in the hysteria and conspiracy theories offered by the network's evening hosts. Having heard, for decades, that Democrats were evil socialists bent on destroying their country, they embraced the extreme-right agenda—antiscience, antiabortion, antigovernment—with a holy-war fervor. In their view America was under attack, and this justified the most ruthless kind of politics.

No one was more ruthless than Kentucky senator Mitch McConnell, who became majority leader as Republicans took the Senate in 2014. McConnell, who had ridden Ronald Reagan's coattails into the Senate in 1984, had been the subject of a new biography titled *The Cynic* by the widely respected writer Alec MacGillis. As revealed in the book, he had been a rather liberal Republican—pro–abortion rights, pro-union, pro–civil rights— who saw where the party was headed, shed the weight of his convictions, and raced to get to the front of the parade. Once there, he studied how to use the rules, like the filibuster, to exercise power even when he was in the minority.

As majority leader, McConnell didn't need to even consider the filibuster when, in early 2016, Supreme Court Justice Antonin Scalia died. As McConnell saw it, an Obama appointee who replaced Scalia could defeat the right's long-running project to use the courts to concentrate their power. But thanks to ballots cast by a distinct minority of the voters, he had the power to stop this from happening.

When Obama nominated appeals court judge Merrick Garland to the court, McConnell just refused to let the Senate act. It wasn't because Garland was some flame-throwing liberal radical. Indeed, Orrin Hatch, the senior Republican in the Senate, had said that he wished Obama would appoint someone like Garland, who was chief of the United States Court of Appeals for the District of Columbia Circuit. However, just as the extreme right had set fire to normal politics in Congress, it was determined to burn down the normal process for filling the court. McConnell's cover story was something about how the country would elect a new president in nine months and that person should make the appointment. Though it held the power to advise and consent to court nominations, the Senate was under no obligation to do so, and in this case McConnell would refuse.

Later in the year, the majority leader pulled a similar move when Obama notified him of rampant Russian interference in the presidential election. Hints of this trouble had swirled around Washington since the start of the year, when the *Guardian* first reported that the Russians would do all they could to help Trump, whom they deemed an unstable figure who would sow unrest in America, over his rival Hillary Clinton. As secretary of state, Clinton had made an enemy of Russian autocrat Vladimir Putin when she showed support for Russians who protested for greater freedoms. As a senator she had even joked that she doubted he had a "soul."

After the *Guardian* report came news that the Russians had hacked both the Democratic National Committee and the Clinton campaign. Multiple American intelligence agencies confirmed that Russian security forces were involved in both the cyber-attacks and efforts to use bots, trolls, and fake websites to influence US voters. In every instance they sought to boost Trump or damage Clinton. The American experts even identified the specific military units in charge of these campaigns and the address of the building where many of the hackers worked. Concerned that Americans needed to know that much of what they were reading on Facebook and elsewhere was fake and intended to mislead them, Obama asked McConnell to issue a bipartisan statement. Well aware that Moscow's assault on the election benefited his side's candidate, Donald Trump, McConnell refused.

In the case of Donald Trump and the 2016 election, it's not likely that McConnell believed the profane, dishonest, and disrespectful TV host/developer was qualified to be president. Trump's record included multiple bankruptcies, public displays of racism, more than a dozen accusations of sexual harassment, and abuse of tenants, workers, vendors, and wives. McConnell surely knew about all of this and recognized the danger in the emotions Trump unleashed as he declared Hillary Clinton a criminal and encouraged people at his rallies to use violence against protesters.

The menace and mendacity in the Trump campaign was like nothing our country had ever seen before, but we should have seen it coming. The constant alarms about traitorous Democrats; the barely disguised racism, misogyny, and anti-LGBTQ rhetoric; the combustible alliance of religion and politics. For years the right had been piling up the tinder that an arsonist like Trump could set ablaze. In retrospect we should thank people like Mitt Romney and John McCain for delaying the crisis.

Hindsight also reveals that we Democrats failed in both our performance and our messaging. During the years of GOP obstruction, we didn't call them out on their tactics, and we let them blame us for congressional gridlock when they had control. Things didn't get done and we often didn't explain well why— Republican obstruction. Finally, some Democrats failed to connect to voters on their core concerns—economic insecurity.

Rhode Island, despite what the Gilded Age mansions of Newport might suggest, is a state of hardworking families. Having lost most of our textile and manufacturing facilities, we have struggled to stay in the middle of state rankings for economic opportunity, and in 2016 our poverty rate was slightly higher than the national average of 12.7 percent. I could look out the window of my district office in Pawtucket and see acres of vacated redbrick mill buildings that no longer supported the community with thousands of jobs. However, in Democratic Rhode Island, government did enough to help folks that despite our struggles, life was manageable for most. We had the seventh-lowest crime rate in the country and ranked near the top in both health care and the quality of our environment.

Knowing my constituents, I recognized the very moment when Hillary Clinton opened the door for Donald Trump to become president. It was September 9, 2016, and some elite New Yorkers had gathered for an LGBTQ fundraiser in Manhattan. In her speech she recognized the struggle our community faced against prejudice that made us victims of legal and illegal discrimination and mistreatment including violence and murder. She noted Trump's support for rolling back marriage equality, making discrimination legal, and in stating other policies she called "deplorable." Then, perhaps because she got caught up in the moment, she crossed a boundary and attached the world *deplorable* to actual people.

"You know, to just be grossly generalistic," she said, "you

could put half of Trump's supporters into what I call the basket of deplorables. Right? The racist, sexist, homophobic, xenophobic, Islamophobic—you name it. And unfortunately, there are people like that. And he has lifted them up."

Later in her talk Hillary noted the "other basket" of Trump supporters, those "who feel that the government has let them down, the economy has let them down, nobody cares about them, nobody worries about what happens to their lives and their futures, and they're just desperate for change.... They don't buy everything he says, but he seems to hold out some hope that their lives will be different.... Those are people we have to understand and empathize with as well."

If you've ever given a public talk in front of a friendly crowd that responded to everything you said, then you know how easy it might be to get carried away. In this case Hillary was speaking off the cuff, as she was about to introduce Barbra Streisand. Her enthusiasm must have been sky high. However, no one running for office should ever talk about voters as deplorables, and when this was reported by the press on September 10, I felt a sense of dread. It would be too easy for the other side to up its expression of outrage to the highest level and then rally supporters around the insult. Soon Trumpists would appropriate the term *deplorables* for themselves, putting it on T-shirts, buttons, and bumper stickers to signal their commitment.

Of course, no one mistake determined the election outcome, but the "deplorable" thing was significant because it suggested the Clinton campaign had failed to understand how voters were feeling and had written off swathes of the country. She subsequently lost millions of working-class white voters who had backed her husband and then the Obama-Biden ticket. While the campaign could have been managed better in some respects, it's hard to overcome the undemocratic hurdle of the Electoral College. And then, near the end, the campaign failed to conduct polls to sense where voters were headed and neglected voter turnout efforts in key states.

Despite all of this, Clinton won the popular vote, which means that in any other developed country she would have become the head of state. She was also the victim of an astounding level of interference by Russia, which leveraged newly powerful social media channels in ways that were impossible to counter. As later confirmed, during the campaign Putin's online army created more than a million anti-Clinton or pro-Trump social media posts that were viewed by more than 125 million people. Millions of Americans, including the candidate, his sons, and his top advisers, engaged with fake Russian posts and amplified them on their own accounts.

What was the effect of the Russian propaganda? Social media experts note that regular users of platforms like Facebook or Twitter became far more likely to trust information they receive from online contacts than to trust what they learn from the press. In this case an analysis by data scientists at the University of Tennessee, Knoxville, found that as the election neared, American voters were very busy reposting the Russian stuff. When the reposts reached twenty-five thousand in any given week, they were followed by a 1 percent rise in Trump's poll numbers.

The problem of social media was not new to me. I had been watching its influence grow until its unfiltered postings began to overwhelm the news media as a source for many voters. At the same time platforms like Facebook had taken so much advertising revenue that used to go to newspapers that the ones that survived did so by cutting staff, and therefore coverage of important events. In Rhode Island our one big daily, the *Providence Journal*, which had won the Pulitzer Prize as recently as 2004, began a steep decline. Subscriptions dropped by 80 percent. It stopped putting out editions featuring news for specific areas of the state. With no one providing real news, people posted their own reports on what they thought was happening in their communities and, along the way, spread huge amounts of misinformation.

No matter how much local newspapers tormented politicians with their investigations and tough questions, I knew the press provided a necessary public service that Facebook and the like were never going to replace. In fact, given that extreme posts attract the most user clicks, and clicks equal revenue, the company was not much interested in curating its platform's content to remove the fakers and the frauds. Without a reason to change, Facebook would never become a source of reliable news but remain a wonderland for conspiracy theorists, hucksters, and liars.

But in a country where free speech is a cherished right and government was never supposed to interfere with the press, it was hard for many to see a role for Congress in this sphere. So it was that people in my office devoted inordinate amounts of time responding to calls from constituents who had "seen something on the internet," and everywhere I went people asked, "What can be done?" about technology's troubling effects. My answer was, "Rein in Big Tech and restore competition."

20

NEITHER SYMPTOM NOR CAUSE

Separating the scandals and perversions of Donald Trump's presidency is a task akin to sorting individual snowflakes in a blizzard. There are so many of them and they come at you so fast that focusing on just one is impossible. As his strategist Stephen Bannon revealed with the help of a term borrowed from football, this was by design.

As Bannon explained during the campaign, Team Trump intended to "flood the zone with shit" so it could overwhelm anyone who might hold it accountable. In office it followed the same game plan, operating at a furious pace, heedless of morality and tradition, and breezing past the inevitable crises. It began on inauguration day, when First Lady Melania Trump advertised her jewelry line on the White House website, and it never stopped. A few of the many things Trump did in his first eleven days were:

- Lying about the inauguration crowd, which White House counselor Kellyanne Conway spun as presenting "alternative facts."
- Demanding personal loyalty from FBI director James Comey.
- Imposing an illegal travel ban on people from Muslim-majority countries.

- Firing the acting attorney general for her failure to defend the travel ban.
- Ordering a raid in Yemen in which thirty civilians and one Navy SEAL died and that produced none of the promised intelligence.

Although more would be revealed as Trump's secrets were uncovered, the abuses of the first eleven days were followed in February by a stream of public scandals highlighted by the forced resignation of National Security Advisor Michael Flynn over lies he'd told about improper contacts with Russia's ambassador. In this month the president leveled personal attacks on the press and the judiciary, and his counselor Conway used a TV appearance to hawk Ivanka Trump's fashion brand. "I'm going to give a free commercial here," she said. "Go buy it today, everybody."

While the zone was flooded with norm-busting craziness, in the same month the Trump administration moved rapidly to muzzle federal scientists who dealt with climate change, cancel regulations protecting rivers and streams from pollution caused by mines, void a rule governing the handling of toxic mercury waste, and open more federal land to coal mining. These quick actions and others benefiting internet providers and private prison companies rewarded the business interests that bankroll the GOP. They would also benefit from Trump's nomination of the decidedly probusiness Neil Gorsuch to fill the Supreme Court vacancy created by Mitch McConnell's blocking Obama's choice. These were the fruits of minority rule, gained thanks to the anti-democratic Electoral College.

Minority rule seemed never to be far from Trump's mind as he abused the dignity of his office to announce, falsely, that Hillary Clinton's victory in the 2016 popular vote had been the by-product of three million illegally cast ballots. The source of this lie seemed to be Trump's imagination. A day later, on February 12, White House adviser Stephen Miller told a national TV audience, "Voter fraud is a serious problem in this country," but then declined to explain what he meant. Trump also inflamed the fears of his base with lies about crime rates and by banning mainstream news organizations from the press room, alleging they were purveyors of "fake news."

Taken together, Trump's extreme public rhetoric and his policy moves signaled two things. The first was that he would reliably follow the established Republican program, which meant denying climate change and other environmental concerns while doing all he could to help corporations and the rich. The second and more ominous thing was that Trump was willing to attack the foundation of democracy—public faith in voting—and to divide the American people with fear based on lies.

In the months that followed, the scandals and scandalous behavior continued apace. Without evidence Trump accused Obama of wiretapping him. He tried to cut $18 billion from programs such as school lunch aid and mental health services to fund construction of an anti-immigrant border wall. He telephoned FBI director Comey to ask him to cease an investigation into Russia's meddling in the 2016 election. He made the long-public White House visitor logs secret, and he said the Constitution's system of checks and balances, which prevented a president from acting like a king, should be junked. "For the good of the country," he said, "things are going to have to be different."

Amid the chaos, which included record-setting turnover in the administration, old-fashioned politicians and members of the press became almost obsessed with what it meant that the country faced such political turmoil. The two main answers found

Trump to be either the cause of the problem or a symptom of it. In fact it would have been more accurate to recognize Trump as the ultimate *product* of a deliberate plan to alienate the American people from their government and exploit the flaws in our system that permit minority rule.

For decades those on the extreme right had pushed the Republican Party to be ever more hostile toward the basic functions of government, making it all but impossible for Congress to address public needs. At the same time a ferocious culture war, led by demagogues and amplified continuously by a propaganda press, divided the country into those who believed America was being destroyed from within and those—liberals, Democrats, LGBTQ citizens, feminists, etc.—whom those citizens regarded as traitors. The fear felt by those who felt imperiled drove them toward politically infused religion, which told them that God was on their side, and into a search for a savior.

All that had stood between the country and the arrival of a leader like Trump was the integrity of conservatives who respected the unwritten rules that preserved our democracy. Those people of integrity were hard to find in the Trump era, and the few who raised their hands to object were met with a furious negative reaction. In response they became meek and withdrawn. As they did this, they confirmed a concern that had grown in my mind. Once our rivals in policy, Republicans had become social warriors who viewed us as enemies.

A similar dynamic prevailed in the Senate, where almost no one stood up against the extremism. Republican Bob Corker of Tennessee complained about Trump's methods but did not rally to challenge him with any vigor. Instead of staying to fight for what he knew was right, he resigned. Senator Jeff Flake of Arizona had been more outspoken as he tried to shake his fellow senators free of Trump's influence, but in the end he decided to cut and run too. His choice bothered me more than Corker's because when he explained it, he made it clear that he had studied the crisis and understood it fully.

Flake announced his retirement in October 2017, more than a year before he would have to win an election to remain in office. In his speech he recalled Madison's writing on the separation of powers, which Trump would destroy. Flake said that the Founders' scheme was based on Madison's statement that "ambition counteracts ambition." Then Flake asked, "But what happens if ambition fails to counteract ambition?" Of Trump he concluded, "I have children and grandchildren to answer to, and so, Mr. President, I will not be complicit."

It was all well and good for Flake to reject the accomplice role, but why would he not stand and fight? A small hint of the real reason was buried in a glancing reference to his belief that people who, like him, favored immigration and free trade had "a narrower and narrower path to [the presidential] nomination in the Republican party."

There it was. As the old joke goes, like every senator, Jeff Flake saw a future president in the mirror, and he was quitting the fight to keep his options open. I wonder if he was paying attention two days later when Senator Corker, another president-in-the-mirror, said he wouldn't rule out a challenge to Trump in a 2020 primary. By the way, this was the same fellow who, sixteen months prior, had said he wouldn't rule out being Trump's running mate.

Weak as Republicans were in the Senate, they were even weaker on our side of the Capitol, where so-called moderates who had once presented themselves as firebrands departed in greater numbers and with less fanfare. The exception in the House was the Speaker who had replaced John Boehner. Paul

Ryan of Wisconsin was as far to the right on most issues as a person could be. Heavily influenced by the greed-is-good writings of the polemicist Ayn Rand, he approached the poor as if they were morally deficient and undeserving of care. He regarded the wealthy with the view that their riches indicated their superiority. Hardly opposed to Trump's legislative agenda, he had been instrumental in getting Congress to approve the one big piece of legislation Trump would ever see passed: a massive tax cut for the rich and corporations.

With the Trump tax cut, the GOP once again promised the whole economy would benefit and failed to deliver. While Trump's director of the Office of Management and Budget, the former Freedom Caucus member Mick Mulvaney, said the lost revenues would be made up by increased taxable growth, instead a deficit of $2 trillion loomed. In the meantime the number of corporations paying zero taxes doubled. Hello Netflix, Chevron, Eli Lilly. Did these companies use their savings to reward workers as Trump predicted? No. A study of the top five hundred companies found they spent most of the money, $149 out of every $150, buying back stock, which rewarded investors. The wealthiest individual taxpayers reaped a bonanza of 10 percent more income from the Trump cuts, while everyone below the top 90 percent saw a bump of less than 2 percent.

Having done his tax-cutting duty, Ryan faced a growing tsunami of public opposition to Trump that would surely wash him into the minority and out of the Speaker's chair. So in early spring 2018 he held a brief press conference to say he was leaving Congress, citing the timeworn explanation that he wanted to spend more time with his family. Then, after the voters gave Democrats enough new seats to take control of the House, Ryan gave a long speech in which he took obvious jabs at Trump by complaining about politics that "starts from a place of outrage and seeks to tear us down from there. . . . It is exhausting. It saps meaning from our politics. And it discourages good people from pursuing public service."

Ryan, who was still a prominent leader of his party, could have said something to show he understood that Trump and Trumpism represented something more than one man's deranged political style. But this would have required abandoning his own cruel policy positions and acknowledging that we were suffering from a crisis that both major parties had created. In its drive for power at any cost, the GOP was largely responsible for producing the first would-be autocrat ever to occupy the White House. The Democrats' share of responsibility could be found in our failure to explain that we didn't get more done for the American people because of Republican obstruction and our inability to recognize the seriousness of the extreme right's power grab and the threat it posed to our democracy.

I'll confess, as someone who had long worked in politics in Rhode Island and Washington, I had been unable to imagine that Americans would be vulnerable to the antidemocracy messages of those who ranted about immigrants, the decline of white power, and a never-ending state of emergency caused by phantom criminals and traitors. This lack of imagination meant that I failed to anticipate leaders who, in the words of Jeff Flake, would be "complicit" with a demagogue like Trump who sought to conquer by dividing.

We House Democrats had begun to plan our effort to save democracy the moment Trump was declared the winner in the presidential race. Understanding we had no power to stop him in the moment, we nevertheless tried to rally public opinion, which was expressed in massive protests across the country, and we looked for ways to go beyond opposing Trump to putting forth our alternative policies and ideals. I had made it a point to get involved in developing our agenda by running to be one of the cochairs of the Democratic Policy and Communications Committee. I then worked with Hakeem Jeffries of New York and Cheri Bustos of Illinois, who were the other cochairs, to come up with an agenda.

Democrats are inclined to make detailed proposals for addressing complex problems and failing to sell them in the way Republicans sell their program of tax cuts and obstruction. (I daresay that someone who became a GOP member of Congress in 1980 would have been able to coast along for forty years without having to learn anything new.) Hakeem pushed us to keep it simple and then encourage Democrats to repeat the message across the country. The way he put it, we would know our message had begun to get through right about when we were sick of repeating it.

Called "For the People," our agenda included lower health-care costs and prescription prices, a big infrastructure program, and cleaning up the corruption of the Trump administration. When asked, incumbents and candidates could elaborate on a dozen more ideas that would directly affect all Americans. They could talk about lowering drug prices by allowing Medicare to negotiate and rebuilding infrastructure to improve everyone's lives and make us more competitive in the world economy. On the third item, dealing with Trump, voters were already ahead of us.

Despite all the noise made on the right, a huge number of Americans—likely the majority—recognized that democracy itself was threatened by Trump and his rage mob. In the time since he'd begun his campaign, authorities had logged many

violent incidents in which attackers used Trump's name or justified themselves by citing Trump themes. (Anti-immigrant hostility was popular with these supporters.) A month before the
election, one of these agitated Trumpists sent pipe bombs to
Democratic Party leaders, liberal financier George Soros, and
CNN. Thankfully, all were intercepted before they were opened.
All of this occurred in a political environment that had become
palpably tense. In this time militant groups like the Proud Boys
and the Oath Keepers, who had taken to carrying guns, added an
air of menace to pro-Trump rallies.

Millions of Americans—more than Trump counted in his
camp—were distressed by what was happening and knew the
Constitution had provided a system of checks and balances that
required that Democrats control the House. With this power our
committees could use their oversight authority to probe what
was really happening inside the administration. We could expose
what was happening, and, if warranted, impeach the president.
A voter turnout that exceeded anything seen in more than a century gave us the power and a mandate. The question was how we
would use it.

21

IS HE WORTH IT?

In the beginning of the Trump era, most House Democrats tried to find comfort in the idea that he might be restrained by the so-called grown-ups in his administration like Secretary of State Rex Tillerson, Secretary of Defense James Mattis, and economic adviser Gary Cohn. Then those grown-ups began to run out of patience, or strength, and gave up. James Mattis, White House Chief of Staff John Kelly, Gary Cohn, Rex Tillerson—one by one they decided Trump wouldn't be contained and departed with leaks to the press that confirmed the president's derangement.

Trump replaced the departed with people who would be easier for him to push around. Many of them were incompetent, so it was hoped they lacked the skills to do too much damage. This hope was misplaced. The proof came in the deaths of children in federal custody after they were separated from their parents on the southern border and in ruptured relationships with longtime allies abroad. Having seen in Buddy Cianci's crowd what even a bumbling wrecking crew could do, I knew things would keep getting worse until Trump was stopped.

I wasn't the only one who understood the Cianci/Trump type. Al Green, a Black congressman from the Houston area had seen his share of abusive, power-mad public officials growing up in the Jim Crow South and recognized the danger posed by Trump. He proposed impeaching Trump shortly after the president praised white nationalists who conducted a violent rally in Charlottesville, Virginia, where they killed a young woman who had marched to show her opposition to the racist hate. Trump said there were "good people on both sides." This happened in August 2017.

In quiet conversations about how Trump might be removed, I was among the group that believed he wouldn't be stopped in any other way. As cochair of our Policy and Communications Committee I was on Nancy Pelosi's leadership team and most of these conversations were internal. She controlled the official caucus position, and after I had my say, I was expected to defer to that position.

In public and in private, Pelosi took the position that even discussing impeachment at such an early point in Trump's term made no sense. She considered impeachment a kind of nuclear option so damaging to the country that it should almost never be used. In Richard Nixon's case, while he was extremely unpopular, hearings alone were so traumatic that some Republicans never stopped seeking revenge for his forced resignation. The impeachment of Bill Clinton, for lying about an affair, damaged Congress more than the president, who was found not guilty. In that case House Republicans came off as petty, vindictive partisans who had abused the power to impeach.

"He's not worth it" Pelosi would say whenever she spoke about impeachment. Besides, we weren't likely to win the power to do it until 2018. And talk of it now might even alienate so many voters that we wouldn't gain control of the House then. Then where would we be? The country would have a madman in the

White House with no one holding the power to at least investigate and expose his wrongdoing.

Pelosi's position made some sense, but I thought it underestimated the crisis we faced. My constituents surely felt it. Whether I was at the supermarket, at the Davis Jewish deli, or at the Italian food place called Tony's Colonial on Federal Hill, I could barely walk ten feet without someone grabbing my elbow and saying something like, "Is he out of his mind?" On the Jewish East Side, they were shocked that an American president would openly attack Muslim and Hispanic people and perform like a Mussolini for social media.

"He scares me, David," said a friend who was standing near the automatic doors as I walked into Whole Foods in the summer of 2017. "The people in his crowds scare me," she continued. "This is America. This is the place people come to escape that, and now he's doing it right here."

In addition to impeachment, the Constitution permits removing a disabled president in a process described in the Twenty-Fifth Amendment. It requires action by the vice president and the cabinet, so there was no direct role for Congress. However, members who knew what they were talking about were free to share their views. One of my closest friends in the House, Representative Jamie Raskin of Maryland, was a professor of constitutional law who understood that the Twenty-Fifth Amendment had been drafted with this kind of problem in mind. Removal would take place if the vice president and cabinet found a president "unable to discharge the powers and duties of his office." Trump might have been able to use his powers, but as he bonded with America's enemy Russia, tore at our alliances, and disturbed the peace at home, he was clearly unable to fulfill his duties.

Jamie was not the only expert talking about the Twenty-Fifth Amendment solution. In late 2017 twenty-seven mental health experts published their views, including the suggestion that Trump might need to be confronted under the Twenty-Fifth Amendment's provisions for replacing a disabled president. The best-selling book *The Dangerous Case of Donald Trump* presciently forecast that if left in office, Trump would grow more erratic and threatening to our democracy.

You didn't need to be a psychiatrist to recognize that whatever his mental status, Trump actively abused his office while neglecting his duties. The chorus of alarms grew louder as Trump persisted in siding with Vladimir Putin over American intelligence agencies in the matter of Russian election interference and threatened to disrupt the work of special counsel Robert Mueller, who was investigating Moscow's cyberattack. Revelations of Trump companies benefiting from business with the government and other countries raised the possibility that he had violated either the Constitution's Foreign Emoluments Clause or Domestic Emoluments Clause. Public threats he made against private citizens, including calls for them to be imprisoned, only highlighted his derangement.

The Speaker had been observing Trump's temperament carefully from the first few days he took office, especially when she and other congressional leaders had their first meeting with him as president. She had gone through this with four previous presidents and recalled quiet sessions in the Cabinet Room where presidents reflected on the weight of their new responsibilities. Some had quoted Scripture and others referenced the Founding Fathers. Trump did none of this. According to Pelosi, the new president chose to meet in a less formal space in the East Wing instead of the Cabinet Room and after greeting the congressional leaders immediately began talking about how he had actually won the popular vote. The moment, as she described it, went something like this:

> TRUMP: You know, I won the popular vote by millions of votes.
>
> PELOSI: No, you didn't, Mr. President. You lost, you know, by three million votes.
>
> TRUMP: Well, there were five million illegal votes in California.
>
> PELOSI: No, Mr. President. That's not true.

Given the way Trump's aides were contorting themselves to support his bonkers claims about the crowd at his inauguration, it was likely that Pelosi was the first person ever to confront him, inside the White House, with actual facts. On this day she wasn't alone. Later in the meeting, Trump said he had plans to spend $1 trillion on infrastructure that he was sure could be approved by Congress "right away." When he looked to Senate Majority Leader Mitch McConnell for support, the senator replied, "Not unless it's paid for." The subject was dropped.

Trump never displayed the kind of humble reverence for his job that indicated he understood what the country and the world needed from him. (He also never showed the kind of serious focus that would have led to success with an infrastructure bill.)

As our first gangster-style president, Trump used a combination of plots and intimidation to get his way. In many cases, as with his public ravings about firing Attorney General Jeff Sessions or special counsel Robert Mueller, he committed his offenses brazenly in public, signaling others that they would face a similar fate if they crossed him. Trump had time for this scheming because he had no real legislative agenda and depended on others to drive his main governing activities: executive orders and judicial appointments. Outside groups submitted proposals for the orders, and judicial candidates were suggested by the right-wing Federalist Society, which had developed a roster of judges who were antiabortion, were pro–big corporations, and otherwise favored Republicans. With these appointments he would attempt to insulate himself against future legal troubles (he expected his appointees to be loyal to him) and further the party's drive to control American public policy without gaining a majority of the votes cast in national elections.

Nothing in Trump's extreme approach to the courts or his executive orders, which he issued at a higher rate than his five most recent predecessors, could be deemed impeachable. Likewise, he was within his rights to indulge in his racist talk—remember that he called Haiti and African nations "shithole countries"—verbal attacks on allies, and lies and distortions issued at a rate of more than twenty per day. But like Trump's obstructions of justice, these offenses amounted to attacks on our democratic spirit, a fact that was being decried in serious books by historians, political scientists, and others who warned that something terrible was happening. With titles like *On Tyranny* and *How Democracies Die*, these books showed how America was on the road to authoritarianism. In fact, Trump and Trumpism ticked most of the boxes in a fourteen-point fascism checklist published by the philosopher Umberto Eco in 1995. The list includes:

The cult of tradition.

The rejection of modernism.

Action for action's sake. (Thinking is a form of emasculation.)

Disagreement is treason.

Fear of difference.

Appeal to social frustration.

The obsession with a plot.

The enemy is both strong and weak.

Pacifism is trafficking with the enemy.

Contempt for the weak.

Everybody is educated to become a hero.

Machismo and weaponry.

Selective populism.

Newspeak. (An impoverished vocabulary . . . to limit the instruments for complex and critical *reasoning*.)

In barring certain press outlets from the White House, persecuting Latino immigrants and Muslim visitors, siding with Russia over his political opponent, inciting violence, and firing insufficiently loyal civil servants, Trump seemed to be deliberately checking off Eco's criteria as if they were a to-do list. His obsession with military men and parades ticked the "machismo and weaponry" box. The Trump slogan "Make America Great Again" signaled both his rejection of modernism and his longing for tradition. Go ahead, review the list, and consider for yourself whether he satisfied all the criteria.

Experts who use data to measure democracy found that Trump was governing so radically that for the first time they judged our country to be a faltering democracy. With Trump in office, we slipped from "full democracy" to "flawed democracy" in the Economist Intelligence Unit's annual report. Freedom House, which considers civil liberties and political rights, downgraded the United States, noting, in dry language, the new president's self-dealing, lack of transparency, and attacks on institutions key to democracy like the press and the courts. Sadly, given its status as an American institute devoted to democracy, Freedom House reported a global decline in freedom made worse by "the withdrawal of the United States from its historical commitment to promoting and supporting democracy." In other words, the country that founded Freedom House to uphold democracy was, itself, in democratic decline.

————

Republicans had had their chance to deal with Trump. Some had seen him standing by our blazing politics, gas can and matches in hand, and called out an alarm. Senator Lindsey Graham labeled Trump "a race-baiting, xenophobic bigot" and Senator Ted Cruz said he was "a pathological liar." Former Texas governor Rick Perry said of Trump, "Demeaning people of Hispanic heritage is not just ignorant, it betrays the example of Christ." Representative Mick Mulvaney declared Trump "a terrible human being." In October 2016 nineteen Senate Republicans told *USA Today* they would not vote for Trump come November.

Then Trump won. Mulvaney accepted the terrible human being's offer to be his director of the Office of Management and Budget. Perry joined the new administration as secretary of energy. Graham and most of the others who recognized the monster in Trump suddenly found him quite acceptable. Senator Cruz even brought his wife, whom Trump had attacked in a viciously personal way, to a private dinner at the White House.

As the only people with the inclination to do something to stop the authoritarian slide, we House Democrats began 2019 arguing about it. One of our newly elected members, Michigan's Rashida Tlaib, stated one side of the argument succinctly when she declared, "We're going to impeach the motherfucker."

Tlaib, the first Palestinian American ever elected to Congress, spoke at what she thought was a private party *before* she was sworn in. She also recalled a conversation with her teenage son, who had talked to her about bullying and asked how she would respond to Trump. The reaction—from our side!—included criticisms of Tlaib's language, her supposed lack of respect for her office, and her apparent recklessness. "That is not the position of the House Democratic caucus," said Speaker Pelosi. A colleague from Illinois said Tlaib should have been aware that "when you are a member of Congress there's always someone listening," and that she hoped the freshman's hot mic moment wouldn't distract from serious business. Representative Eric Swalwell of California said we needed to avoid making "a martyr" out of Trump by going after him too hard and too soon.

I'll confess that was my initial response too, but in retrospect she was right. Our margin of victory in November had come from people who wanted us to stop the madness. In a word, or rather *three* words, they wanted us to "impeach the motherfucker." These voters were not just Democrats or Democrat-adjacent voters who may have been among the millions who protested against Trump at the rallies that occurred in every state. The 2018 margin of victory, especially in swing districts, had come from voters who had taken a flyer on Trump in 2016 and were disgusted and alarmed by what he had done while in office.

When I argued that even in swing districts people wanted Trump held accountable and impeached, the Speaker remained focused on what she believed voters expected most from us—help with problems like health care and jobs. This was what our For the People agenda had been about, and she had gone on to promote a dozen specific legislative proposals to fulfill it. This approach was very Democrat-y. We have always been the party devoted to researching problems and creating solutions. The trouble was that whatever we passed in the House the Republican-controlled Senate and White House would kill, and in so doing they would make our efforts seem meaningless.

The Speaker was also keen to protect swing-district Democrats, whom we called "frontliners" as if we were involved in trench warfare. Among them were Josh Gottheimer of New Jersey and Cheri Bustos of Illinois, both of whom I spoke with directly about impeachment. They said that they needed to proceed carefully to protect our House majority because without it no one would be in a position to challenge Trump. This struck me as a circular argument: we Democrats had been given the power to check Donald Trump in the 2018 election, but we shouldn't use it because that might cost us in a future election.

I felt that if we immediately backed away, fearing what the voters would say in 2020, then we were not doing our duty. Besides, if we acted swiftly because we believed our democracy was at stake, we would have the better part of two years to tell voters why we had acted as we had. If at that point they disagreed with our actions, then they had every right to communicate that in the next election. But at least we would have acted with the understanding of the emergency we faced. Also, what problem did our country face that was bigger than the destruction of our democracy by a monster who was unmoved by the suffering he caused and growing stronger by the day?

In this moment, we didn't seem to understand the demon who would attempt to devour democracy. Always eager to deliberate, seek the facts, and consider all sides, we wanted to continue to model good behavior.

Where had this gotten us in the years since Newt Gingrich had begun his scorched-earth campaign of lies? From Bill Clinton's pivot to the center to Barack Obama's professorial cool, we had failed to develop the organizations and tactics to match the conservatives as they built fake populist movements like the Tea Party and powerful probusiness political and legal organizations.

We couldn't match the other side dollar for dollar because its funders considered their donations to be down payments on tax cuts and deregulation that produced more revenue than almost any investment outside politics. The result was that a large number of older voters accepted the propaganda that painted us as too liberal to be trusted, and a large number of younger voters considered us so insufficiently liberal that we never got anything done. In the meantime the planet grew warmer, sea levels rose, and Donald Trump threatened to destroy the democratic institutions that represented our one real hope for getting anything right in the future.

22

THE PLAYING-NICE
IMPEACHMENT

Instead of showing purpose by diving into impeachment investigations and hearings, we Democrats joined millions who anxiously awaited special counsel Mueller's final report, as if it would settle things. This idea that Mueller would bring justice was stoked by the dozens of indictments and criminal referrals produced by his team, which had led to the prosecution and conviction of Trumpworld figures like his campaign manager Paul Manafort, his former lawyer Michael Cohen, and his onetime national security adviser, Michael Flynn. For a while Mueller was regarded as one part western sheriff and one part Eliot Ness: the silent, persevering lawman who would carry the burden of saving us from Trump. This was the hope of my colleagues who thought we could wait out the crisis and escape a difficult decision.

The folly of the passive, playing-nice approach was proved when Attorney General William Barr accepted Mueller's report and then, instead of making it public, immediately issued his own four-page synopsis, which was his effort to spin the counsel's findings in a way favorable to Trump. Barr wrote that Mueller did not "establish that the president committed an obstruction-of-justice offense." As Trump and the press seized upon this conclusion, the whole world seemed to accept that after nearly two years of effort, Mueller had found nothing incriminating the president. At the White House and Fox News, they celebrated as if it were New Year's Eve. In the meantime Barr kept the report itself secret, explaining that it would undergo a lengthy review and redaction.

Since Barr had previously declared that the whole Mueller investigation was "fatally misconceived," his take on the report was no surprise. However, when we finally got the full two volumes, we could see that Barr had acted as an appallingly brazen partisan. I spent five hours reading the entire report and saw that Mueller did not "establish" that Trump had committed crimes because he didn't consider that part of his charge. But he wrote, in clear terms, that his own findings "do not exonerate him" either. In fact, the report cataloged hundreds of contacts between Trump's campaign team and Russians and Trump's repeated attempts to interfere with investigations into these contacts.

A close reading of the report showed that Mueller had found that on at least ten occasions, Trump might have tried to obstruct investigations. Among the most egregious examples was his demand that White House Counsel Don McGahn lie for him. Mueller also documented numerous instances in which Trump and his people lied about the president's obstructive acts, including the firing of FBI director Comey.

As a by-the-book federal officer, Mueller accepted a long-standing Department of Justice position that says presidents cannot be prosecuted while in office, even though the rule had never been tested and affirmed by any court. This immunity would end when Trump left office, which meant that prosecutors could go after him then. In the meantime the responsibility for dealing with him rested with Congress, which had the power to investigate and impeach any president for what the Constitution termed "high crimes and misdemeanors."

Did we investigate?

No.

Instead we argued among ourselves. On one side were the Speaker, the frontliners, and others who didn't think Trump was worth it. I stood on the other side with many fellow members of the Judiciary Committee, which would be the logical committee to lead an impeachment process. A New Yorker who had known Trump for decades, Chairman Jerry Nadler was certain we should proceed but met a wall of resistance. Madeleine Dean of Pennsylvania, who is an attorney, and former Orlando chief of police Val Demings knew criminal behavior when they saw it and wanted to act. So did my two closest friends on the committee, a former state regulatory official named Joe Neguse and constitutional law professor Jamie Raskin. (Joe, who is both thoughtful and quick on his feet, is the American-born son of refugees who came to America, and he's a rising star in our party.)

Always ready to recite passages from *The Federalist Papers* or make a historical reference that explains why Congress itself defines "high crimes and misdemeanors," Jamie Raskin, a brilliant scholar of the Constitution and the law, had long considered Trump worthy of impeachment. Trump's most obvious crimes were violations of a clause in the Constitution that prohibits presidents from accepting "foreign emoluments," by which the Founders meant anything of value or benefit from a foreign government. With the Saudis and others gobbling up rooms at various Trump hotels, Trump violated the Foreign Emoluments Clause pretty much every day. When Jamie talked about this as a crime most Americans could understand, once they got past the arcane term *emoluments*, I agreed with him.

The three of us—Neguse, Raskin, and Cicilline—made nuisances of ourselves as we kept pressing our leaders, and our caucus, to act. In light of the full Mueller report, everyone pretty much agreed that Trump had committed impeachable offenses. The pushback came in two forms. One involved the fact that polls showed only about half the American people believed impeachment would be a good idea. I didn't see this as a problem because I believed that the process would reveal facts that would bring more people around. The second objection focused on the fact that impeachment was a kind of indictment that would lead to a trial in the Senate. Since Mitch McConnell and his GOP majority would guarantee a not-guilty verdict, why bother? Trump might actually be emboldened as a result.

In my work as a defense lawyer, I'd had lots of clients who were charged with crimes, went to trial, and were acquitted for various reasons including, I hope, my good lawyering. However, the verdict didn't mean they shouldn't have been charged. Our whole system says that when there's evidence you broke the law, you should get charged for it. Then the process begins. There was value in teaching the president there were consequences for his behavior and in demonstrating to the public that presidents should be held to certain standards. And as most Americans understand, no one is above the law.

I said all of the above, and more, in conversations with other members of House leadership. When it seemed we were winning the argument on one element of the problem, the other side would raise a new concern about, for example, getting some GOP support. With Trump making their party into a cult of personality, the notion that even a single Republican would risk the backlash that would follow his or her support for impeachment seemed an impossibility. Then it happened. Having studied the

Mueller report, Justin Amash of Michigan, a founding member of the Freedom Caucus, took to Twitter to say Trump "has engaged in impeachable conduct."

With Amash on board, several of us on the Judiciary Committee shifted into a new gear. The committee had summoned McGahn to testify, but the White House had ordered him to stay away. When he didn't show up, I used a TV interview to introduce the notion of an impeachment "inquiry" rather than an "investigation" as the first step we could take toward holding Trump accountable. This early-step idea was something that Jamie Raskin, Joe Neguse, and I had devised so that we could continue to press the Speaker a little harder on impeachment. Though I went first, Joe and Jamie quickly followed.

To say that the Speaker did not appreciate our tactic would be an understatement. The three of us were on her leadership team, which meant we were supposed to present a united front. She might forgive those who break ranks, but she wouldn't forget.

We weren't the only rebels. Chairman Nadler would leave meetings where the Speaker had ruled out impeachment and say, almost immediately, that Trump's behavior was "making it harder and harder to rule out impeachment." Meanwhile members of the House Permanent Select Committee on Intelligence also began making noise about impeachment, which meant a contest was developing over who might play key roles in any future effort.

It's common for House committees to jostle for jurisdiction, especially when issues of great public interest arise. Nothing Congress does is higher profile than an impeachment, and the standard for modern proceedings was set by the two committees that investigated the Watergate scandal and cover-up. On the Senate side Chairman Sam Ervin became a historic figure as he led the

Select Committee on Presidential Campaign Activities, which uncovered the extent of the effort to cover up the Nixon campaign's break-in at the Democratic National Committee headquarters at the Watergate Office Building. White House lawyer John Dean would be their star witness. In the House, Peter Rodino led the Judiciary Committee, which approved three articles: obstruction of justice, abuse of presidential power, and contempt of Congress for defying the committee's subpoenas. Remarkably, each of the articles received Republican support. Facing impeachment and possible conviction in a Senate trial, Nixon resigned. In the decades that followed, those who had been part of the drama were featured in books, documentaries, and dramatic films.

In the case of Donald Trump, GOP control of the Senate meant we would have no investigating partners there. Since his abuses revolved around Russia's interference in our election, the Intelligence Committee could logically investigate events while the Judiciary Committee could work on the articles that would set the charges in a Senate trial. But to reach this point we would have to agree impeachment was necessary. By "we" I mean that Speaker Nancy Pelosi would have to agree because once she did, our caucus would fall in line. (The way she would put it was that she had listened carefully to everyone and knew when it was time to move forward.)

A month after we got the full Mueller report and began to digest it, the number of House Democrats who said they would move forward on impeachment had increased from a handful to nearly fifty. The Speaker then appeared on a late-night TV talk show where she explained how the Senate would inevitably find Trump not guilty and he would take a self-serving victory lap. This meant the House needed to be "as ready as you possibly can be" because impeachment would be about revealing him to the

American people, not removing him from office. When the TV host asked, "Will you be ready [before the 2020 election]?" the audience applauded, and the Speaker said, "Yeah, we will."

She said it so quietly that when I saw a clip of the interview online, I had to rewind and listen to it again to be sure of what I'd heard. In fact she had indicated a change of heart, and from this point forward the House would try to hold the ever-slippery Trump accountable. It was not an easy process. When we on the Judiciary Committee heard from Mueller, the whole world seemed to be watching on TV as he announced that he would answer our questions with the information in his report. What ensued was a three-hour display of hesitation, stammering, and sometimes even confusion. At age seventy-five Mueller was no longer a confident prosecutor with a command of the facts. Instead he sometimes seemed unable to detect who was speaking to him from the dais and often declined to answer questions by saying, "I refer you to the report."

At our first break, which allowed our star witness a chance to use the restroom and stretch his legs, we went to a back room, looked at each other in shock, and concluded that Mueller was not going to help us make a case the American people could understand. I heard someone say, "This is a disaster." My thoughts and feelings ranged from sympathy for the witness, who was a hero for his service to our country but was clearly a different witness from the time he last came before Congress in 2014, to frustration over the fact that Mueller would not help clarify things for the American people.

In the afternoon Mueller appeared before the Intelligence Committee to discuss Russia-related issues in greater detail and once again struggled with the questions. The chairman of the committee, Adam Schiff of California, was a Pelosi favorite whose manner was very different from that of judiciary chairman Nadler. At age fifty-nine he looked ten or twenty years younger thanks to his devotion to long-distance running. A product of Stanford and then Harvard Law (cum laude), in his life before politics he had been a federal prosecutor. Nadler was seventy-two years old. He was a born fighter. He had come up hard in the New York of the 1960s and 1970s, attending Fordham law school at night and working days at a state offtrack betting parlor. Chairman Nadler is a progressive champion with an extraordinary intellect and a long record of success. He knew the substance of the case and he knew the Constitution and he had the strong support of the members of his committee.

In what became an obvious contest for the leading role in our defense of democracy, Schiff's California charisma, aided by his personal relationship with the Speaker, gave him the advantage. Jerry lost the competition after a hearing where Trump's former campaign manager Corey Lewandowski testified.

A thuggish character who sported a military-style haircut and a constant smirk, Lewandowski had once been caught attempting to bring a handgun into a House office building. He had more recently become notorious for having manhandled people at Trump campaign events. When he testified before the committee, which is the second-oldest committee in the history of Congress, he appeared in a wood-paneled room where a great deal of history had been made. It was here that the major civil rights bills of the 1960s had been crafted. It was here that freshman representative Barbara Jordan had captivated the nation with a speech that marked the beginning of the end of Richard Nixon's presidency.

When history summoned Lewandowski to room 2141 in the

Rayburn House Office Building, he chose to respond like a clown, repeatedly mocking the committee and refusing to answer questions on the grounds that he was acting under orders from the White House. (To be clear, the White House can't order a private citizen like Lewandowski to do anything.) As he tried to run out the clock by demanding to see documents and insulting Representative Sheila Jackson Lee by suggesting "you can have a conversation by yourself," his purpose was clear. He was planning to run for Senate and anticipating help from inveterate TV viewer Donald Trump, who was watching at the White House. Sensing this, Hakeem Jefferies told him, "This is not the campaign trail yet. This is the House Judiciary Committee. Act like you know the difference."

As the circus continued, Nadler and the committee had the option of holding Lewandowski in contempt. At one point I interrupted the chaos to say, "Mr. Chairman, I ask that if the witness refuses to answer the questions, you hold him in contempt." This caused a small uproar as Republicans on the committee interrupted often, and loudly, because they too were playing to Trump. As Nadler brought the room to order, a staffer came to me and discouraged me from doing this again. It was infuriating to watch this obnoxious man act so disrespectfully and know there was nothing that could be done about it.

After the hearing Speaker Pelosi was reportedly livid over the witness's behavior and Nadler's failure to control him. Jerry would later acknowledge publicly that before the hearing the Speaker had advised him that he should not hold Lewandowski in contempt. Contempt-of-Congress charges are hard to enforce. It had last happened in the Reagan era when an official was found guilty and imprisoned for six months. That case was handled by the Department of Justice. In 2019, with Trump and Barr having politicized the DoJ, Congress couldn't hope for a federal prosecutor's help. But we could have proceeded under our rarely used "inherent contempt" power. This would have sent the sergeant of arms to arrest Lewandowski and bring him to the House Chamber, where he could have been punished by imprisonment for up to a year.

There is no doubt that we have the power to charge and confine people. In 1796 it was done without much debate when a man was suspected of attempting to bribe a member of the House. It happened again in 1800 when the Senate briefly imprisoned a witness for failing to appear when summoned. Inherent-contempt cases arose with regularity until the last one, in 1935, when a resistant witness was sentenced to ten days' confinement, which he served in Gilded Age splendor at the Willard Hotel. Afterward congressional leaders decided that arresting and detaining people was time consuming, distracting, and unseemly.

The problems that had led Congress to abandon inherent contempt remained in 2019, but it was still rather compelling to consider flexing some muscle in response to the Trump crew's defiance. Congress has allowed its power to be chipped away by presidents from both parties, and it's been infuriating to watch them get away with it. In the case of Trump, we feared that Lewandowski's defiance foreshadowed a long process in which we could be disrespected. In this time there was a lot of talk about reviving inherent contempt. One widely shared argument noted that if the executive branch defied requests and subpoenas for documents and testimony, as the Trump administration had more often than not, we couldn't fulfill our Constitutional responsibility to conduct oversight of the government. Invariably these discussions led to questions about whether there was a jail in the Capitol building.

The spot most people mistake for an abandoned jail is an unused tomb, closed by metal bars, that was designed to be a resting place for George Washington's remains. (His descendants honored his wish to be buried at Mount Vernon.) However, the architect of the Capitol has reported that at various times Congress has maintained cells in the Capitol where people have been held for various reasons, including findings of contempt. The last person confined in the Capitol was a witness who refused to cooperate with a Senate committee in 1889. The cells have, since then, been repurposed for use by the sergeant of arms and the Capitol physician.

I don't care whether we have cells where we could confine people or whether we would need to send them to local jails or a hotel where a guard would be posted at their door. I am in favor of the House using its inherent-contempt power to compel testimony and the production of documents. If we use this power a few times, executive branch officials will get the idea that our democratic republic depends on the checks and balances created by the Constitution and that they can't just defy an equal branch of government.

Colleagues who oppose this idea worry about alienating voters who may support a particular president or tempting Republicans to use this power when they control the House. My response to the first argument is that we might impress more voters than we alienate if we show we aren't wimps. As for what might happen with the shoe on the other foot, I'd say that a Democratic administration that defies Congress should be held accountable too. I'm not much worried about this prospect because in their sixteen years in office neither Obama nor Clinton ever fully defied a congressional demand. They may have negotiated and dragged their feet, but in the end Congress got what it needed.

———————

It didn't take long for us to forget Corey Lewandowski and inherent contempt. Two days after his bizarre hearing appearance, the press reported that the president had tried to either bribe or extort the government of Ukraine for help with his 2020 reelection campaign. To be specific, he'd wanted Ukrainian officials to tell some damaging lies about his presumed opponent, Joe Biden, and to say that their country, and not Russia, had messed with the 2016 election. If they refused, Trump would delay delivery of the equipment they needed to defend themselves against Russian military forces they were fighting in the eastern part of their country.

Thanks to a whistleblower who was never named and a number of officials who sacrificed their careers by coming forward, the Ukraine scandal was revealed in Intelligence Committee hearings conducted in just two months. What we learned was that what we impeachment hard-liners had feared—that Trump would escalate his criminal behavior until someone stopped him—was true. In fact, Team Trump's scheme to manipulate Ukraine had started before Democrats took control of the House. While Speaker Pelosi resisted impeachment discussions and everyone was waiting for Mueller's report, Trump's political operatives had been looking for officials in Kyiv who could be corrupted. After the report was made, while we were studying it to determine our next steps, administration officials had been maneuvering to delay aid shipments so the matériel could be a bargaining chip.

The lesson here is not that I was correct in my evaluation of Trump but that he represents such a radical departure from the American experience that it was extremely difficult to understand fully the threat he posed. I relied a bit more than others on insights from mental health experts who warned that he was not someone who would ever stop on his own, but I was still subject to the people-are-mostly-good idea that informed my view of humanity. This is another one of those beliefs that is a classically Democratic trait. We believe in the goodness of people, in Martin Luther King Jr.'s notion that the arc of history bends toward justice, and that when properly informed, the American people will act wisely.

Since convicting Trump and removing him from office was the remotest of possibilities, informing the people would be the main benefit of impeachment. I think we did a remarkable job of it through the Intelligence Committee hearing process, which I was able to join when it was held behind closed doors due to the national security secrets discussed in those sessions. I think the public could have been served by watching the disruptive behavior of certain Republicans, including Jim Jordan, Matt Gaetz, and Lee Zeldin, who behaved like pro-Trump hecklers. However, the important points made in secret were repeated when the Intelligence Committee held public hearings that were televised from start to finish.

In the Judiciary Committee we had the essential task of writing the articles. Before we got underway, we had a weekend session with the constitutional law expert Laurence Tribe. No one in the country was more respected than Tribe when it came to all aspects of the Constitution, including impeachment. Having taught at Harvard for decades, he counted many members of Congress, including Jamie Raskin and Adam Schiff, as former students. He had also taught President Obama, Supreme Court Justice Elana Kagan, and Chief Justice John Roberts. In addition, the Speaker trusted Tribe and frequently consulted him.

In our weekend, Jamie pushed for an article on emoluments,

citing all the payments foreign governments had made to Trump businesses and arguing that it would be easy for Americans to see the betrayal committed by a president who profited from his office. Others thought that Trump could be impeached for offenses unrelated to Ukraine, including the obstruction of justice noted in the Mueller report, his abuse of his pardon power, and his violation of campaign finance laws as he hid hush money payments to women.

As we worked on the options, the choice came down to a throw-the-book-at-him approach or something more narrowly strategic. Here Tribe nudged us toward a position he had likely discussed with Speaker Pelosi. She didn't want the American people to think we were piling on. Better to keep things simple, he counseled, by focusing on Ukraine. We had incriminating transcripts of his calls with Ukraine's president and reams of recent testimony to cite as evidence.

I thought a narrow set of charges seemed the wrong way to go even though I understood we might not have the votes. If we were going to tell the world that Trump was a bad guy, better to demonstrate that he was a *really* bad guy by presenting all of it. Besides, most people couldn't tell whether Trump had tried to bribe or extort the Ukrainians. I began to think that our best opportunity had come with the release of the Mueller report and we had blown it. I remembered how I had shut the door to my office, read the document in one five-hour go, and recognized that Mueller had laid out a case for impeachment and invited Congress to act. However, being Democrats, we had again chosen to be deliberate, cautious, and consummately fair while forgetting that people were expecting us to act decisively.

Put yourself in a typical citizen's place. You have a world of demands on your time and depend on the people you elect to mind things in Washington. The Democrats have been howling about Trump's lawlessness, Mueller plunks down the evidence, and we do nothing.

The American people took that as a signal indicating that either Barr's spin on the report was correct, or we weren't all that serious about Russia helping Trump in the election and his outrageous obstruction and abuse of power. We had wanted to be fair and judicious but lost the trust and confidence of too many people.

Given a second chance to go all in to protect our democracy, we followed our usual—and decent—instinct, which was to be fair and precise. Jamie's emoluments charge and all the others that would have related to Trump's pre-Ukraine behavior were out. So too were the easy-to-grasp words *bribery* and *extortion*. The reason given was that these two words referenced real-world crimes and once they were thrown into the debate, lawyers would demand that we prove that Trump's behavior met all the legal standards that define them. I disagreed. The Constitution leaves it to Congress to determine what constitutes a "high crime or misdemeanor." If we wanted to charge bribery or extortion, we were free to do it, and those terms would mean something to everyone.

Neguse, Raskin, and I made repeated efforts to expand the articles, and I know that Chairman Nadler brought it up in the meetings where the Speaker's leadership team reviewed the options. Speaker Pelosi had come a long way from wondering if Trump was worth impeaching to authorizing impeachment proceedings, and it would be her responsibility to bring the articles to the House floor. Her goal was to reach a majority vote on impeachment, which would demonstrate to the country that accountability was still possible. This couldn't happen without almost every Democratic member's support, and here the so-called frontliners could wield real power. Like the Freedom Caucus on the GOP side, the frontliners had enough votes to block impeachment. And since their swing districts determined control of the House, their opinions mattered more to leaders looking toward future elections. They believed their voters would respond very negatively if we threw the book at Trump, and so they wouldn't support more than the Ukraine articles.

Pelosi's choice was easy to understand, but I still disagreed with it. I think we could have had some witnesses testify on a range of pre-Ukraine issues and then committee members could have written half a dozen additional proposed articles. These could then have been considered by the committee in the normal way with those who made it through the process going on to and up or down by the entire House. This work would have at the very least demonstrated that prior to the Ukraine scandal, we had been justified in our condemnations of Trump, and it would have focused the national press and through it the country on the way Trump threatened democracy.

When Pelosi named seven House members "managers" of the impeachment trial, Adam was designated their chief. Jerry ranked second to him as judiciary chairman. Among the five others were her close friend from the San Francisco Bay Area Zoe Lofgren and the eloquent Hakeem Jeffries, who is my close friend on the Judiciary Committee and is chair of the Democratic caucus. Val Demings, a dynamic and serious person, sat on both Judiciary and Intelligence Committees, and Jason Crow of Colorado was a frontline freshman. The team was rounded out by Sylvia Garcia of Texas, another freshman, who was on the Judiciary Committee and had experience as a judge.

Although all senators swore an oath to function as impartial jurors, and the rules required their presence, attention, and silence in the chamber, many Republicans seemed eager to show their disregard. Marsha Blackburn of Tennessee read and under-lined passages in a book while several senators played with little toys called fidget spinners, which they had been given by their colleague Richard Burr of North Carolina. When the manag-ers played a 1999 video clip showing Senator Lindsey Graham insisting Congress itself defined impeachable offenses, he got up and left the room. Together the Republicans voted to prevent the managers from issuing subpoenas to obtain testimony from wit-nesses and documents. At the time polls showed that as many as 70 percent of the public wanted to have those subpoenas issued.

In the end the impeachment trial followed the course deter-mined by the quality of our politics in this tragically partisan era. The managers persuaded just one GOP senator, Mitt Romney of Utah, to vote for one of the articles. He was convinced that Trump had abused his power in his attempt to strongarm Ukraine for help in the upcoming election. He called this "an appalling abuse of public trust." As she made excuses for not joining Romney, Susan Collins provided unintentional comic relief when she said she believed Trump had learned "a pretty big lesson." A day later, after Trump conducted a televised celebration of the vote, Collins adjusted her view, telling the press she didn't "believe" but rather "hoped" Trump had learned from the impeachment experience.

23

THE LESS NICE IMPEACHMENT

No one had thought that Donald Trump would be removed from office in the first impeachment trial. However, it was reasonable to expect that the GOP, and the American people, would recognize that he had brought a dangerous, autocratic mindset to the presidency. The problem, once again, was that too many wouldn't, or couldn't, see what was going on. Like those GOP senators who fidgeted while our democracy burned, the vast majority of voters didn't watch the trial. Partisanship, apathy, and cynicism led them elsewhere.

Ever sensitive to TV ratings and political polls, Trump reacted in a way that was diametrically opposed to the hopes expressed by Senator Collins in 2020. At the time she had said Trump had learned "a pretty big lesson," and would be "much more cautious" going forward. I thought that she was dead wrong. Indeed, he had only been emboldened. Presented with a chance to lead the country through the COVID-19 pandemic, he brutalized our understanding of the crisis with lies, and scorned science and the principles of public health in order to protect himself, politically. As cases spread and fatalities soared, he played the skeptic, the snake-oil salesman, and finally the troll as he took the GOP's anti-science attitude to a deadly extreme.

In refusing the advice of public health officials and making the pandemic into a political issue, Trump added 461,100 excess deaths to America's COVID casualty count. This figure comes from a study published in the *Lancet*, a prestigious British medical journal, which compared our record with that of other wealthy countries and found we did the absolute worst job of protecting people.

Because leadership counts, and political acts have consequences, I'm comfortable saying that leaving Trump in office, where he rather predictably doubled down on his worst instincts, was a lethal mistake. Many in his base, especially the millions who believed in the QAnon conspiracy theories, regarded his escape from conviction as new proof of his infallibility. Among these extremists were militants in groups such as the Proud Boys, the Oath Keepers, and the Three Percenters, who believed that Trump was heaven-sent to save them from some sort of existential threat. (Though it was rarely expressed in these terms, the emotion behind this fear was often driven by the decline of the white majority in our population and by rising diversity.)

Those willing to see what was happening as Trump followed impeachment with divisive pandemic politics should have awakened to the crisis when he unleashed federal forces who used low-flying helicopters, horses, tear gas, flash grenades, smoke canisters, batons, and rubber bullets to force peaceful protesters from Lafayette Square near the White House. The protest was part of a nationwide movement calling attention to police killings of Black citizens, including George Floyd, whose death in Minneapolis, recorded on video, outraged people worldwide. The bloody spectacle of the protest, broadcast live on TV, was capped by Trump's ceremonial walk, with aides and a uniformed General Mark Milley at his side, to a church that faces the square.

There he posed for photographers while holding up a Bible. (He was so unaware that he was holding a holy text that he held it upside down.) And we later learned Trump even asked Defense Secretary Mark Esper why he couldn't shoot citizen protesters.

Overall, the scene at Lafayette Park had a Leni Riefenstahl feel to it, as if someone had considered the protesters—mostly young Black people—symbolic extras representing an enemy that could be vanquished with military might and a flashing of Christian emblems. Before the day was done, the White House had released a propaganda video featuring Trump, the walk, the Bible, the church, and a driveway lined on both sides by uniformed men in riot gear, posing with their shields raised to protect their bodies. Walking ahead of General Milley and others, Trump pumped his fist to signal his status as the victor. The video ended with a shot of the American flag waving over the White House.

The Lafayette Square episode established a new appalling first for Trump. Never before had a president ordered up a paramilitary assault on peaceful protesters so he could insert himself in the moment and produce a political set piece featuring cinematic violence, militaristic patriotism, and religious themes. Chilling to everyone who wasn't a part of the Trump cult, this made-for-TV event showed how far Trump was willing to go to assert his power. It was a signal to the extreme element in his base, the men and women who hoarded weapons and tactical gear in anticipation of a call to arms.

———

It's almost impossible to overstate the level of crisis we faced as the 2020 election approached. Unwilling to address a tidal wave of conspiracy theories and violent rhetoric, social media companies let their platforms become clubhouses for those who spread

bizarre lies about Democrats, Joe Biden, the "Deep State," and
the security of our elections.

When you added in the similarly awful stuff being said about
the COVID pandemic, the civic environment was less stable than
it has been in generations, and many thoughtful experts were
beginning to warn of armed conflict. The simplistic and wrong-
headed way some people talked about the mood hearkened back
to the Civil War, as if somehow an army of rebellion would be
formed by so-called red or conservative states to fight against the
United States government. This was not going to happen. However, it became evident to many of us in Congress that groups
of people—officials said the main threat came from the extreme
right—might carry out small attacks. This is how civil war is
done in most places around the world as people become agitated
by extreme ethnic, racial, or religious propaganda that turns
neighbor against neighbor.

Weeks before the election, as the president repeatedly warned,
without any basis, that the election would be stolen, the FBI and
police swooped down on members of a paramilitary group who
called themselves the Wolverine Watchmen, who were planning
to kidnap Michigan governor Gretchen Whitmer and attack the
state capitol. The fourteen men held various extreme right-wing
political views. One was a leader of the antigovernment Three
Percenters, who believe a force of 3 percent of a country can overthrow a tyrannical government. According to their social media
accounts, guns were extremely important to these men, and
many believed false claims that somehow the government was
about to confiscate all the privately held firearms in the country.

The firearms fetish expressed by the Whitmer plotters is
common in many corners of the Trump movement. The year
2020 would see more than fifty political demonstrations in which

people showed up dressed like soldiers and wielding military-style firearms. Nearly all of these events were organized by Trump-favoring right-wingers. Intimidation is the point of these armed protests, and the fact that people of all political stripes seem willing to brandish arms is frightening.

The guns came out again after Trump lost the election and a Stop the Steal campaign—preplanned by key operatives including Steve Bannon and Roger Stone—sprang to life. (One notorious pro-Trump activist had revealed preparations for this effort in September with a Twitter message that read "#StoptheSteal 2020 is coming...") Normal political leaders recognized how a massive effort to persuade Americans that their elections were rigged would have a grave impact on our political culture. Republicans had already spent forty years teaching people to mistrust first the government and then anyone, Democrat or Republican, who thought it might accomplish good things for the country. With public confidence already weakened, it wouldn't take much for Trump, aided by activists with money and organizations, to draw millions of people to Stop the Steal groups. Protesters who truly believed that someone was trying to steal the election from Trump flocked to places where votes were being counted and clamored for proof that the balloting and counting were fair.

————

Although the Trump administration's own experts declared the 2020 election the most secure in history, and every recount and court case ended with the results unchanged, the monstrous ideas loosed by Trump and his helpers led, inevitably, to the January 6 attack. This was obviously a violent attempt at a coup, the first in American history, but one that they saw as a rescue mission.

Knowing that accountability would be essential to any return to a politics of peace and trust, I immediately worked with Jamie Raskin, Ted Lieu, Joe Neguse, and other House Democrats to push for the second impeachment of Donald Trump. Within two days our lone article of impeachment, for the crime of "incitement of insurrection," was supported by more than one hundred members of Congress. Included was Speaker Pelosi, who, I was told, had stopped Adam Schiff as he began to write his own draft article to compete with ours. Within four days we had 210 official cosponsors. On January 13, a week to the day after the attack, the House impeached Trump with the votes of every Democrat and ten Republicans. Among the latter were prominent figures like Liz Cheney, the former vice president's daughter, and Adam Kinzinger, a rising young GOP star. Both were stalwart conservatives who had resisted the Trump cult.

Whatever happened next, in a Senate trial, would matter to Trump, of course. We who had voted to approve the impeachment article were eager to see him convicted so that the world would see the rule of law and democracy upheld. But there was one thing we had accomplished all on our own. We had, with a record number of the opposing party's assent, made him the only president ever to be impeached twice. This stain would be indelible and, along with his shameful behavior, assure him last place in every ranking of American presidents well into the future.

————

The many differences between this impeachment and the one that had preceded it began with the fact that we had a much simpler case to present. Trump's words of incitement had been broadcast live on TV, as had the ensuing battle between the Trumpists and the police. Senators and House members were themselves witnesses as well as victims of the attack, which made it far more difficult for Republicans to simply ignore the facts, as they had in the first impeachment. (This explains Lindsey Graham's emotional rebuke of Trump: "All I can say is count me out. Enough is enough.")

Video of Trump presenting Stop the Steal propaganda and then sending the mob to "fight" on January 6 could be located with a Google search. Five people died as a result of the attack, including four police officers. More than 140 people were injured. And hundreds of senators, representatives, and staff were traumatized from being driven into hiding. Add the damage done to Americans' sense of security, and the negative effect the attack had on our international reputation, and the effects of the insurrection were obvious. In fact, the issues at hand weren't much more complicated than those presented when police watch an assault occur in front of their own eyes. In some jurisdictions magistrates hear these cases within days of the event.

Since we could put on a case almost immediately, we asked Senator McConnell to call the Senate into session and permit the trial to happen before Trump left office on January 20. McConnell refused to act and cited a tradition that requires every senator to agree to interrupt a recess to return to Washington. Trouble was, in 2004 the Senate had created an exception that allowed the majority and minority leaders to agree to an emergency session. McConnell conveniently ignored this change, hid behind the fig leaf of a no-longer-relevant tradition, and signaled, on January 8, that he would not allow us to bring swift justice to a defendant whose crimes had been committed before the millions of witnesses who had watched on TV.

Though we were denied the quick action the situation

seemed to demand, the delay would allow the House to develop an even more persuasive case. This thought came to my mind as the Speaker called to ask me to be part of the managers' team. Those of us in the group selected by the Speaker to present the second case against Trump were, on average, ten years younger than those in the first managers' group. I think we were also less burdened by the expectations that sometimes comes with certain ranks—not one of us chaired a committee—and more committed to collaborating.

Jamie Raskin would serve as lead manager with me, Ted Lieu, Joe Neguse, Diana DeGette of Colorado, Joaquin Castro of Texas, Madeleine Dean of New Jersey, Eric Swalwell of California, and Stacey Plaskett, a nonvoting delegate from the Virgin Islands. Eric Swalwell would be the lone Californian member of the team.

Jamie was one of those rare members of Congress who was liked, and in some cases loved, by everyone in the Democratic caucus and quite a few Republicans. Unfailingly kind and attentive, even when he is listening to someone on the other side of an issue, he possesses a rare level of brilliance that he leavens with respect for others. He's idealistic to such a degree that he's often surprised by political duplicity, and it's hard to imagine anyone more different from Donald Trump.

Two days prior to the January 6 attack, members of Congress and a wide range of people in the Washington region were shocked to read that Jamie and Sarah Bloom Raskin's son Thomas, age twenty-five, died by suicide on New Year's Eve. The family had shared this tragic news in an open letter in which they discussed Tommy's long struggle with depression and shared his sad message that his "illness won today."

There may be no loss greater than a parent's loss of a child. If there is, I can't think of it. In this case Jamie and Sarah had raised a young man who was tenderhearted enough to ask his survivors to "look out for each other, the animals and the global poor" and so intellectually gifted that he had been a champion public speaker at Amherst College. When he died, he was a law student at Harvard University, where he also taught an undergraduate course called Justice: Ethics in an Age of Pandemic and Racial Reckoning.

When Jamie returned to the House on the day when members and their families typically celebrate being sworn in, many members wanted to see him and support him. Majority Leader Steny Hoyer lent a space near the House floor where Jamie received colleagues. Joe Neguse and I spent much of the day there with him. I've never seen someone so stricken with grief manage to be so caring to so many others. Of course he was in shock. But he was nevertheless both vulnerable and generous. These hallmark Raskin traits—vulnerability and generosity—got him through the first difficult days following Tommy's death. They allowed him to endure what happened on January 6, which he came to describe as a coup attempt carried out by the violent extremists who attacked the Capitol from outside and the manipulative extremists who sought to block the certification of Biden's victory from inside the process.

A week after the day that Trump's forces tried to kill our democracy, Jamie would again apply his strengths. This time he worked with the eight of us who had also been named to the impeachment managers team. Together—decisions would always be made jointly—we recognized that we could make our case by presenting the evidence of Trump's incitement, the purpose of the attack, and the proof that he had committed a very high crime. We could do this with the aid of a vast collection of video evidence that would allow us to display events in a way that would be incontestable, except in the minds of politicians who saw something to be gained by denying the facts and betraying their country.

24

PROOF IS NOT ENOUGH

Images of the January 6 attack on the Capitol saddened—and in some unfortunate cases thrilled—people across the country. These, respectively, were the reactions of the people who had a well-grounded regard for America's enduring values and of the deluded Trumpists who were lost in conspiracy theories and fantasies of rebellion. A third group, self-interested cynics in the United States Senate, downplayed the fact that they had been driven by the mob from their own chamber and searched for political advantage.

Although the Republicans' leader, Mitch McConnell, had once said he might vote to convict Trump, he abused the rules of the Senate to delay scheduling the trial. With the Senate evenly divided and Vice President Kamala Harris the tiebreaking vote, Democrats would take control on January 20. After Harris and Biden were sworn in and Democrat Chuck Schumer of New York became majority leader and the one who would set the Senate's agenda, a slew of Republicans began protesting the very idea that a government officeholder who had left office could be tried at all.

This argument, that a president could not be tried for an impeachable offense after leaving office, was a classic example of an appeal to common sense made in bad faith. Since most people understand impeachment and the trial that follows as a way to get rid of a president, they might hear this appeal and think, "If he's already gone, isn't the whole thing over?" Senator Josh Hawley of Missouri, whose raised-fist salute to the January 6 attackers had become an emblem of the tragedy, said, "I think that this impeachment effort is, I mean, I think it's blatantly unconstitutional. It's a really, really, really dangerous precedent."

As Hawley and the forty-four other Republicans who voted to prevent a trial knew, or *should* have known, impeachment and the prosecutions that follow have more than one purpose. In addition to leading to removal, conviction can bar a person from ever holding public office in the future. This happened in the case of Secretary of War William Belknap, who thought he had evaded trial for accepting bribes by racing to the White House to resign. Senators, realizing that this ploy could be used by anyone seeking to avoid punishment for crimes committed in office, proceeded anyway. So did we.

————

Our preparation for the trial was driven by our determination to tell the full story of the January 6 attack and the events leading up to it, which some very gifted House staffers and consultants were able to piece together from video broadcast by news outlets and from scenes captured by the fixed cameras that are part of the Capitol security system. After an initial in-person meeting with the Speaker in her conference room, she gestured to a portrait of Abraham Lincoln and reminded us that the Confederate battle flag had been waved by the attackers both inside and outside the Capitol. "You have the chance to bring accountability back to government," she said, "to rescue Congress and the Constitution and the country from this insurrection and this president."

The Speaker, who has a very keen sense of history, was not

exaggerating. Trump loyalists were already downplaying the seriousness of what had happened and deflecting blame. We could correct them with an effort that, while unlikely to yield conviction, would persuade enough Republican senators to show the strength of our democracy. This was one of our main goals as we used videoconferencing to meet daily while staying safe from COVID. At these sessions we often viewed video clips showing much more shocking levels of violence than news cameras had captured, including scenes of rioters gouging police officers' eyes, ripping off their face masks to spray chemicals into their eyes, and leaving them bloodied and unconscious.

Some of our first meetings also involved discussing what senators had shared with some of us about what went wrong in the first impeachment trial. They'd said, "Remember that when an impeachment trial is underway, we are required to be in the Senate Chamber. We cannot have our phones, we must be in our seats. For a busy person, that's really hard. The only thing worse than that is being forced to sit there and hear things repeated." Every senator we consulted said that the repetition had been harmful to the prosecutors' case, like the many moments of oratory when managers who thought they were inspiring senators were, instead, alienating them.

————————

On January 25 we managers were charged with delivering the article of impeachment to the Senate. This is a ceremonial process that required us to assemble on the House side of the Capitol, where we were given copies of the ornately printed article inside blue leather folders. With Jamie first, followed by the rest of us in pairs, we assembled behind Clerk of the House Cheryl Johnson and Sergeant at Arms Timothy Blodgett. (His predecessor had just resigned amid criticism of his leadership on January 6.)

The walk took us through National Statuary Hall, which occupies the original House chamber space, where we were greeted by Ethan Allen in marble, Chief Standing Bear in bronze, and dozens more. With the path cleared by police, the space was so empty I could hear the sound made by the footsteps of some of the women in our group. As we entered the rotunda with its soaring dome, we passed under the two-hundred-year-old marble statue of Clio, the Muse of history, which was designed, sculpted, and placed during the reconstruction of the Capitol after British forces burned its interior. John Quincy Adams once wrote a poem in which he imagines Clio joining a House floor debate on the side of those who would abolish slavery.

Jamie stopped at the door to the Senate Chamber, and we stopped behind him, holding our two-by-two places. I noticed immediately that the door looked very much like the glass-and-wood door to the House Chamber, which had been smashed by the January 6 mob.

After a few seconds' wait we were greeted by Sergeant at Arms Jennifer Hemingway, who wore a simple black dress that evoked the solemnity of the moment. She led us inside, where we could see Senator Patrick Leahy presiding from a chair high above the floor. I thought of the ridiculous character who called himself the QAnon Shaman, half-naked with his face painted and racoon tails hanging from his horned fur hat, sitting in the same chair. I looked at the one hundred senators' desks, some dating to 1820, arranged in an arc before him. Five weeks earlier, attackers in distinctive red Trump caps had rifled through many of these desks, spilling papers on the floor. After one of the mob shouted, "This is our House!" another, attempting to be less disrespectful, had answered in equal ignorance, "No it's not, it belongs to the vice president."

Each door in the Senate is crowned by an inscription. Among them are Novus ordo seclorum ("A new order of the ages [is born]"), and E pluribus unum ("Out of many, one"). It is much smaller than the House chamber, and the sound is muffled a bit by thick carpet that is a slightly brighter shade of blue than the carpet covering the floor of the House. Instead of the 446 brown leather seats used by the delegates and members of the House, we faced the one hundred antique desks used by the senators. I could see the setting would have the intimacy of a courtroom, where you can look into the jurors' eyes and even notice when they are impressed by something that has been said.

As we waited just inside the door, Hemingway stood in the aisle and said, in a loud, steady voice:

Mr. President and members of the Senate, I announce the presence of the managers on the part of the House of Representatives to conduct proceedings on behalf of the House concerning the impeachment of Donald John Trump, former president of the United States.

The only suggestion of nervousness in Hemingway's presentation was the slight trembling of the paper she read from. As she paused, Senator Leahy said, "The managers on the part of the House shall be received and escorted to the well of the Senate." Hemingway then led us to stand between the senators and Leahy, facing him. After Leahy commanded her to "make the proclamation," Hemingway walked confidently to the small rostrum that faced the senators, rested her hands on the lectern, and said:

Hear ye, hear ye, hear ye.

All persons are commanded to keep silent on pain of imprisonment while the House of Representatives is exhibiting to the Senate of the United States an article of impeachment against Donald John Trump, former president of the United States.

The scene was more solemn than most religious services and seemed fashioned to function a bit like one. We were there to affirm our commitment to the Constitution, to declare the truth of our experience, and to deliver judgment upon a person who had violently defiled our shared endeavor. Then, standing at the same lectern where Hemingway had stood and reading the article aloud, Jamie spoke words that honored the historical moment but also used plainer language that fit the crime. The relevant parts included, first, a reference to the fact that as the body established to most directly consider the will of the people, that was what we were expressing:

> Article of impeachment exhibited by the House of Representatives of the United States of America in the name of itself and of the people of the United States of America, against Donald John Trump, President of the United States of America, in maintenance and support of its impeachment against him for high crimes and misdemeanors.

Whether those who opposed the impeachment liked it or not, our action *did* reflect the will of the people. As the article asserted, Trump was being impeached for insurrection and rebellion against the United States "by willfully inciting violence" intended to interfere with the House and Senate as Congress counted the votes of the Electoral College. In its vernacular passages, the article quoted Trump's preattack speech, in which he said, "If you don't fight like hell, you're not going to have a country anymore," and it noted that he'd pressured Georgia's secretary of state to "find" enough votes to give him a victory there.

Finally the article addressed, head-on, the main objection that would be raised, namely the idea that Trump couldn't be impeached because, thanks to Mitch McConnell's delays, he had left office. The article dispatched that argument by citing the Constitution, which said a conviction would bring "disqualification to hold and enjoy any office of honor, trust, or profit under the United States." As the Senate had previously established in trials of others, this passage can refer to officials no longer in office, and its intent is clearly to keep such wrongdoers out of government forever.

At the end of the reading, we were escorted out of the chamber, where we were met by the House sergeant at arms, who led us as we retraced our steps to the House. There we sighed our collective relief and thought about what was to come. We would need seventeen Republican votes to convict, and this was, in the eyes of most experts, an impossible task. Acting as partisans and not jurors, many Republican senators had said their minds were already made up and that they would find Trump not guilty no matter the evidence. Still, we had been, each of us, infected by Jamie Raskin's boundless optimism and confidence that the senators would act as reasonable people of goodwill. We would, therefore, conduct the trial as if we could prevail. And we were sure that even if the vote went against us, we would win by establishing the facts of what had occurred. Eventually the Trump cult would recede, and all Americans would need a record of the events that also showed how we'd sought accountability.

Before we presented evidence, we had to deal with a defense motion to have the charge dismissed because Trump was no longer in office and therefore not covered by the impeachment process. We began our argument with a jarring thirteen-minute video that recalled the events of January 6, which, by the looks on the senators' faces, brought them back to that traumatic day. It included scenes of the crowd pressing on a revolving door where a screaming officer, caught between the door and its frame, was being crushed. It also included video of a mob chasing an officer up flights of stairs, where he cannily led them away from the Senate Chamber. When they saw the video of a plainclothes Capitol police officer shooting a rioter who tried to vault through a glass door panel to reach the House Chamber, some of the senators gasped audibly. This clip ended with Trump's video message to the rioters. "Go home," he said. "We love you. You're very special."

In his opening, Jamie explained the most relevant previous impeachment, that of Secretary of War William Belknap, who had resigned to escape impeachment for taking bribes. He had been impeached, tried, and convicted. In the case of Trump, said Jamie, a president should not be given a "January exception" that permitted illegal behavior on the grounds that it was absolved by the inauguration of a new Oval Office occupant. Joe Neguse quoted many prominent conservative lawyers whom GOP senators respected, all of whom recognized our argument. In my turn at the lectern, I would continue the argument against the motion to dismiss, which would also include reminders of the crimes Trump had committed.

It may be hard to accept this, but I felt calm as I got up from my chair and walked to the lectern to address the Senate. Some of my equanimity came from decades of speaking in forums as varied as the Italian Workingmen's Club of Woonsocket and the House of Representatives. More importantly, I had been prepared by long days and nights working with colleagues and staff lawyers who had labored as if we were presenting a landmark case to the Supreme Court. (Some might say the case was more important than but a handful of those.)

I began by telling the senator-jurors, "Impeachment is not merely about removing someone from office. Fundamentally, impeachment exists to protect our constitutional system." I said that a president must be subject to impeachment, "from the very first day in office to the very last day" and that the whole purpose of the power to impeach "would fail if you created a January exception." I reminded everyone of the tragedy that had occurred and, following our strategy, used the words of a Republican, Senator Lindsey Graham, to punctuate the point. Speaking shortly after the attack, a shaken Graham had said, "They could have killed us all." And I concluded by noting that if the senators declined to even conduct a trial, they would signal any future president that he or she could act with impunity to overturn a lost election and claim power as a dictator.

As I spoke I noticed that nearly all the senators seemed to be quietly focused on what I was saying. During this impeachment no one played with a fidget spinner. The most attentive person in the room was Senator McConnell, who sat directly in front of me in the first row on the center aisle. As we would each notice, he barely moved during the entirety of the trial. He was either a master of marathon listening or one of those people who can meditate with their eyes open.

My final task as a manager defending against the move to throw out our case was to address the other side's plan to present examples of other politicians using incendiary language—calling on people to "fight"—to create false equivalency. I countered by saying, "President Trump was not impeached because the words he used, viewed in isolation without context, were beyond the pale." He had been impeached because "he sought to overturn a presidential election that had been upheld by every single court that had considered it. . . . He summoned an armed, angry, and dangerous crowd that wanted to keep him in power that was widely reported to be poised on a hair trigger for violence at his direction. . . . It was foreseeable that those statements would spark extraordinary imminent violence. He then failed to defend the vice president. . . . He issued statements during the insurrection targeting the vice president. He issued a tweet, five hours after the attack, in which he sided with the bad guys. . . . After a betrayal like this, there cannot be unity without accountability."

When their turn came, the president's lawyers, who were representing someone who had been, weeks before, the most powerful person on Earth, appeared unprepared and unserious. They offered baseless attacks on our effort, arguments devoid of legal underpinnings, and casual talk of the sort that would get you thrown out of a municipal court hearing. Their intent was obvious. They wanted to show contempt for us and loyalty to the former president, who was, no doubt, watching on a television somewhere in his gilded Palm Beach resort.

Michael van der Veen, a personal injury lawyer known for TV ads that solicited clients for slip-and-fall lawsuits, began by apologizing for the fact that he had to "clean up" the "mess" that we House managers had made as we laid out the facts of January 6. Van der Veen than leaned on the lectern as if he were leaning on the bar at a tavern and went on to echo Trump's claims that impeachment was a "politically motivated witch hunt" that was "divorced from the facts" and "an unjust and blatantly unconstitutional act of political vengeance." As he went on I began to think of all the ambulance chasers I had seen in courtrooms back home and how so many had thought they could use hype, histrionics, or charm.

The president's lead counsel, Bruce Castor, infamous for refusing to prosecute the serial sex offender Bill Cosby, tried to use the charm approach. He stumbled out of the gate as he introduced himself as the "lead prosecutor," which was not, technically, a role anyone had been assigned. Of course if anyone could be considered a "lead prosecutor" it was Jamie Raskin. And as was obvious to everyone, Bruce Castor was no Jamie Raskin.

Once he got his bearings, Castor made a bunch of folksy observations—"We are generally a social people"—that weren't attached to any legal purpose. He also delivered the kind of word salad that made him sound much like Donald Trump himself. Nebraska was, in his words, "quite a judicial-thinking place." He also said, "Many of you are lawyers, probably lawyers, some of you—I have been a lawyer thirty-five years—longer than me, many longer than me, probably."

The last of the president's trio of lawyers, David Schoen of Alabama, was the most serious of the three. Specializing in federal criminal defense, he had done some high-profile work, including the defense of Trump crony Roger Stone, who had been convicted of obstruction of justice, witness tampering, and lying to law enforcement. (The charges had grown out of the Mueller investigation, and Trump pardoned Stone before he reported to prison.) When he addressed the Senate, Schoen spoke more soberly than his colleagues, but he couldn't overcome the weakness in his arguments. At one point he complained that the House had been too slow in transmitting the article of impeachment to the Senate. Then he contradicted himself by saying we were engaged in a "rush to judgment." Schoen suggested that when we quoted the Framers who had feared mob rule, we were expressing an "elitist view," as if most Americans were OK with being ruled by violent hordes. He also tried to place the president above the law, saying that impeachment wasn't necessary because the voters had thrown Trump out of office. Of course the crime we had charged him with involved his scheme to subvert the election, and it had all been captured on video, but hey, Schoen had to say *something*.

We managers, split between the few allowed at a table in the Senate and the rest watching on televisions in a nearby reception room, could hardly believe what we were hearing. Apparently Trump, notorious for not paying his legal bills and obviously guilty, had failed to attract first-rate lawyers. What he'd gotten instead was guys who relied on the fact that we needed the support of seventeen Republican senators to achieve the supermajority required for a conviction. There was little to no chance we would win over that many GOP senators. This reality may have persuaded the members of the defense team that they didn't need to do much more than show up. The only other explanation for their performance was that they were incapable of doing better.

The vote to continue the trial was fifty-six to forty-four. The six Republicans who went with the majority were Bill Cassidy of Louisiana, Susan Collins of Maine, Lisa Murkowski of Alaska, Mitt Romney of Utah, Ben Sasse of Nebraska, and Pat Toomey of Pennsylvania. Cassidy was a surprise, as was the praise we received from other GOP senators. Add what others said about the power of our presentation, especially the videos, and it was hard to resist feeling hopeful. From the outside this surely seemed ridiculous. It was hard to imagine that we could prevail. But we had a duty to do our job well, and that required believing that we could win. Most of us did.

*   *   *

We got ourselves into a competitive mindset by imagining how seventeen Republicans could vote to convict Trump and drive a stake through the heart of America's first authoritarian movement. One argument stressed the defense of democracy. The other, which we couldn't make directly, related to their own political futures. Convicting Trump would end the chance that he could run again for any office and greatly diminish his political standing. Did they want him to continue his takeover of the Republican Party and drive out everyone who wasn't loyal to him personally?

One person, Senator McConnell, could have led sixteen others to convict Trump. As the top Republican in the Senate, he had always been a brilliant tactician focused mainly on preserving his own power and key to the party's success for many years. McConnell had often expressed a distaste for Trump and his cult of personality. He was also widely regarded as an institutionalist who valued the GOP and the Constitution. Finally, as Joe Neguse would point out after reading a biography of McConnell, he had taken risks to do the right thing before. Without naming them, Joe noted that two men currently in the Senate had, in 1986, voted to override Ronald Reagan's veto of sanctions Congress had imposed on apartheid-era South Africa. Every senator surely knew he was talking about McConnell and Leahy, who was presiding over the trial.

————

As we clung to the belief that victory was possible, we continued to work feverishly on our statements and our arguments against points raised by the other side. All of this work took place in an ornate ceremonial room just off the Senate floor where big TV screens showed us what was happening in the trial and laptops set on a long wooden table made it possible for us to do research. The space was painted a soft yellow and featured a marble fireplace topped by a huge mirror with an equally ornate gold frame. It was lit by a huge crystal chandelier and by the light streaming in from a window that opened on a view of a nearby office building. An American flag and its staff stood in a corner to the right of the window, and a low filing cabinet had been placed in front of it. On top of that rested a copy machine that I would use as a lectern as I stood to face the window and the flag and practice my remarks.

I think that at one point or another everyone on our team practiced before the window and the flag because we had so little space for work that it was the only spot where you could get out of the buzz of activity. In the corner you could hear yourself think and avoid distracting everyone else. It was hard for me to stick to practicing a speech because what was going on around me was exciting and energizing. Between the managers and the staff, which included impeachment specialist Joshua Matz and impeachment trial attorneys Barry Berke and Sarah Istel, we had a million volts of legal brainpower in the room, and not one of the other side's misrepresentations, distortions, or propaganda techniques escaped our notice. In fact, since the defense lawyers spoke a lot like Donald Trump, they made so many of these false arguments that we couldn't possibly address them all.

One that did get addressed was caught by delegate Stacey Plaskett. Our opponents tried to counter the problem of Trump directing folks to "fight like hell" moments before the attack with an everybody-does-it claim. They accompanied their argument with a video that showed Democrats using the word *fight* in interviews, remarks in Congress, and speeches to peaceful groups. Stacey noticed, of course, the absence of context. Not one of the speakers had tried to incite people to march off to accomplish a goal by force. She also noticed that women like her were overrepresented in the film, to exploit stereotypes about angry Black women.

In one of her turns at the lectern, she took the defense to task, saying, "It was not lost on me" that so many in the film were "Black women like myself who are sick and tired of being sick and tired for our children, your children, our children." After referencing the multiracial protests against police brutality in Black communities, she said she once thought that the country was "moving past" the kind of stereotypes in the film. "I thought we were past that," she concluded. "I think maybe we're not."

Throughout the trial senators would use breaks in the proceedings to tell us how well we were doing. Among them were many Republicans, including Lindsey Graham and Ted Cruz, stalwart Trump supporters who had already said they were voting not guilty but who admired our lawyering. Since they said that we were making our case successfully and since they were sworn "to do impartial justice," these approaches from senators had a through-the-looking-glass quality to them. If we were prevailing, and they were acting as impartial jurors, how could they not support our case?

The answer, of course, was that they weren't honoring their pledge to act impartially and were not much like jurors at all. In one of the strangest moments in the trial, Senator Mike Lee of Utah sprang up from his seat in the second-to-last row and began objecting loudly to something I had said. I couldn't tell what he was upset about, and for a moment my mind flashed to a little ploy I used to use in trials. I would tell the jurors about a prosecution claim I expected they would hear during closing and say, "If you hear that, stand right up and say, 'Where is the evidence of that?'" In truth jurors aren't supposed to do this—and not one ever did!—but my words to them invariably persuaded prosecutors to avoid whatever topic I had flagged.

I had never seen a juror actually stand up and object until I participated in the Senate's trial of Donald Trump. It happened at the very start of the trial, when I referenced "the first call we are aware of that he [Trump] made to anyone inside the Capitol during the attack." I noted that he hadn't called the vice president or leaders in Congress but "instead he attempted to call Senator [Tommy] Tuberville" of Alabama. As had been reported widely in the press, Trump apparently connected instead with Senator Lee. I described how Lee had realized the mix-up and "handed the phone to Senator Tuberville." I then described how Trump had wanted Tuberville to make sure GOP senators tried to stop the counting of the Electoral College votes. Suddenly I heard, off to my right, the sound of an angry voice. I thought to myself, *Is a juror objecting?* If that was the case, I really wanted to savor what came next.

Indeed, a juror was objecting. It was Senator Mike Lee of Utah asking that something that I'd said be stricken from the record of the trial. Since I had said only that Lee had received an errant call from Trump and handed the phone to Tuberville, I couldn't imagine what Lee was upset about. Given a chance to explain, he said, "Statements were attributed to me moments ago by the House impeachment managers. Statements relating to the content of conversations between a phone call involving President Trump and Senator Tuberville were not made by me, they're not accurate, and they're contrary to fact."

Lee's request was denied by the presiding officer, but he was adamant, and quite agitated, and demanded a vote on it. All of this seemed quite strange because no one had said anything about Lee revealing the content of the call. I had only said he'd taken the call and handed off the phone. As we managers stepped back to watch, Lee got himself red in the face asking to correct something that hadn't been done in the first place. Gradually I realized that Lee wasn't actually addressing the Senate. Upon hearing his name mentioned, he had recognized that Donald Trump, watching on TV, might associate him with something bad. He'd then seized the opportunity to perform as the senator who was angry at the managers and insist that what we had said was "false." Lee's voice quavered as he did this, and he continued to complain as the Senate devolved into a confused consideration of what had been said and whether there was a way, under the rules, for Lee to object.

As senators called out their concerns and struggled to figure out what they were being asked to do—strike something that hadn't been said—it was hard to believe that I was standing in the well of what is often described as the most powerful deliberative body on Earth. I decided to sit down at our table with Jamie. We discussed what was really happening. Lee was terrified of Trump. He needed to win some concession. We'd wanted to mention the incident to show that Trump had been more concerned about stopping the vote count than stopping the attack. Jamie figured he could graciously say I had "correctly and accurately" quoted a newspaper account that included statements made by Lee himself. He then said that since this incident wasn't a significant element in our timeline, we could just leave it out of our presentation. Lee, still emotional, heckled Jamie like a half-drunk customer at a comedy show, calling out, "You're not being the one cited as a witness, sir." For a moment it seemed he was going to burst into tears.

Since there should be no crying in impeachment trials, we were very happy to move along. Over the course of five days, we worked long days and into the night, making sure we presented a complete and persuasive case. Pizza became a meal of choice, and every morning I marveled at how, after we managers went to sleep, Sarah, Barry, Josh, and others continued writing into the early-morning hours.

Coming after a period of several weeks when we had kept a similar schedule compiling the evidence, this heavy load seemed, in a way, quite normal. However, we were also aware of the dangers of burnout and quite concerned for our leader, Jamie, whose grief over his son's death was still fresh. There were nights when, despite his feeling that he was doing what Tommy would have wanted, we insisted that he go home to be with his family.

Ultimately we produced such a volume of evidence, which was never refuted by the defense, that no fair person committed to acting impartially would have found Trump not guilty. But before we finished our case, we heard about a development that McConnell had sent a note to his colleagues informing them that he would vote to acquit. This meant they were free to do the same.

Jamie the optimist—some might say the *cockeyed* optimist—wouldn't accept that this was true. He noted that McConnell had been listening the whole time, never moving a muscle. How could he take in all we had presented and not vote to convict Trump? With this in mind Jamie clung to the belief that McConnell would do the right thing and the GOP senators would give us the margin of victory. The problem was that if McConnell had ever possessed a moral compass, he had long ago lost it. For decades he had consistently opted for whatever move preserved or increased his own power. In the case of Trump's trial, McConnell apparently saw that the most rabid people in the party backed the former president and that he was already dominant in the Republican National Committee. Add the number of GOP senators who might reject McConnell as their leader if he voted to convict, and the self-interested senator had decided to put his country second.

With McConnell failing to lead his senators to convict, the outcome was obvious. We were going to lose. But we still couldn't accept it. When Richard Burr of North Carolina, Bill Cassidy of Louisiana, and Susan Collins of Maine each voted guilty, I found myself thinking, *We're still at the start of the alphabet. Maybe we can get those seventeen!* Then we heard James Lankford of Oklahoma, John Kennedy of Louisiana, and Rob Portman of Ohio say, "Not guilty," and reality dawned. Lankford and Kennedy were smart guys who had been outraged by the attack. Portman had been publicly critical of Trumpism, and he was retiring. Why he chose to protect Trump was beyond understanding. Nevertheless, seven Republicans had voted guilty, making the result the most bipartisan in history.

Jamie had been the most hopeful and was therefore the most disappointed by the result. Throughout the trial he had talked about how he couldn't believe that the senators would fail to recognize that the Constitution, which he so loved, and the rule of law, which he revered, needed to be protected from men like Trump. When we made it to our room off the Senate floor, we embraced, and Jamie asked us to form a circle, as we had before when we had made key decisions or needed mutual support. "I'm sorry I let you down," he said, choking a bit with emotion. We wouldn't hear of it and instead gave him a round of applause as thanks for being our leader.

As we talked over what had happened, Eric Swalwell produced a bottle of whiskey, and we each had a shot. Madeleine

Dean, coincidentally, gave out souvenir flasks decorated with the Great Seal of the United States. I said something about how with fifty-seven votes, a clear majority of the United States Senate had found Trump guilty of inciting insurrection against the government of the United States. I said this in part to comfort myself because, like Jamie, I had had my own moments of hope when I considered how well we had argued and believed that we could win a two-thirds majority.

One of the strangest and most infuriating moments in this whole experience occurred after we had left the chamber and begun packing our personal belongings into boxes. Mitch McConnell took to the floor and delivered a twenty-minute speech that began with the words, "January 6th was a disgrace." He then proceeded to say, "Former President Trump's actions preceding the riot were a disgraceful dereliction of duty" and "There is no question that President Trump is practically and morally responsible for provoking the events of that day."

On and on McConnell went in his syrupy drawl, excoriating Trump and confirming everything we had said in our case. At some point Jamie said, "Hey, he could have been an impeachment manager." It was as if he was trying to prove to future historians that he had actually listened during the trial. He knew we had proven Trump's guilt, but that wasn't enough. He couldn't support conviction, he said, because he didn't believe an official who had left office could be impeached.

To be clear, McConnell had some nerve claiming the high ground after he'd voted to let Trump escape accountability. The Senate had taken up the question of whether the trial was proper and determined THAT IT WAS! (Sorry for all those capital letters, but unlike Donald Trump, I reserve them for the most important points.) Since the Senate had conducted a trial, an explanation drawn from the courtroom is useful. In many trials judges have to rule on questions that arise as a case is being argued. For example, judges often rule on whether certain evidence will be admitted. Once the court issues a ruling to allow this evidence, the jury is not permitted to disregard the court's decision and refuse to consider it. It's what the legal profession refers to as "the law of the case." Of course, McConnell wasn't sincere. He was making an excuse, which he hoped the American people would accept, for playing dice with our democracy.

————

On the last night of the trial, after the verdict was issued and we had gulped some whiskey, commiserated, and accepted thanks from senators Cory Booker, Amy Klobuchar, and others, we walked over to the House side of the Capitol for a press conference that Jamie began by saying, "Trump stormed our house with the mob he incited, and we defended it." With our captain at the lectern and us members of the team lined up behind him, the scene resembled the losing side's postgame "press availabilities" that follow some big football games like, say, the Super Bowl. Although Trump had not been convicted and barred from future office, Jamie claimed credit for "reviving" and protecting our democracy and debunked the excuse used by McConnell and others who'd shielded Trump. Sounding very much like the coach who thought the referees had cheated his team, he added, "But it is what it is."

In an appearance that, given her casual attire, was obviously unplanned, Speaker Pelosi also spoke of a "cowardly group of Republicans who apparently have no options" for employment outside the Senate, who in their fear put their careers above the Constitution. As Pelosi spoke I saw her gestures grow more expansive as

she lit into McConnell for refusing to accept the article of impeachment before Trump left office and then refusing to find him guilty
because the proceeding occurred after he departed.

The questions from the press resembled the sort that second-
guessing sports reporters throw at losing coaches. Our response
was to note what we'd realized as McConnell made his posttrial
remarks. We had made our case and there was nothing we could
have done to win conviction from senators who were willing to
deny the evidence. It was as if we were prosecutors trying to convict a gangster who had threatened to kill half the jury.

After answering the reporters, we walked back to the Senate
to collect our belongings, taking care to leave behind work product that would go to the National Archives. We said our goodbyes to each other and to the room that had, for a time, been the
frenzied center of our lives. I carried under my arms two large
binders of materials that I had used to stay on top of my parts of
our presentation.

My route took me from the grandeur of the Capitol to the drab
basement tunnels that lead under the grounds and Independence
Avenue to the Rayburn House Office Building. I was exhausted
though proud and, since it's possible to have two feelings at once,
I also felt a little depressed. As I walked alone through the tunnels, I thought about what we had proved. Trump had plotted to
bring the mob on January 6 with the purpose of interrupting the
certification of the election. He had then wound them up with
outrage and sent them to the Capitol to "fight like hell." The senators who had heard the case had, six weeks prior, been targets
of the attack. That so many hadn't been able to convict Trump
meant they either feared him or approved of him. These motivations indicated weakness of character on the one hand and moral
depravity on the other.

By the time I reached the office I had begun to decompress and shift a bit from trial mode to regular-life mode. Soon I would be back in Rhode Island, where, aside from giving me occasional words of gratitude, people wanted to tell me about their lives and their ideas for how government might make things better.

25

STATE OF EMERGENCY

After the second impeachment trial of Donald Trump ended, Jamie Raskin tried to take some of the blame himself for the outcome. As crazy as it sounds, he said he should have pushed harder to have the senators seated alphabetically rather than in partisan groupings so they would chat across party lines. He also blamed himself for not demanding a secret ballot and for ending our presentation without using all our allotted time. And he wondered if he should have made more of Trump's refusal to testify. Why would someone with nothing to hide refuse to answer questions?

It was true to Jamie's character that rather than feel satisfied with how many votes we'd captured he considered himself responsible for how Trump had evaded conviction. However, all the blame for the trial's outcome belongs to Republican senators who had a chance to guarantee that Trump would never return to the presidency.

Republican obstruction in Congress has caused most of the public frustration with Washington and had allowed Trumpism to grow. On gun violence, voting rights, climate change, health care, immigration, and support for families, people wanted progress. We in government—and I include Democrats here—gave them too little of it. Sometimes members of our party even joined the obstructionists to derail our efforts. A glaring example arose in 2021 when Senators Joe Manchin of West Virginia and Kyrsten Sinema of Arizona helped block President Biden's "Build Back Better Plan." Both said they were acting on principle. However it also seemed they were worried about getting re-elected and thought their positions would help. And so they talked about the need for "bipartisanship" as they deprived Americans of their basic rights and support for their families. They were, to my mind, largely looking out for themselves and preserving undemocratic Senate rules like the filibuster so they might use them themselves one day. Thus they blocked the policies that would have done the most to help Americans and restore their faith in their government.

In 2022 to be successful we must remind voters that despite the odds, our response to the COVID pandemic saved their lives and saved their jobs, and now we are trying to save our democracy. For its part the GOP no longer has positions that voters can consider. The Republicans chose not to have a party platform in 2020, and in 2022 Senator Mitch McConnell has declared the party will campaign with no ideas at all. Their primaries have become contests over who is closer to Trump—*I am! No, I am!*—and who can be more hateful in their campaigns. I nominate the Arizona candidate whose TV ad showed him shooting actors portraying Joe Biden, Nancy Pelosi, and Senator Mark Kelly. Kelly's wife, then Congresswoman Gabby Giffords, was shot in the head by a would-be assassin in 2011. That someone would shoot at Kelly, even in an advertisement, should be disqualifying.

With opponents who stand for nothing beyond one man's violent drive for power, we have reached a state of emergency that too many Americans, even members of Congress, don't seem to recognize. Perhaps the blood and excrement smeared on the floors of the Capitol on January 6 were cleaned too quickly.

Or perhaps the need to deny the trauma of that day has caused a kind of political amnesia. Whatever the reason, they downplay a threat that is screamed at them every day.

Don't believe me? Consider that as I write this, Representative Jim Jordan and Donald Trump are suggesting that certain government officials and former aides to presidential candidate Hillary Clinton are traitors deserving of execution. I needn't tell you why they are saying this because there is no reason other than a desire to inflame their followers with homicidal fantasies. Remarkably, no one responded with a public rebuke after Fox News aired Jordan's remarks on the network's morning show. It was regarded as just another comment, as if talk of murder is now part of normal discourse. Actually, a week before the call for executions, the Republican National Committee declared the attack on the Capitol "legitimate political discourse" as it censured the two Republicans, Liz Cheney of Wyoming and Adam Kinzinger of Illinois, who accepted appointments to the congressional committee investigating the January 6 attack.

One year into the investigation, no one can reasonably doubt that what happened on that day was an attempted coup. No one can sensibly ignore that as soon as the smell of tear gas faded, the Republican Party began a concerted effort to normalize what had happened. With Trump using his evil charisma to rally the rank and file and his money and influence to support primary candidates, he transformed the Republican Party into a cult devoted to his authoritarian dream.

Sadly, the party that has, since Lincoln, promoted conservative values, policies, and principles is dead. (I say *sadly* because, like Speaker of the House Nancy Pelosi, I think our country needs two responsible parties.) In its place has arisen a fascist movement that uses modern propaganda techniques to captivate believers and old-fashioned violence, and threats of violence, to terrify, bully, and silence everyone else. Fear is a normal response for anyone who sees the uniformed and heavily armed militias that appear at Trump rallies and protests. In addition to the paramilitary groups, Trump's fascism comes with the menace of white nationalists, neo-Nazis, and black-shirted thugs who call themselves Proud Boys. Their presence in our political life is so jarring there's a temptation to deny their significance and to fail to confront what they represent.

————

Since bullies who get their way only push harder for more power, Trumpism must be confronted and not appeased. Federal agencies like the FBI and state and local police should deal with the violence-prone extremists. The worst response would be the rise of civilian anti-Trump militants, and this should be discouraged. However, we must use every other means of resistance and opposition against this threat. This should include massive voter turnout and campaigns to:

Demand voting rights laws to overcome the GOP's efforts to limit voting.

"Out" antidemocracy extremists.

Educate Americans on the value and history of their democracy.

Invite others into the prodemocracy movement.

Reform or abolish the filibuster.

Support democracy's guardians, especially Republicans who stand with us.

Help those who are lost in conspiracy theories with respectful conversations.

Make online platforms accountable through persuasion and
   new antitrust laws.
Support election workers in their effort to conduct fair elections.
Confront white Christian nationalists as truly anti-Christian
   and anti-American.
Expand the Supreme Court and require that justices adhere
   to ethics rules.

The last item on my list, reforming the Supreme Court,
would be difficult, but given the court's ethical problems and
its politicization, few things are more urgent than restoring
the court's credibility. That the court is riven by politics—and
increasingly captive to conservative religious ideology—is evi-
denced by its many decisions favoring that point of view. Time
and again laws covering health care, public health, education, and
other issues have been decided in favor of religious institutions
seeking exemptions. In the meantime, the court has favored gun
owners and corporations, two pillars of the right-wing agenda, in
almost every case in which they were involved. Add the increasingly conservative profile of justices appointed by Republican
presidents—since 1969 they have named fourteen out of eighteen
appointees—and it's easy to see why the balance has shifted. (It
should be noted that the fact that four of today's nine justices
were appointed by presidents who lost the popular vote affects
public trust in the court.)

In correcting the imbalance, we could follow one of two
courses. The first would impose term limits, which may be a
good idea. The second would expand the number of justices on
the court, which is something I support wholeheartedly. Congress has the power to change the number and did so many times
before settling on nine in 1869. With nine circuit courts of appeal

each justice was assigned to one and tasked with deciding certain issues in cases these courts consider. Today there are thirteen circuit courts. Each one considers roughly 24,000 cases every year. This is about double the number counted fifty years ago, when officials said the courts were in a "crisis of volume." Adding new justices would reduce the pressure on each one and, we should hope, make the court more balanced and less a body for imposing hard-right decisions on a country that doesn't support them.

The other reform—imposing a code of ethics on the justices— would bring them in line with all other federal courts as well as the executive and legislative branches of government. This would, I hope, put an end to the luxury junkets justices take as gifts and the troublesome political activities of their spouses. The latter problem has been highlighted by revelations of Justice Clarence Thomas's wife's support for the January 6 effort to block certification of Joe Biden's election. Ms. Thomas has, for years, subtly traded on her husband's power. Ethics rules to stop such practices would, like expanding the court, begin the restoration of the public's confidence in the court, which polls show is in steep decline. A bill I cosponsored would move the ethics requirements forward but will likely be filibustered to death in the Senate, where my fellow Rhode Islander Sheldon Whitehouse is the chief sponsor. This reality explains why we need overwhelming support for an end to the filibuster.

In addition to enduring the rulings of a Supreme Court that no longer holds our confidence, Americans are also challenged by unaccountable Big Tech companies whose social media platforms destroy our trust in basic facts, institutions, and one another. As chairman of the House Subcommittee on Antitrust, Commercial and Administrative Law I've been leading the effort to rein in Big Tech and confront its role in degrading public discourse and aiding election interference. This process has taken more than two years and involved many hearings both in and outside Washington. The suite of bills were developed with the help of top experts on anti-trust.

Few outside the industry, or for that matter inside it, said there was not a problem. Our legislation focused on the largest platforms: Amazon, Apple, Facebook, and Google, who due to their market share and size, behaved like monopolies. Their business plans and size stifled competition, discouraged innovation, and squeezed many smaller companies to the point where they could not survive. Our bills would require Big Tech companies to prove that acquisitions would not hurt competition and consumers and would bar them from favoring their own products and services over others identified in search engines or on their e-commerce websites. We also would require that companies make it easy for people to switch from one platform to another without losing their data.

In a bit of old-fashioned bipartisanship, I had collaborated closely with the ranking Republican on the Subcommittee on Antitrust, Commercial and Administrative Law, Ken Buck of Colorado, to get Republicans on board. We had enough GOP votes to win majority support in the subcommittee and the whole Judiciary Committee and to prevail in a future House floor vote. Unfortunately, we ran into significant opposition from Democrats where Big Tech companies dominate local economies, the most outspoken of them was a high-ranking member of the Progressive Caucus who has twenty-six years in the House and enjoys a close friendship with the Speaker.

Zoe Lofgren's district included part of the region called Silicon Valley, which is home to the headquarters of Facebook, Google, and Apple. More than fifty thousand people worked at these three locations, and smaller-but-still-big tech companies employed another two hundred thousand or so. These were some of the richest companies in the world. They were spending tens of millions of dollars on lobbyists, advertising, a misinformation campaign, and political contributions to stop all reforms and to maintain an ecosystem that allowed them to make profits at a level never seen in the history of the world.

————

This is not the first time Congress has struggled over regulating big business. During the Gilded Age several senators proudly protected the oil, steel, and railroad trusts, which were smothering competition while they raised prices at will. Those who defended the trusts emphasized how they had made the United States a world power. America's Big Tech companies play an even bigger role in the world than our oil companies did back then, and they are more problematic. Like the oil trusts of the past, their size permits them to snuff out potential competitors, and just as the drillers and refiners harmed the natural environment, Big Tech harms our social environment by favoring clickbait political conspiracy theories and crackpot assaults on science and medicine.

Zoe showed her commitment to the cause of Big Tech near the end of our work on the bills, which were based on a sixteen-month bipartisan investigation and a 450-page subcommittee report. As the finishing touches were put on the legislation, she began saying that we were rushing the process and the bills were not well written. She did this at one of our hearings, where she added that one of our bills "would essentially, metaphorically, take a grenade and just roll it into the tech economy and just blow it up."

Her arguments, which could be refuted, shortchanged the majority of Americans who are sick of Big Tech's behavior.

Others on the subcommittee told me to refuse Zoe's request to delay the hearing on our bills, saying she wanted to kill the bills. I did not want to believe this and decided, out of respect for her, to compromise and give her an additional week. She spent the time attacking the bills by echoing industry-generated talking points. One top Google executive said we would "break" services consumers liked and "undermine America's technology leadership." He offered no evidence to back this claim. Over at Amazon they said that provisions to stop Amazon from bullying small businesses and copying their product designs would hurt small businesses. (Try to wrap your mind around that one!) And everyone in Big Tech whined that we were somehow punishing innovators. Soon Big Tech would be campaigning against us on TV, suggesting we were destructive traitors who were selling out to China, Russia, and Iran.

When we went to the Congressional Progressive Caucus to describe the legislation and answer questions, Zoe demanded equal time to attack our work. These presentations are never followed by rebuttals, but she grabbed her chance to talk and warned that our bill would destroy tech companies.

In my response I didn't mince words, saying:

It's just not true that these companies will be destroyed. They're just going to have to play by the rules and operate fairly, which is something they would soon be required to do in the European Union under their Digital Markets Act. Even under these rules, they will continue to be wildly profitable.

I was very confident in the legislation we had developed. The members of the subcommittee were very knowledgeable and careful people and had developed real expertise. Our chief counsel, Slade Bond, is a brilliant lawyer with world-class expertise in this area of the law. Lina Khan is an internationally respected expert in the field and had joined the subcommittee staff to help with our investigation and the drafting of our report. She now chairs the Federal Trade Commission. We also received help from Columbia University professor Tim Wu, who is a leading scholar on technology and competition.

Zoe was a lawyer, but her expertise was immigration law. She had no background in antitrust regulation, she hadn't participated in the investigation, and she'd waited to speak up until the last minute, as we were preparing for the markup of the legislation. Even then, we had accepted some of her suggested modifications, and *still she was going to vote against us.* This kind of politics is what alienates voters and hurts our party's effort to win their support.

I was glad when the leader of the caucus, Pramila Jayapal, a principled and strategic leader, interrupted to say, "Zoe, this is not about you."

As I write, polls say a huge majority of the American people support the regulation of Big Tech.

If we don't act, we'll give voters one more reason to believe Washington isn't working. In this case we have the public with us because everyone knows Big Tech is too big, and we have more than enough Republican support to overcome the no votes from tech-district Democrats. If the bipartisan effort fails, we will be guilty of bad politics and bad policy.

———

The words *politics* and *policy* have the same Greek roots. Politics relates to the competition for government power. Policy is what government does (or doesn't do) in the exercise of that power. In their political campaigns, individuals and parties make promises about policy. If they win but don't follow through, they may get thrown out of power. Republicans have it easy. Other than cutting taxes and bulking up defense spending, they don't have a serious policy agenda. We Democrats want to do a bunch of serious things, including protecting the planet, supporting working families, making the free market function fairly, and developing the nation's infrastructure. President Biden proposed to do all of the above with what became known as the Infrastructure Investment and Jobs Act and the Build Back Better Act, which focused on fighting climate change and supporting working families with better and more affordable childcare, education, paid family leave, and eldercare and by transforming child tax credits into a permanent child allowance for millions of families. In repeated polls almost 70 percent of Americans said they supported these policies. When pollsters focused only on Republicans, the number was still a remarkable 50 percent.

As much as Americans wanted us to reach our goals, we were generally blocked by that hard-to-understand Senate filibuster rule, which lets forty out of a hundred senators kill just about anything the House approves. Some budget bills are considered exceptions, and with rulings from the parliamentarian, who had final say on Senate procedures, the Biden proposals qualified. Then we Democrats commenced to undermine ourselves.

As Joe Biden started his presidency, he proposed three big initiatives. The first dealt with the COVID-19 crisis. The second addressed huge infrastructure repair and development needs. The third dealt with reducing costs for working families in childcare, eldercare, health care, prescription drug prices, and much more. This plan was called Build Back Better. However, our congressional majorities were so slim—six votes in the House and one vote in the Senate—that every Democrat had to join the effort.

The terrible thing about holding such slim majorities is that it can allow a very small number of people to make demands with the threat that they'll defy their fellow Democrats, including congressional leaders and the President, and kill an important proposal. With Biden's agenda we all worked together on COVID relief but then ran into a terrible intramural squabble.

In 2021 we gave President Biden an early victory, approving his Covid-19 relief plan, which quickly became law. Then for months Democratic senators Joe Manchin of West Virginia and Kyrsten Sinema of Arizona refused to say they would vote for both of the remaining Biden bills. They both liked the bipartisan infrastructure plan. But they weren't sure about Build Back Better. Without Sinema's and Manchin's votes getting us over the fifty-vote threshold, the bills would die. In this event, voter reaction could hand the GOP control of the House—and perhaps the Senate—in 2022. As for the White House in 2024? We could lose that too.

Manchin's resistance seemed to come from the fact that his state is quite conservative and had gone for Trump by more than two to one. He didn't think West Virginians wanted to spend trillions of dollars the way Biden wanted, but to his credit he kept negotiating with the White House. Sinema's opposition was harder to explain. Her state had gone for Biden in 2020. Arizona had two Democratic senators and five Democrats in Congress compared to four Republicans. Then there was Sinema's biography. The second openly LGBTQ woman ever elected to Congress, she had started her career as a member of the superliberal

Green Party. She had also been a social worker. One would think these experiences would incline her to favor bills that would help so many people. Unfortunately, however, Sinema has a tendency toward self-interest that is noteworthy even in the political world. Before reaching the Senate she had served in the House, where I had observed her closely. In that time she had seemed more committed to reelection than policy making. She spent a great deal of time fundraising and was below average as a cosponsor of bills. However, she was a very effective attention-getter whose national press appearances made her into a celebrity.

The intransigence of Sinema and Manchin led to months of bruising conflict within our party. At one point, members of the House proposed that the two bills be considered together, which meant that those who wanted only infrastructure wouldn't get it without the programs in Build Back Better. With Sinema and Manchin resisting, they, and the rest of the Senate, moved ahead on infrastructure, approving it in the Senate in August 2021. In the House it was held up by progressives who wanted some sort of guarantee that Build Back Better would get a fair chance in the Senate.

Given how Manchin and Sinema had sent conflicting signals for months on end, the progressives were right to be wary. We wanted to help President Biden but didn't like how the senators had behaved and feared that they would renege on the arrangement. Meanwhile millions of Americans were watching us to see if we could get anything done. In an interview in the *New York Times*, Pramila Jayapal, the House progressives leader, mentioned her twenty-four-year-old child whose friends don't vote because "they are so cynical about anybody actually fighting for them."

After meeting with Whip Jim Clyburn and the pragmatic chairperson of the Congressional Black Caucus Joyce Beatty, the Speaker decided to bring things to a head. She scheduled a

vote for Friday, November 5, which would force the Congressional Progressive Caucus into a decision. When the day came, we
gathered in the morning in a wood-paneled subterranean theater
that was part of the Capitol Visitor Center. With no windows and
a plush blue carpet absorbing sound, the space had an intimate,
almost secretive feel, which seemed right for a session at which
we hoped to speak honestly, as family might when a big decision
was at hand. Then, as Pramila was about to start us off, Speaker
Pelosi entered the room. She wore a magenta suit and matching
shoes with stiletto heels, which made her impossible to ignore.

In general the Speaker takes members' input in private or
in big Democratic caucus meetings. Although she is a legendary progressive, she rarely attends Progressive Caucus meetings.
We usually meet without members of the senior leadership team
so that we can speak freely. In this case, the need to be frank,
especially about the Speaker's strategy, was significant. Pramila
reacted quickly, saying: "Madame Speaker, you know you always
are welcome at our meetings, but not this one."

The Speaker, moving as if she hadn't heard Pramila, took a
seat. Then, as the discussion began, a number of caucus members expressed, as politely as they could, that they couldn't support seperating the infrastructure and Build Back Better bills.
Her good friend Jan Schakowsky of Illinois emphasized this point
in an earlier caucus meeting. Pelosi's fellow Californian Mark
Takano, chairman of the House Committee on Veterans' Affairs,
put it succinctly, saying, "Madame Speaker, you know I love you,
but I can't in good conscience support separating these bills."

After a few more such comments, the Speaker quietly
departed, and members of the caucus continued the discussion. For two hours we discussed the merits of the two bills—
infrastructure and Build Back Better—as well as the agreement

being hammered out with the reluctant senators and House members and, finally, the importance of achieving something tangible for the American people. Infrastructure was relatively easy to consider. Everyone in the country knows we have bridges, roads, highways, airports, and rail lines in need of repair, and the work would employ lots of people at relatively high wages. When it came up for a vote it passed easily. Build Back Better, on the other hand, had been stripped of some key items, including Medicare for all people and the president's plan to provide free community college for all students. It was hard for most of us, but especially the younger outspoken progressives, to accept such a diminished bill. It was harder still for them to accept a deal without getting firmer assurances that the House and Senate would also move on Build Back Better.

After a break for lunch and a little work back in our offices, the caucus resumed its meeting. This time we gathered in a room on the third floor of the Longworth House Office Building. First used when the building opened, during the height of the Great Depression, room 1334 featured a magnificent two-level horseshoe-shaped dais. Behind the chairperson's seat loomed a giant mural that had been completed in 1996. In it four angels, their wings shaped like V's for *Victory*, hovered above three propeller-driven airplanes. Underneath the blue sky was a green agricultural landscape divided by a modern highway and a blue river navigated by ships. The angels represented the "four freedoms" that FDR had said America sought to protect: freedom of speech, freedom of religion, freedom from want, and freedom from fear. It seemed quite fitting that above us was this picture of an idyllic America with gleaming infrastructure, calling upon us to relieve people of their fears and help them satisfy their needs.

Except for Pramila, who would hold on to hers as she ran the meeting, we all left our cell phones on a table outside the room, which would be guarded by a caucus staff member. This guaranteed that we would stay focused on the work at hand and that no one would leak reports of what was happening in real time. We then resumed our discussion. Gradually it became clear that too many of us were not confident that if we passed the infrastructure bill, that we would ever pass the Build Back Better legislation.

Our meeting took a long time because we wanted everyone to have a chance to speak. What none of us knew at the time was that Speaker Pelosi was planning to begin the floor process for a vote on the infrastructure bill, which meant she had to pass a preliminary "rule" to set things in motion. These procedural votes are usually pro forma, but since the ninety-five progressives were meeting behind closed doors, they were not near the floor to cast their votes. Most of the caucus members had left their phones outside the meeting room, so they did not receive any of the calls or texts that the Speaker, Majority Leader Steny Hoyer, and Majority Whip James Clyburn were making to bring people to the floor. As the clock ticked, the Republicans reveled in the prospect of either defeating Pelosi or forcing her into the embarrassing position of holding the vote open. This was permitted, and it could go on for hours if the Speaker chose.

———————

Back in the hearing room, Pramila decided to call the White House. Soon President Biden came on the line. Given the woeful state of our technology, the best she could do was put her phone in speaker mode and hold it up as we crowded around to listen. The president said he was sure that Manchin and Sinema would support the two bills and that both would be moved along quickly. He was confident he had 50 votes in the Senate.

Most but not all of us were reassured. Missouri representative Cori Bush, a freshman, asked the president, "Why are you speaking to nearly one hundred of us when there are really just eight people who could clear things up?" She was talking about some of the members of the Problem Solvers Caucus, which were meeting four floors up from where we had gathered, in the office of Stephanie Murphy, who represented a frontline district in Florida.

Biden didn't answer the question, but he did urge the caucus "to get this done." It was at about this moment that I turned to Joe Neguse and suggested we just go talk to the Problem Solvers. Sheila Jackson Lee of Texas and Mondaire Jones of New York joined us as we went upstairs and found them gathered around the table.

In the conversation that ensued, we stressed the idea that we needed to get something done on infrastructure but that without a firm commitment from them on Build Back Better, it wouldn't happen. They expressed valid concerns about what the voters in their districts wanted them to do. Still, they wanted to help the president.

We opened a laptop computer and wrote a statement that they could accept, saying they would vote for the infrastructure bill. Joe, Sheila, and I left the office in a hurry, but as we raced downstairs, we ran into Sara Jacobs, another freshman from California, who said rather urgently, "The Speaker's about to pull the bill. I'm not going back there—she already yelled at me once—but someone needs to."

This was drama at a level rarely seen in the House. The Speaker's withdrawing a bill from consideration would be an even greater embarrassment for all of us, and in the time that it took for us to get the legislation ready again, some unforeseen snags could develop.

I raced to the Capitol and found Speaker Pelosi, Hoyer, and Clyburn fuming in a small room off the House floor. The Speaker demanded to know what was going on. "Why is no one answering my calls and texts? Why are they keeping all these people who work for us so late? They are tired, they have families. They want to go home."

Steny Hoyer and Jim Clyburn threw their two cents into the conversation and were also clearly miffed. I explained that the Problem Solvers had finally given the progressives what they needed, so everything was out. This didn't really lower the temperature much. The Speaker was in the kind of mood that drives mothers to send every child in the family to their rooms. The difference was that she had 222 children. And each one felt obliged to serve constituents who had certain interests, and each one worried about delivering to those constituents.

Ultimately seven hours would pass between the rule being proposed and our final approval of the infrastructure bill. As we voted I could see that the Speaker was still upset and wanted to know all that had occurred out of her view. It took quite some time for her to let go of this issue.

By the end of the night, the infrastructure bill was ready for the president to sign, which he did on November 15. Three days later a slimmed-down version of Build Back Better was offered on the floor and, as the Problem Solvers had promised, nearly all got behind it. The disruption came this time from Minority Leader Kevin McCarthy, who, since he couldn't defeat the bill, decided to delay its approval for as long as he could stand on his feet and speak.

According to the press, McCarthy's futile stunt, which began around 9:00 p.m. and ended after 5:00 a.m., was intended to capture the attention of Republican members, who would vote to elect a Speaker should they regain control of the House. McCarthy, who very much wants that job, did his very best to imitate Donald Trump as he delivered a stream-of-consciousness rant decorated with distortions, half truths, and full-on lies. Among the lies was the false claim that we were spending more than FDR had during World War II, that we were siccing the IRS on middle-income Americans, and that somehow we would be putting one million people out of work. None of these claims were true, and there were many more like them.

Almost no one was present when McCarthy ran out of energy, but the press dutifully noted that he had set a new record for the duration of a House speech. The headline in the *Washington Post* read: "'Can I be speaker?' Kevin McCarthy asks—for eight hours straight."

Later in the morning we approved Build Back Better, and dispatched the bill to the Senate. After we had accepted huge cuts to the bill, including the elimination of priorities many of us had pushed for decades, all that remained was for Joe Manchin and Kyrsten Sinema to make good on their commitment to the President while we waited, and waited, and waited.

It is now spring 2022, and we are still waiting. Back in Arizona, Sinema has been subjected to protests, and her approval rating fell to single digits. Two House Democrats likely to challenge her in a primary would defeat her handily if she runs for reelection in 2024. I say "if" because it's not clear that she wants to be the Democratic senator from Arizona anymore. Given her service to pharmaceutical companies that don't want to see the federal government negotiate drug prices for Medicare and

Medicaid, she could find a high-paying job in that industry. She's also quite telegenic and reliably conservative, so perhaps a show on Fox News is in her future. In West Virginia, Joe Manchin's Republican-in-Democratic-clothing act earned him praise and a bump in his popularity. He could stay in his seat indefinitely, I think. Or perhaps, given that every senator sees a president in the mirror maybe that's what he sees.

————

Our first year in control of the government revealed some institutional problems—in Congress and in our party—that needed immediate attention. In the House, too many Democratic members of Congress felt their talents were wasted and they often felt as if they didn't know what was happening because top House leaders played things close to the vest. The old style of top-down leadership that had caused these problems seemed to have run its course. For a century that had begun with Speaker Champ Clark's partnership with Woodrow Wilson, dominant figures have guided Washington with a strong, top-down style. In that same time the Democratic Party has become astoundingly more diverse and more accustomed to collaboration. This evolution matches what is happening across the business sector, in academia, and even in the nonprofits. Today people everywhere expect open, collaborative processes and power sharing. This is especially true for those under forty, who simply leave if they don't get these things.

One way to ease the frustration of congressional Democrats would be to move up some people who have shown their ability to work well with a diverse group of colleagues and are inspirational voices. In the Senate I would consider Mark Kelly of Arizona, Chris Murphy of Connecticut, Tammy Duckworth of Illinois, Cory Booker of New Jersey, Amy Klobuchar of Minnesota, and Jon Tester of Montana to be this kind of Democrat, but there are others. In the House I could name thirty people who demonstrate the dynamism and cooperative spirit that will take us into the future. Included, in no special order, are Hakeem Jeffries of New York, Jamie Raskin of Maryland, Pramila Jayapal of Washington, Katherine Clark of Massachusetts, Raul Ruiz of California, Joe Neguse of Colorado, Robin Kelly of Illinois, Colin Allred of Texas, and Veronica Escobar of Texas. These people would lead with the transparency that would allow everyone—most especially the American people—to see whether the House and Senate are working for them.

At the presidential level I am, of course, glad that Joe Biden has stabilized our democracy after the ravages of the Trump years and that he has done what no one else could have done on the world stage. Before he was elected, *Politico* reported that Biden had told close allies he expected to serve one four-year term. More recently he has said he will seek reelection. Even though repeated polls have indicated Americans don't expect him to run again in 2024, when he will turn eighty-two. Political forecasters are split, with many saying Biden's stated intentions allow him to decide later and avoid becoming a lame duck.

I think that even if the president leaves office in 2024, he will conclude a fifty-four-year political career without equal in his lifetime. His successes as senator, vice president, and then president mark him as a great public servant, and his character, proven at moments of diversity and enormous challenges, are a lasting example of what's possible in politics and government. Behind him stand more than a dozen high-qualified Democrats who would, I think, appeal to the majority of American voters.

But whoever is president, he or she must devote real energy

to changing the two other elements of national politics that erode the quality of our democracy. The first is the Senate filibuster, which must go. This rule—and it's only a rule!—can be changed by the Senate itself. The presidential candidates must campaign with the promise to push hard for this change, and, while we're at it, we must pressure Senate candidates to pledge that they will abolish it. If it had already been abolished, the Senate might have enacted a slew of House bills favored by the American people, such as the Bipartisan Background Checks Act pertaining to gun purchasers, the Equality Act for LGBTQ people and the George Floyd Justice in Policing Act. The Senate might have raised the minimum wage, made it easier for people to join a union, and protected the right to vote. Along the way we would have proven that Democrats can do what the people want and deserve their support.

The change in the filibuster is going to come eventually. Senators who argue that the rule is somehow sacrosanct should recall that when Republicans wanted to ram through judicial nominations and pack the Supreme Court with conservatives, they did it by abolishing the filibuster for Supreme Court nominations. Add new rules that eliminate the filibuster from budgetary work, and it becomes clear that there's nothing sacred about this arbitrary rule. If our party is truly committed to enacting the will of the American people, the majority of whom support us and want us to act, we must act boldly against the minority rule that freezes the Senate into inaction, and if we're not willing to use every lever of power to deliver for the American people, we don't deserve to govern.

Reform or elimination of the Electoral College is the second must-have if we are going to call the United States a true democracy. Today a number of states, including Rhode Island, have agreed that they will appoint electors to the candidate who gets the most votes nationwide in any election. However, this agreement has not been tested in the courts, and if it is, it may be found unconstitutional. The other and far better option would be a constitutional amendment to eliminate the Electoral College altogether. There may have been a time when this system made sense, and the rule now serves only to create the possibility that someone will become president without the support of most voters. This is not democracy.

A truer American democracy, in which our votes are equal in presidential elections and minorities cannot control the Senate, can be achieved but will require citizen action at a level not seen in many decades. This includes organizing and voting and mass protests against the hate, lies, incitement, and intimidation practiced by the Trumpists. We must make sure Americans understand that the once-peaceable GOP has come to accept violence and coup plotting as it pursues a white nationalist future. This isn't true of everyone in the party, and the dissenters must have our support. But as I have discovered in private conversations with them, more reasonable House Republicans fear the old party of genuine conservatism is lost.

Today, Republicans have reengineered election systems in many states to empower partisan politicians to throw out the results tabulated by election boards. In nearly twenty states access to voting has been restricted, voters' names are being purged from the registration rolls, absentee and mail-in ballots are being sharply curbed, and the election infrastructure—the number of polling places, their hours of operation, and the availability of drop boxes—is under attack. All of this is being done in service of the GOP's Big Lie that the election system is flawed.

As someone who helped fashion the successful 2018 Democratic agenda, which was all about returning America to normal politics, I feel I have the standing to say that in 2022 we need to make the defense of democracy our new priority. Republican Trumpists—almost all Republicans are Trumpists now—are for mob attacks and against fair elections. They are in favor of waving the Confederate battle flag over fallen police officers. They are in favor of overturning elections when they lose and of curbing the rights of citizens when they win. They are the party of chaos, corruption, and destruction, and no Democrat should ever pass up the opportunity to say so.

It's time for specific Democrats to take a stand, even if it means losing the next election. House members from places where Big Tech looms large must, nevertheless, help us regulate companies that insist they can't afford to police hate speech and the incitement of violence. Last year the top five American tech companies made more than $300 billion *in profit* on $1.4 trillion in revenues. They paid 3.4 percent in taxes on those revenues. All this business depended, of course, on a World Wide Web developed by the government, or rather you, the taxpayer.

Frontline Democrats who fear voter reaction should remember that they are not attacking conservatism or criticizing conservative constituents. Genuine conservatism seeks to moderate change, to preserve what is good in society, and to protect rights while reinforcing responsibilities. Conservatives created a national park system and the Environmental Protection Agency. They have been essential to the coalitions that backed civil rights and voting rights laws, and they have worked tirelessly to defend America from foes like Russia. Genuine conservatives and independents are the ones who gave you the margin of victory in the past two elections, and they will do it again if you remind them that the Republican Party is now the Trump Party.

True American conservatives would not flock to Hungary,

as Trumpists have, to celebrate the creeping authoritarianism of Prime Minister Viktor Orbán. As leader of a party that blends extreme religion with autocratic policies, Orbán has packed the courts with crony judges, changed the rules to let ethnic Hungarians who have never lived in the country vote, destroyed independent media, and installed party spies in the civil service.

————————

True American conservatives would have supported Ukraine unequivocally as it faced an unprovoked invasion. By mid-February 2022, Vladimir Putin had massed more than one hundred thousand troops and thousands of armored vehicles on Ukraine's border. It was obvious that after years of threats and speeches about re-creating the empire the Soviets had built, he was trying to do it. Nevertheless, a remarkable number of the new, Trump-era conservatives in politics and the media sided with the autocrat against the democracy we supported. Support for Russia had grown in the Trump camp ever since Putin helped him win election in 2016. From this beginning, his followers began to admire his militarism, his machismo, his support for Russian nationalist Christian leaders, and his harsh treatment of LGBTQ people.

On Fox News, host Laura Ingraham mocked Ukraine's president for imploring Russia to forego the invasion it had planned. Her colleague Tucker Carlson asked, rhetorically, if Putin had promoted "racial discrimination" in schools, made fentanyl, attempted "to snuff out Christianity," or eaten dogs. "These are fair questions," he told his Fox News audience with a straight face. "And the answer to all of them is 'no.' Vladimir Putin didn't do any of that. So why does permanent Washington hate him so much?"

Permanent Washington, which must mean the defense and diplomatic establishment, hated Putin because he ruled as a dictator at home—ordering his opponents be assaulted, arrested, and killed—and acted as a similarly violent thug abroad. Few world leaders were more brutal and more dictatorial. Fewer still dared to attack the American election system as he had.

Before the invasion I went to Ukraine to convey support from the American people and to affirm our nation's commitment to Ukrainian autonomy. In what was then a calm and beautiful Kyiv I met with government officials who politely but firmly insisted that they are on the front lines of democracy's defense against authoritarianism. As we talked in elegant government conference rooms that would soon become Russian targets, they said they were grateful for America's military and economic aid but noted the size of Russia's active army—nearly one million soldiers and twelve thousand tanks—and asked for more, especially antitank weapons.

On the streets of Kyiv, where shops, cafés, and restaurants operated as normal, I met people who were trying to carry on with their lives even as they imagined a terrifying future. (In fact President Volodymyr Zelenskyy was advising calm as his military quietly prepared for an invasion.) Ordinary Ukrainians told me they were determined to fight, street by street if necessary, to preserve the freedoms they had realized since their county became free of the collapsing Soviet Union in 1991. In thirty years they had become so certain in the value of their democracy that they couldn't imagine giving it up. "Slava Ukraini," "glory to Ukraine," was something people were beginning to say to each other as they came and went.

The Russian invasion began on February 24 with missiles, bombs dropped by aircraft, and assaults by tanks and infantry. Then, to the surprise of many military analysts, Ukraine began using arms supplied by the West—including antitank rockets that could be fired by a single soldier—to halt attacks across their country. Although the Russians would turn to attacking civilians, killing thousands and leveling entire cities, their invasion would be stalled. World leaders, appalled by the mass killing of Ukrainians—especially of women, children, and the elderly—began to talk of war crime trials.

On the seventh day of the war, I joined another delegation that went to eastern Europe to signal American support for NATO allies and their humanitarian relief efforts. I was happy that all the Republicans who joined this mission had voted to certify our past election. These were not fired-up Trumpists.

In Poland we traveled to the busiest border crossing, an agricultural town called Medyka, which is about forty miles west of Ukraine's sixth-largest city, Lviv. Extreme cold weather meant that many of the arriving Ukrainians, some of whom traveled on foot, were shivering almost uncontrollably. Upon arrival they received coats and blankets. Children were given stuffed animals, and everyone had a hot meal.

What we saw made every person in our delegation weep. Women, children, and elderly men arrived in a state of shock. They carried little or nothing from their homes, uncertain of where they were going and how they would survive. They struggled to grasp why Russia would attack Ukraine and how its military could even think of bombing homes and apartments.

The two million who fled in the first ten days of the war left husbands, sons, fathers, and brothers to fight. As afraid as they were about what these men might face, no one expressed any uncertainty about their joining the fight. "We love our country," they told me. "We fought to get our democracy. We can't give it up." They also knew that one of Putin's motivations had been to destroy a neighboring country where his people could see the freedoms that come with the democratic system.

I couldn't think about what was happening in Ukraine without wondering how Americans would respond in a similar situation. Do we understand that it's only by accident of birth that we are citizens of a democratic government? Could we recognize real threats to our way of life? What would we sacrifice for our democracy's preservation?

Having seen the deluded self-described patriots attack the Capitol, I found it obvious that the defense of democracy depends on separating propaganda from reality. Years of lies had persuaded millions that they should fear amorphous enemies including liberals, Democrats, immigrants, the Deep State, non-Christians, even a pedophile cult of the powerful. Then came Donald Trump, who affirmed their fears, declared, "I alone can fix it," and summoned his followers to action. They believed they were fighting for democracy when in fact they were fighting to keep in power a man with authoritarian designs.

The most bizarre thing about January 6 was that the marauders believed, like the Ukrainians fighting Putin, that they were fighting to save their country. But they were nothing like the Ukrainians. They had been drawn, by Trump, into a shared delusion, but I doubt that he really believed the stories he told. (The planning for the Stop the Steal campaign preceded the election.) He only wanted power and was willing to use the presidency to delude supporters who came to believe in a fearsome fantasy.

Long protected by oceans that keep aggressors like Putin at a distance, Americans have never confronted a foreign power determined to destroy our democracy. However, in this information age we have no oceans to separate us from weapons like the Big Lies told by Trump. The enemies to our democracy spring from among us and wield emotionally charged disinformation. Our fight for our democracy is not like Ukraine's. However, theirs should inspire us to confront lies wherever we see them and devote ourselves to helping those who come under the spell cast by the power seekers and profiteers.

———

Thanks to President Biden and his diplomatic team, much of the world rose to defend Ukraine's freedom by imposing economic sanctions that would quickly affect almost every Russian citizen. NATO rallied to supply a growing stream of arms, and every neighboring country ramped up humanitarian relief. This would be part of Biden's overall effort to show that democracy works.

Meanwhile, the task of protecting our country remained urgent. Listen to people outside Washington, and outside the Trumpist cult, and they ask, continuously, why Democrats are not shouting from the rooftops about the political mob threatening our democracy. They feel that freedom is slipping through their fingers, and they are right. Freedom House, which has documented our country's decline as a democracy, found that in the 1930s a consistent 75 percent of young Americans said it was "essential" for people to live in democracies. Today the number is around 30 percent. In 2016, on the eve of Trump's election, 46 percent of Americans said they either "never had" or "no longer had" faith in democracy.

The whole world is watching, and worrying, as our country— once the unshakable proof of democracy's strengths—decides whether our experiment in self-governing will continue. The most moving expression of this international concern was voiced in May as Prime Minister Kyriakos Mitsotakis addressed Congress on the matter of our shared commitment to "freedom over tyranny" and democracy over authoritarianism. He noted that ancient Greece inspired our founders and then modern America showed the way for the Greeks to achieve independence and establish its democracy.

Today, said Mitsotakis, he is most worried about "internal fragmentation of our democracies." He said that the "sirens of populism" are being heard by people who have been left behind by income inequality. And though he admitted it is "a tall order" he insisted that reinventing our democracies for the twenty-first century, so that they work for all people, is "the mission of our generation."

The time to fight is now, before the fascists get too far. If they win in 2022, they will act to further erode freedoms and rights. They will set the stage for a Trump comeback in 2024 that will be aided by state officials willing to meddle in the vote counting and, if necessary, throw out a tally that finds Trump on the losing end.

If you think the level of political conflict we're experiencing today is bad, imagine what will happen if the Trump cult is powerful enough to either return him to the White House or throw the 2024 election into chaos. Reliable information will be impossible to find. Trust will collapse. Militancy will rise on both sides. In eight short years, puppet master Vladimir Putin will have succeeded in bringing America to a state of crisis it hasn't experienced in more than 150 years. We must not let this happen.

ACKNOWLEDGMENTS

There are so many people to thank for the fullness of my life and to the experiences detailed in this book. First, my incredible family: my parents, Jack and Sabra, whose love started it all, and my siblings, John, Roberta, Susan, and Stephanie, who all taught me about unconditional love and the importance of devotion to family. And my brothers-in-law and nieces and nephews, who have added so much to my life. My grandparents, Ruth and Irving and Lucy and John, who were such important influences in my life.

Childhood friends, especially Karen Watts, Paul Caprio, Philip Carrozza, Robbie Rice, Lisa Battista and Ken Silva, who helped shape me in so many ways, and I'm so grateful for the ongoing encouragement and support of friends Ken Zarrilli and Josh McKinney-Zarrelli and Jack and Sara McConnell and so many others.

My best friend who knew me from birth, Harriet Quinn, who passed away before this book was completed, and my dear Gail McGowan, who has provided consistent love and support to me.

I've been lucky to benefit from the political skill of great campaign managers and other professionals like Mandy Grunwald, Diane Feldman, Mike Donilon, Chris Bizzacco, Eric Hyers, Nicole Kayner, Jeff Larivee, and Amy Gabarra.

In each of my work in government, I have been blessed by colleagues and staff that have inspired me every day. In the state legislature, powerful examples of public service like Nancy Benoit, Edie Ajello, Paul Sherlock, Maryellen Goodwin, and the late Barbara Burlingame.

In the mayor's office, I was lucky to have the most dedicated and talented team ever in Providence City Hall and I am grateful for people like Dean Esserman, George Farrell, Alix Ogden, Mike Mello, Deb Brayton, Carol Grant, John Simmons, Andy Andujar, Gonzalo Cuervo, Xiomara Gonsalves, and so many others who remain important faces in my life.

The contributions of my extraordinarily dedicated congressional staff have been so remarkable: Peter Karafotas, Chris Bizzacco, Megan Garcia, Roger Suchite, Slade Bond, Joe Van Wye, Rita Murphy, Annie Pease, Rich Luchette, Andre Herrera, Colin Driscoll, Leo Confalone, Larson Binzer, Jenn Bell, John Myron, and Luke Zakedis. All have contributed so much to the story of my life.

One of the greatest joys of my life has been the privilege of working with giants like the late John Lewis, the incomparable Speaker Nancy Pelosi, my great mentor, Rosa DeLauro and dear colleagues, with particular gratitude for the friendships of Jamie Raskin, Joe Neguse, Val Demings, Ted Deutch, Janice Hahn, Mark Takano, Terri Sewell, Karen Bass, Frederica Wilson, and Hakeem Jeffries.

Special thanks to Michael D'Antonio, without whom this project would not have been possible and whose patience and grace were invaluable. Thanks to Mel Berger for his careful guidance, and much gratitude to Sean Desmond and his team at Hachette Book Group for helping me complete this project.

Final thanks to the people of the First Congressional District of Rhode Island and the residents of the capital city, Providence, for giving me the privilege and honor of representing them and standing with me during my best times and my most difficult moments.

ABOUT THE AUTHOR

David N. Cicilline serves Rhode Island's First Congressional District in the US House of Representatives. Cicilline is a leader in Congress on issues of core American values, serving as chairman of the House Subcommittee on Antitrust, Commercial and Administrative Law, chair of the Congressional LGBTQ+ Equality Caucus, and vice-chair of the Congressional Progressive Caucus. Prior to his election to Congress, Cicilline served two terms as mayor of Providence, where he rooted out the corruption of his notorious—and imprisoned—predecessor Buddy Cianci. He is a graduate of Brown University and the Georgetown University Law Center and resides today in Providence.